UNEXPECTED
AWAKENING

22 Days at a Buddhist Monastery
Freed Me from Abuse

BLUE
SKY

ISBN: 979-8-9916923-1-1 (Paperback)
ISBN: 979-8-9916923-0-4 (Ebook)

Library of Congress Control Number: 2024926099

These events, as well as the conversations with others and my internal musings, are portrayed to the best of my memory. Although all the accounts in this book are true, names and some identifying details have been changed to protect the privacy of the people involved.

Book cover and Interior Design by Philip Alcock.

Published in the United States by Blue Sky Press LLC.

First printing edition 2025.

Blue Sky Press LLC
419 Birchside Circle
Locust Grove, VA 22508

www.lauriesjacobson.com

For Philip, my partner, my love, my superhero,
my knight in shining armor

For Carl, my dear friend and teacher

And for all the women who suffer in silence
with an abusive partner

Contents

PART Three: *Return to Darkness*

PART FOUR: *Open to Love*

Preface

It was the winter when I began to breathe again—when the snow opened my eyes, love healed my heart, and the escape I only dreamed about unexpectedly became reality.

Looking back, this wondrous adventure seemed nothing short of divine intervention, and for this gift, I am eternally grateful. Wishing never to forget, and to preserve and honor what existed only in memory, I've set down the seemingly magical events of the winter of my forty-third year—a time when I was transported from a place that felt like death into a marvelous new life.

What follows is the story of how it all came to be.

PART ONE

Uncharted Territory

1

Lu's Place

(Day 1, Morning)

Bells chimed as I opened the front door of the diner.

I'd been driving for three hours straight, up and down narrow, winding mountain roads in the middle of nowhere West Virginia—just trees, icy highway, and the occasional small town. It was early February, and we were in the midst of a cold, snowy winter.

"What in the world am I doing?" I muttered, doubting this last-ditch effort for the hundredth time.

I didn't have an answer. I didn't even know who I was anymore. At that moment there were only three things I knew for sure: I'd left my home with only a packed suitcase and sleeping bag, I was in bad shape, and I was scared to death.

I was also running out of options. I'd been to medical doctors, reiki healers, psychiatrists, yoga teachers, social workers, and chiropractors. I'd tried swallowing various herbs, vitamins, even anti-depressants. I fasted. I decluttered my environment. I went vegetarian. I tried meditating. I borrowed a mountain of self-help books from the library on topics ranging from nutrition to cognitive behavioral therapy, from

Zen to the power of positive thinking, and everything in between. Nothing helped relieve my pain. But I'd never been to a Buddhist monastery before. There was still hope—even though it was only a glimmer.

My bladder about to explode, I made a beeline for the "Restrooms" sign at the back of the dining area next to the kitchen. Seated on the toilet, I let my head drop. The oppressing weight of the past decade was like a concrete vest strapped to my chest, sinking my body deeper into the toilet bowl as I stared blankly at a spider crawling across the tile floor. *How did it all happen? How has my life come to this?*

I squinted, recalling the bizarre coincidence only a few minutes earlier when my eyes locked on the sign above the diner in utter amazement. The sign said "Lu's Place." Fifteen years earlier, my husband Mack had given me the nickname "Lulu," and he usually called me "Lu." *Out of all the names in the world, what were the chances this run-of-the-mill diner located in a backwoods town where I happened to stop to pee on my way to a Buddhist monastery would have my own name?*

At the sink, I gasped at my reflection in the mirror. Not long ago, I'd been complimented on my youthful forty-three-year-old appearance and healthy complexion. Now a pale, exhausted old woman with dark hair graying at the temples stared back at me with lifeless brown eyes. Despair inundated me as a flood—my sadness so heavy it was as though my heart and soul mourned the entire world. Silently, I cried out for help, then rubbed my aching cheeks. That morning my occasional TMJ flared up and I woke up with sharp pain and stiffness in my jaw.

I washed my face, took a deep breath, closed my eyes, and reassured myself with the only thought that had kept me going all these years: *I haven't given up.* Not yet. I was still holding on to this last sliver of hope—this meditation retreat would save me. The Buddha would save me. I'd read that Buddha was the Great Physician. His teachings were supposed to be medicine for the mind—medicine that promised to end pain and suffering. There was still a chance. And who knew? Maybe I'd be lucky. Maybe during this retreat I'd taste the Buddha's special elixir; the magic potion that would end my suffering and help me find my way back to the person I used to be.

The scent of fried food dominated the dimly lit diner. A row of booths with cracked red upholstery lined one side of the large room, and a weathered wooden counter ran the length of the far side. Half the booths were occupied. A few hefty men wearing hunting jackets sat on stools at the counter. It seemed like a place where everyone who walked in knew each other intimately, and where coffee and conversation flowed freely and regularly.

As I approached the counter, a warm sensation washed over me. I sensed a close presence and turned around. A woman wearing a short-sleeved white dress and black apron tied around her slim waist stood beside me.

"Can I help you, hon?" the waitress asked. She was about my age and height. Her face was pale, her dark hair tied in a bun. Oddly, as though I'd known her for years, I felt an immediate connection to this woman. But that was impossible. I'd never been to this small West Virginia town before. Her presence emanated warmth, tenderness, and empathy; her dark eyes overflowed with kindness. But it was her sweet, knowing smile that drew me in.

Then, right before my eyes and to my utter amazement, she was suddenly transformed; her face appearing radiant, incredibly beautiful, almost angelic. I gawked as her hair unraveled from its bun and cascaded to the waist of her glowing, ankle-length white gown. An aura of magnificence surrounded her brilliant white figure. She stood barely two feet away from me, beaming, smiling, and melting my heart. I blinked several times, thinking, *This can't be real. I must be hallucinating.*

"You okay, hon?" she asked in a faraway voice. "Can I help you?"

I didn't know what to say. I certainly did need help. I swallowed hard, searching for words. I blinked several times, and suddenly she was back to normal. Staring at the woman's ordinary face and figure once more, I was relieved, yet also slightly disappointed.

"Oh, I'm okay, thanks. Could I please get a cup of hot water to go? I always carry tea bags in my purse."

"Sure, hon." She pointed toward a beverage counter opposite the kitchen. "Go 'head and take it from that red nozzle there. The cups and lids are next to the napkins."

I pulled my wallet from my purse.

"Aw, no charge, hon." She removed a pad and pen from her apron pocket. "You want anything else to go?"

Dazed, I remained perfectly still. What had just happened? Who *was* this woman? She was a complete stranger, yet I was certain I knew her. A surge of gratitude overwhelmed me. I wanted to wrap my arms around her shoulders and embrace her. I wanted to thank her for the hot water, thank her for her kindness, and thank her for simply being here with me in a totally unfamiliar place—in this remote country diner that happened to share my name. I opened my mouth to speak, but all I could manage to say was, "Are you Lu?"

She laughed. "Oh, no, hon," she said. "Lu's not here anymore."

2

Rulebreaker

(Day 1, Afternoon)

I sat in the monastery parking lot frozen to the car seat, seized by fear. My anxiety about attending the retreat had increased with each passing mile, and I'd almost turned the car around to head back home. Although I was glad to escape Mack's criticisms and insults for a week, I had no idea what to expect from a six-day silent retreat at a Buddhist monastery. What if the whole thing turned out to be a complete waste of time? What if nothing significant happened? Even scarier, what if something significant *did* happen? I'd once read in a book about Buddhism that on rare occasions, after sitting for hours upon hours in meditation day after day, some great, internal transformation could occur, changing life as you'd previously known it. I shuddered at the possibility of losing the only life I knew, even though that life was racked with pain.

I'd learned about the monastery several months earlier when I picked up a free brochure at a local coffee shop. I was intrigued. Bodhi Community was a Buddhist monastery located in a West Virginia forest about a four-hour drive from my little rented farmhouse in the Pennsylvania mountains. The monastery held various retreats throughout the year, and the only cost to attend was a donation, which fit my meager budget perfectly.

Tall conifers bordered three sides of the parking area. My hands squeezed the steering wheel until my knuckles turned white. "Don't be afraid," I whispered. "You've got to give this retreat your best shot." I mustered my courage, took a deep breath, and opened the car door.

A few inches of snow blanketed the ground. The afternoon sun cast its brilliance upon the sleeping forest which was wonderfully silent except for the soft crunches of my hikers. Small fir trees lined the long driveway. The crisp air and rich woodland scent invigorated me with each step. Up ahead two buildings with burnt-orange siding were nestled among trees and shrubbery. I headed for a wooden "OFFICE" sign tacked to the door of the smaller building.

No one answered my knock. I opened the door and immediately jerked backward. Inches from the doorway, a man dressed in orange robes and wearing an orange knit cap knelt on the floor, a power tool in his hand, a dust mask covering his nose and mouth. When he turned to face me, the soft, yet penetrating gaze of his Asian eyes held me still.

"Excuse me," I said. "I'm here for the retreat. I called and got permission to come a few days early."

The monk's eyes brightened. They were crystal clear, shining from the inside like diamonds. He pointed in the direction of the larger building directly across the road.

"Oh, okay. Thank you." I remained motionless. His eyes oozed serenity, and my whole being melted into the depths of his gaze. Time seemed to stop. At that moment, my only desire was to curl up inside those diamond eyes and become encased in a tranquil cocoon within them. There, I was certain I could rest in peace and contentment forever.

The monk turned back to his work. I headed across the driveway to the bigger building, shaking my head. I'd always imagined Buddhist monks as lofty, larger-than-life, super-spiritual beings who spent all day silently meditating inside grandiose temples or remote cave dwellings. I never imagined the first Buddhist monk I'd encounter as a dust-masked handyman on all fours. Climbing the short flight of stairs onto the porch of the building, I had a profound sense that even stranger encounters might be awaiting me in the days to come.

Beside the porch railing, a huge brass gong was suspended on an elaborately carved wooden frame with peeling red paint. A basket filled with flashlights and umbrellas was tucked in the far corner of the porch, and to the left of the front door was a small bench. My hand trembled with fear as I reached for the doorknob, somehow knowing that once I was inside, there was no turning back.

I entered a long, narrow hallway lined on the right side with windows—an old porch that had been enclosed. Beneath the windows, a row of low wooden benches spanned the length of the covered porch. To my left, beside a closed door, was a beverage area containing three electric urns and jars of instant coffee, packets of sugar, honey, and powdered creamer. The shelves above it were stacked with dozens of boxes offering a wide selection of teas, along with mugs of various sizes and colors. Several pairs of shoes and sandals lay beneath the bench closest to the door, so I figured I'd better remove my hikers.

Then I saw it—a big, black wood-burning stove set up on bricks in the middle of the porch. I had an affinity for wood burners; I was a country girl at heart, albeit a transplanted one. Born and raised in an urban, solidly middle-class Jewish neighborhood, I'd managed to escape the noise, crowds, dangers, and stresses of fast-paced city life twelve years ago, disappearing into the quiet peace of the countryside.

I'd always fantasized about living in the country. My husband, Mack, thought it was a pipe dream, that I'd never do it. But I was determined. About a year after we were married, when Mack began denigrating me for no apparent reason, it became clear our marriage was on a downward spiral and I needed to take action. One summer day, I came home and announced, "I've rented a farmhouse in the mountains seventy-five miles away. You can either come with me and we can try to make this marriage better out in the countryside, or you can stay here in Pittsburgh. But I'm going."

He was driving a cab at the time and probably figured it was safer and easier for him to tag along, despite the fact we'd be moving to a rural area with limited employment opportunities.

"Okay, I'm in," he'd said. "You Jews are a clever bunch. Your tribe knows how to make money. I'll bet on you, Lu. You won't let us starve."

And I didn't. We were surviving. Barely. The meager income from the cooking business I'd launched and ran out of my farmhouse kitchen supported us both, because for the past ten years Mack had flat out refused to get a job, claiming it was beneath him. He was nearing sixty years old, and his only "job," as he constantly reminded me, was his writing. Nothing else. Well, that and maybe the "job" of lashing out at me and the Jews. He seemed to find plenty of time for that.

Now, I crept closer to the stove. Oh, she was a beauty! A Cadillac compared to the corroding old clunker of a wood burner with broken grates I tended in my first rented farmhouse. I raised my hand a few inches above the stove. She was barely warm, and the temperature outside was below freezing. *Why isn't this baby cooking? She should be blazing hot on a day like today.*

The front door opened. A short man with a full gray beard walked in, took a mug from the shelf, and fixed himself a hot beverage. He sipped his drink while reading notices pinned to a large bulletin board on the wall beside the beverage counter. I approached him.

"Hi," I said.

"Hello."

Dressed in an oversized sweater, work boots, and stocking cap, his appearance and small stature reminded me of one of the seven dwarfs. He peered at a typed list tacked to the board, then turned to me. "Are you Margaret?"

"Uh, no."

Squinting, he moved closer to the paper. "Lori?"

"Yes, that's me." I tried to smile, but my jaw was too painful. He'd mispronounced my name, but I didn't care. Everybody did. I'd long ago given up correcting people, telling them my name was Laurie, rhymes with "sorry." Not Lori, that rhymes with "story."

He pointed to the list. "You're in the Women's Dorm. Room number 3."

"Okay." I waited for more instruction, but he was silent. Finally, he pointed to the closed door near the entrance. A large sign on the door read:

DO NOT WALK THROUGH THE KITCHEN

"The Women's Dorm is located on the other side of the kitchen. There's an entrance to it outside, so you can pull your car up and unload your things, then take your car back down to the parking lot."

"Okay," I repeated. "Will do."

The Women's Dorm was an addition to the main building, connected by a short hallway. It contained four bedrooms and one large bathroom. The rest of the monastery's accommodations were scattered around the grounds. I'd picked up a map of the property on my way out of the main building. *Kutis*—small shelters with no electricity or running water—were placed along various paths through the woods. They were furnished with low, hard beds, oil lamps, candles, a pee bucket, and either propane heaters or wood-burning stoves. There were also two large dormitory-style buildings at the top of the hill: Datta House for women and Janaka House for men. Fortunately, I was assigned a room adjacent to bathrooms and the main building, and close to the meditation hall, perhaps because I was the first retreatant to arrive. But unfortunately, I'd also be the first retreatant to leave.

"You'll have to skip the last day," Mack had insisted. "You need to be home on Monday to start cooking. We can't afford to lose a second week of income." I was annoyed about missing the final day of the retreat, but hoped my early arrival and participation in the monks' daily life would somehow make up for the lost day.

A friendly orange cat followed me in and out of the building as I unloaded my car. I'd brought my sleeping bag and a small suitcase packed with thermal underwear, several pairs of thick socks, slippers, three turtlenecks, two pairs of sweatpants and two sweatshirts, a fleece hat, half a dozen panties, toiletries, and an alarm clock. I'd read in the *Guidelines for Visitors* that the one essential item all retreatants should bring is an alarm clock because morning meditation started precisely at 5:30 a.m.

I'd received my copy of the *Guidelines* several weeks earlier. I'd decided not to tell Mack of my plans until a couple of days before I left for the retreat, afraid he'd erupt as he usually did when I dared to make a decision on my own. Each night, after Mack retired to his bedroom for the evening, I studied the monastery rules and protocols. Afterward, I placed the *Guidelines* booklet back in its hiding place under my mattress in case Mack came into my room to snoop around. We'd maintained separate bedrooms for close to ten years. Mack demanded absolute privacy, even while sleeping. And to my surprise, he also claimed he was no longer interested in sex, insisting he had to save all his vital energy for his writing.

As the retreat grew closer, I worried constantly. Could I rise before dawn? Would I be able to endure hours upon hours of silence and meditation? What if couldn't sit still? Would they ask me to leave? But most of all, I worried about breaking one of the monastery's long list of rules which spanned several pages in the *Guidelines for Visitors*. I was rebellious by nature—a notorious rulebreaker, or at least I used to be. In my youth, I balked at conventional norms, rejected mainstream America, and wasn't afraid to cross the line into forbidden territory. That was probably how I ended up living in a ramshackle rented farmhouse tucked away in the mountains of rural Pennsylvania and running a small cooking business that barely paid the bills, with no savings to mention.

Yet, despite my anxiety about attending the retreat, I was eager to spend some time away from Mack and his perpetual anger. When I finally told him of my plans, instead of throwing a fit, instead of railing against my stupid idea, or demanding I stay home, his response surprised me. "A silent Buddhist retreat, eh? Great idea, Lu. That's exactly the kind of self-discipline you need. Sit on your ass and keep your mouth shut all day long. It'll be good for both of us. You'll be out of my hair for a week, and when you find Nirvana, you'll come home with a smile on your face instead of that ugly gloomy Jewish mug I have to look at every day."

The cat followed me into room number 3. It circled the floor, purring and rubbing my leg while I unpacked. The sparsely furnished room contained two sets of bunk beds separated by a low table beneath a curtained window. A small closet contained a few folded blankets and two round meditation cushions. I chose the lower bunk, unrolled my sleeping bag, set my alarm clock on the table, collapsed onto the bed, and groaned. The thin mattress was hard as cement.

The cat jumped onto the bed and I stroked its soft fur. I loved animals. At home, I cared for seven outdoor cats, plus one big bruiser of a dog—my beloved, broad-chested Booter. I missed him already. I had to admit that at this point in my life, although I had a husband, a mother, a father, and a sister, the one living thing I loved most in the world was that big black dog.

I sat up and set the alarm for four thirty—plenty of time to wash up, have a cup of tea, and make it to morning meditation on time. Staring at the alarm clock, fear grabbed me by the throat. *I must be crazy. I'll never be able to wake up at four thirty every day, let alone sit still on a meditation cushion for hours.* Most mornings, I struggled to haul myself out of bed, and my previous attempts at meditation lasted barely ten minutes. Still, I supposed being here had to be better than being at home with Mack. Most days started with the same old argument. If I wasn't out of bed by 8 a.m., Mack barged into my room and gave me hell.

"What's wrong with you?" he'd shout. "You need to be up and at 'em by five sharp every single morning! You'll never accomplish anything worthwhile sulking in bed all day! Look at me. I'm at my desk every single morning by five thirty sharp. I should be your role model. I know what's good for you. Now get your goddamned lazy ass out of that bed!"

"Lazy?" I'd fire back. "And who do you think is keeping us afloat? Who's single-handedly running 'our' little vegetarian catering business? Who's doing all the menu planning, grocery shopping, cooking, delivering, cleanup, and general schlepping all by herself? Me, that's who! All you do is sit in your room all day and bang on your typewriter. What the hell do you have to complain about?"

"I don't know why I put up with the likes of you, your slothful behavior, and your incessant, loud-mouthed Jewish bullshit!" Then he'd storm out of my room and we wouldn't speak again until lunchtime.

The cat crawled into my lap. Tears welled in my eyes. Angry at myself for staying in a marriage that was destroying me, I dropped my head into my hands. I'd been on the verge of leaving dozens of times. We both routinely threatened to leave. I didn't know why I stayed. God knows I'd asked myself that question countless times, especially after our more horrific fights when I sat bawling on the edge of my single bed, my upper body rocking back and forth, crying to myself, "I can't *do* this anymore! I can't *do* this anymore!"

Consoled by the cat's warmth and gentle purr, I wiped my tears and figured I'd better freshen up. On my way to the bathroom, I noticed a sign near the front door. I gasped as I read it:

DO NOT ALLOW CATS INTO THIS BUILDING. CAT DANDER REMAINS LONG AFTER THE CAT IS GONE, AND IT WILL PREVENT PEOPLE WITH CAT ALLERGIES FROM USING THIS BUILDING. IF YOU SEE A CAT INDOORS, PLEASE PUT IT OUT GENTLY.

I hurried back to my room, scooped up the cat, and practically threw the poor thing out the front door. *Shit! I've only been here less than an hour, and already I've broken one of the rules!*

Unsure what to do next, I headed back to the main building. According to the Daily Schedule posted on the bulletin board, evening meditation would begin at five thirty. If nothing else, I could sit by the woodstove and drink a cup of tea until then.

On the covered porch, an elderly, dark-skinned monk sat on a high wooden chair facing the windows, drinking from a colorful mug. I recognized the elder monk immediately from the back cover of his books. It was Bhante B, the abbot of the monastery. I removed my shoes and stood stock still in the doorway, amazed and anxious that I was face to face with this most enlightened man.

He smiled a gleaming white-toothed smile that seemed to take up half his face. "Hello," he said.

"Hello, Bhante B." I managed a slight smile despite my stiff jaw.

"Have you been here before?" he asked.

"No, Bhante. This is my first time." The *Guidelines* instructions for addressing monks and nuns flashed in my mind, and I awkwardly brought my palms together at my chest.

"Ah, your first time here. Very good." The elder monk nodded. "Where are you from?"

His comforting gaze put me at ease. The wooden chair he sat on was the tallest among the short row of other similar chairs, the only seating facing the windows.

"I'm from Pennsylvania."

"Ah, Pennsylvania." His accent made it sound like Pennsyl-VAHH-nia. "Which direction?"

"The southwestern part of the state. I live out in the country, in the mountains." I always spoke this fact as though it were a badge of honor even though many people, including my own family, thought I was insane for choosing to live way out in the "hinterlands."

"That's not too far from here?"

"Not really. It only took me about four hours to get here."

Bhante B's questions and kind smile beckoned me. I approached the monk and sat in the wooden chair beside him, honored and excited that he wished to speak to me.

"You are here for the retreat?" The elder monk sipped his beverage.

"Yes. I wanted to come early because I have to miss the last day due to work obligations. The secretary gave me permission to arrive today as long as I helped with chores and followed the monastery rules." The air was chilly, and I rubbed my cold hands together.

"Ah, very good. And what is your name?"

"Laurie."

He chuckled.

I cringed. *Did I say something funny?*

"You know, in my country there are many, many Loris. You see them on the roads, carrying heavy things. The name Lori, it means *truck*." He chortled, eyes shining. "So maybe I should call you by a new name!"

Suddenly uncomfortable, I excused myself, moved to the low bench opposite him and stared out the window. I'd expected pearls of wisdom to flow from this wise man's lips. Instead, he was comparing me to a truck and laughing. In the awkward silence that followed, I focused on several chickadees pecking seeds at a birdfeeder hanging from a thick tree limb. I kept birdfeeders at home, and spent long, mesmerizing hours enjoying the birds' daily darts from tree branches to feeders. The flight of those lovely winged creatures never failed to brighten my mood, and their songs, sweet and comforting as a lullaby, somehow told me all was well.

Consoled by the chickadees at the feeders, I turned back in Bhante B's direction. A few feet above his head, a small sign was tacked to the wall. The words made me shudder:

THESE CHAIRS RESERVED FOR MONASTICS ONLY

A wave of nausea swept through me. In less than two hours since arriving at the monastery, I'd already broken not one, but now two rules! Things were not looking good.

3

The Great Hall

(Day 1, Evening)

Alone on the covered porch, I shivered, wishing someone would come along and throw wood on the fire. It was almost time for evening meditation. I glanced again at the clock in the adjacent room which served as a dining hall. The monks ate their meals seated on a platform spanning the right side of the large room. At the opposite end, near the kitchen, were rows of low benches and meditation cushions where everyone else ate. Only two meals a day, both vegetarian, were served at Bodhi Community, keeping with the Theravada Buddhist tradition that monks were not allowed to take food after noon. I didn't think I'd have a problem adhering to that rule because I wasn't normally a big eater.

The front door opened. A stocky figure entered, removing a black wool coat dusted with snow and a pair of rubber boots. It wasn't clear if this person was male or female, but he/she was middle-aged and dressed entirely in white—white trousers, white button-down shirt beneath a white sweatshirt, white socks, and a white fleece cap. As he/she passed slowly and solemnly by me, I noted the bright yellow badge pinned to the sweatshirt. The badge said:

THANK YOU FOR HELPING ME TO BE IN SILENCE

The figure disappeared around the corner. I glanced once more at the clock and followed behind. We entered a long, windowed corridor which led to the meditation hall. A sign on the wall said:

PLEASE WALK MINDFULLY AND WITH METTA

I'd learned from reading Buddhist books that "Metta" meant "loving-kindness." I slowed my pace, trying to walk mindfully, but I had no idea how to walk with loving-kindness. Halfway down the corridor I stopped before a window to admire the view. In the foreground, a large bronze Buddha statue sat on a lotus flower pedestal at the edge of an oval-shaped pond. Beyond the pond, a narrow path twisted its way through the woods, branching off in several directions. Bare tree limbs formed a canopy above the paths and the grounds, landscaped neatly with junipers, hollies, azaleas, rhododendron, and tall bamboo. The Buddha statue's eyes were painted white with black pupils. Wide open, they seemed to stare into the pond and beyond, silently presiding over the peaceful forest.

At the end of the corridor, a sign above a square wooden box said:

PLEASE HELP YOURSELF AND FOLD BLANKETS NEATLY
UPON RETURNING. WITH METTA

Another sign said:

MEN SIT ON THE LEFT. WOMEN SIT ON THE RIGHT.

Two large glass doors were open at the entrance to the meditation hall. Standing in the doorway, I prepared myself for the long meditation period ahead: *Just sit still, stay quiet, and do your best.* The peach and rose colors of twilight shone through the windows lining the right side of the great hall, illumined only by the glow of a solitary candle on a high altar draped with a printed tapestry. Vases of fresh flowers adorned either side of the altar. High above it, tucked in an alcove in front of a tall green and white stained-glass window, was a giant, golden Buddha statue seated in the full lotus pose. Looming high and majestic above the carpeted floor, the Buddha's larger-than-life presence and serene smile commanded my attention. His figure was imposing yet benign, fascinating, and somehow reassuring.

Below the altar I recognized the shadowed outline of Bhante B sitting cross-legged on a cushion facing the center aisle that separated the men and women. I walked down the aisle and chose a cushion in the third row, behind the person dressed in white, obviously a woman. I counted about half a dozen men seated on cushions on the left side of the hall. Half wore robes and knit caps on top of what appeared to be shaved heads. The others were dressed in jeans or sweatpants and heavy sweaters. Carefully, I arranged myself on the hard cushion as quietly as I could, crossed my legs, placed my hands in my lap, and inspected the great hall.

The high vaulted ceiling, arched beams, golden oak walls, and stained-glass window infused the large room with churchlike awe. But it was the presence of the giant Buddha statue high above that filled the magnificent hall with a tranquility that seeped into my bones.

I kept waiting for some signal, but all was quiet. If I leaned to my right, I could see a lighted digital clock which I was sure I'd want to consult as time passed. Evening meditation was scheduled to last for one hour. *Can I make it?* I'd never meditated that long before, but I'd try. I'd concluded weeks ago that in order to get any benefit from this retreat, I'd commit to do every single thing I was asked to do; I'd follow the strict schedule, meditate for hours, eat only two meals a day, keep silent, get up at four in the morning, whatever it took.

When the meditation session ended, nothing much had happened except that I was chilled to the bone. *Next time I'll have to remember to borrow one of the blankets from the wooden box.* On the covered porch, I headed straight for the woodstove and practically wrapped myself around it. But the heat emanating from the stove was faint. My instinct told me to grab a log and feed the fire, but I didn't dare break another rule. A sign above the stove stated:

DO NOT TOUCH THE WOODSTOVE. ONLY PEOPLE ASSIGNED THE JOB OF STOVEMASTER ARE TO OPERATE THE WOODSTOVE.

Just then, a tall man with neatly trimmed gray hair came walking toward me from the direction of the meditation hall. He wore aviator glasses, khaki pants, and a button-down blue flannel shirt, and carried a thick book and spiral notebook. He was slender with broad shoulders; well-built for his age, which I guessed to be in the mid-fifties. He took a seat opposite the stove, opened the book, placed the notebook on the bench beside him, and started reading. Every so often, he took a pen from his breast pocket and jotted something in the notebook. The man's face was ruggedly handsome, the deep creases in his forehead and around his eyes suggesting he'd experienced plenty of life's hardships. Totally absorbed in his studies, he didn't acknowledge me. Yet there was something about his presence that drew me in, and I sat down beside him.

The woman dressed entirely in white appeared around the corner, heading toward us. Her gray hair was cropped short, barely visible beneath her white cap. She shot me a disapproving glance as she passed by on her way to the beverage area. The *Guidelines* mentioned that Theravada monks were forbidden to touch women. I wasn't sure if I was breaking a rule by sitting too close to a man, so I joined the woman at the other end of the porch. She'd taken off the yellow badge, so maybe now I could speak to her. I assumed talking was permitted since the silent retreat hadn't formally started.

She introduced herself as Polly, one of the residents. She was plump, with pudgy, rosy cheeks and alert gray eyes behind her round, wire-rimmed glasses.

"Did you get in all right?" she asked.

"Yes. Thank you." I selected a blue mug from the shelf and scanned the vast selection of teas.

Polly reached through a curtained shelving unit beneath the bulletin board. "Here." She handed me a roll of masking tape and a thick black marker. "Write your name on your mug, and use this mug during your stay here. You're responsible for keeping this mug clean. The dishwashers have enough work to do."

She then launched into an explanation of the monastery's daily schedule and routine. The high, muted quality of her voice, along with her brusque manner, reminded me of a spinster schoolmarm. "Morning meditation begins precisely at five thirty. Please don't be late. It disturbs the other meditators. Breakfast is served in the dining hall at seven. Please make sure to fix your beverage and be seated before the monks make their procession to the kitchen. Never, ever walk across the dining hall when the monks are taking their meals. Puja starts at eight thirty in the meditation hall. We ask that you observe Noble Silence from the time you awaken until after puja. Lunch is served at eleven fifteen. Evening meditation begins at five thirty, and afterward we usually have some type of program, such as Pali class or a book report. Otherwise, you can fill your time here as you wish. You'll have plenty of time for meditation, and we ask that if you are the last one to leave the meditation hall, please extinguish the candle. We also have a large library you're welcome to use. And we do ask that you help out with some basic chores while you're here. There are lots of breakfast and lunch dishes to wash, but there are other jobs too. You'll have to ask Bhante Ganda about them. He's in charge this month of assigning jobs." She smiled.

"Okay. I understand. And I'll be happy to help wash dishes. Actually, that's a job I'm pretty familiar with. I run a little vegetarian catering business. And I teach cooking classes." I ripped off a piece of tape, placed it on my mug, and wrote "Laurie" on the tape. Then I thought, *Maybe I should write "Truck" instead.*

"Oh, a professional vegetarian cook!" Polly squealed. "Maybe you could show me a few tricks in the kitchen if you have time. I'll be cooking for the first half of the retreat. Getting meals together during retreats is a huge job around here. Especially during the large retreats when we have over sixty mouths to feed."

"Wow. That's certainly a lot of cooking for one person. If you need extra hands, I'll be glad to help." I took a box of chamomile from the shelf and prepared my tea.

"It shouldn't be too bad for this retreat. We have about forty people registered. I'm cooking for the first three days, and Charles, our other cook, will be taking the last three days. We've found it's easier on both of us that way. In the past, either he or I cooked for the entire retreat, and we discovered that was one sure way to get burned out." Polly let out a high, delighted chuckle.

"And is Charles an experienced cook?"

"He does a fine job. He's that man sitting over there by the stove." We both turned around, but Charles was gone. "Well, he was sitting there a minute ago. He seems to have disappeared."

"Listen, Polly, I'll be happy to help both of you in the kitchen. I know we're supposed to volunteer for a job while we're here on retreat."

Polly's expression hardened. "As much as I'd appreciate your help in the kitchen, I'd suggest that you volunteer for a job that has nothing to do with cooking. We have many other jobs to choose from. A retreat is a good time to get away from all the things you normally do in your daily life. I believe that if you stay away from the kitchen, it will help your concentration, and bring freshness to your meditation."

Polly was right. The idea of chopping mounds of vegetables, stirring stockpots of soup and beans, and spending hours in front of a hot stove seemed not only counterproductive, but also crazy. I was here on retreat trying to find some peace and contentment, not duplicate my usual routine.

"Thanks for the advice, Polly. Actually, it will be a relief to stay out of the kitchen. Maybe I should volunteer for a job that's the complete opposite of feeding people." I giggled to myself, wondering if I could sign up to clean the toilets!

4

Fears and Doubts

(Day 2)

The shrill, static beeping of the alarm clock awakened me. I'd slept badly. The rigid mattress hurt my back, the pillow was too soft, and despite piling extra blankets on top of my sleeping bag, I couldn't stop shivering.

Groggy with sleep, I hauled myself up and headed to the bathroom. Last night before bed, I'd made it a point to read every single sign posted in the Women's Dorm. The bathroom was plastered with instruction. The sign on the door to the toilet stall said:

TO KEEP FROM OVERLOADING THE DELICATE SEPTIC SYSTEM, FOR LIQUID WASTE, PLEASE PUT PAPER IN BIN AND DO NOT FLUSH TOILET. FLUSH FOR SOLID WASTE ONLY.

On top of the toilet tank were several books of matches, and above it was another printed request:

PLEASE STRIKE A MATCH TO REMOVE ODOR. BE SURE IT'S
COOL BEFORE DISPOSING IN THE BIN.

After washing my face, I couldn't ignore the sign that said:

PLEASE DRY THE SINK THOROUGHLY AFTER USING IT.

"Okay, okay. I get ordered around enough at home! Here, too?" The sound of my own voice startled me. *Oh, shit!* Polly said we were supposed to keep Noble Silence from the time we awakened until after puja, so technically, I'd broken another rule. Fortunately, no one had heard me because that morning I was the only person staying in the Women's Dorm. Polly lived in her own kuti at the top of the hill.

My limbs trembled. *Oh God, I'm screwing up right and left!* Not only had I broken Noble Silence, but after I peed, I'd flushed the toilet out of habit. My temples throbbed, and I rubbed my aching jaw. When I admitted to myself that I didn't even know what puja was, I thought I might cry. I bit my lip, then set my sights on sipping a hot cup of tea on the covered porch. That simple pleasure would surely warm me up and soothe my nerves.

Charles was the only person on the covered porch. He sat directly in front of the woodstove, reading. I placed my slippers under a bench and brewed a cup of green tea. Despite my thick socks, my feet were freezing, my toes like icicles. Wrapping both hands around the mug, I brought it to my lips, took a sip, and winced. The water was barely warm. *Shit. Everything is going wrong! I can't even get a hot cup of tea in this icebox of a place!*

My heart raced as I doubted this whole crazy idea. *Oh, why did I even come here?* I must have been mad to think that attending a retreat at a strict Buddhist monastery where I'd meditate for hours at a time, eat only two meals a day, and not speak a word to anyone might somehow change my life for the better. Was I merely running away from an unbearable situation at home, grasping at straws because nothing else in my life was working? I hung my head. I didn't belong here. I was a tourist without a map in a foreign country. Although I no longer practiced, I was a Jew, not a Buddhist. Judaism was my heritage. I'd grown up in a household where my mother lit Shabbos candles every Friday night. Our family ate brisket, bagels, and chopped liver. I attended Sunday school and learned about the Torah. I fasted on Yom Kippur, sang Hebrew hymns and recited psalms during Temple services, and when I had a personal problem, I spoke to the rabbi. My grandmother would turn over in her grave if she learned I was seeking solace at a Buddhist monastery and practicing spiritual teachings led by robed monks with shaved heads instead of consulting a wise rabbi wearing a yarmulke.

Fighting back tears, I wished I'd never picked up the monastery brochure at the coffee shop and gotten the idea in my head to come here. I wished I was back home taking a long walk down my favorite country lane with my beloved Booter, inhaling the fresh, clean air of Somerset County.

I glanced at Charles. If he were "stovemaster" maybe he'd stoked the fire, and at least I'd soon be warm. I placed my mug on the windowsill and ambled over to a glass-enclosed bulletin board hanging on the wall near the front door. Inside the glass were headshot photos; the top two rows were photos of the monks and residents, and the bottom two rows portrayed the monastery's board members.

There was Bhante B's smiling face on the top row above the longer version of his name, Bhante Bhisamulaladayaka, which I didn't even attempt to pronounce, and his title, Abbot. No wonder everyone called him Bhante B. The monk in the headshot beside him had a long, oval face, hollow cheeks, and large, protruding eyes. He was Bhante Upali, Vice Abbot, who was scheduled to lead the retreat. Another monk, whose skin was darker than Bhante B's, was Bhante Sabbakittika.

Among the photos of the residents, I spotted Polly and Barry—the man who resembled one of the seven dwarfs. Beside Barry's headshot was a photo of Charles. He had an impish grin and a twinkle in his eyes as though he knew a privileged secret.

The front door opened. Along with a burst of cold air, in came Polly wearing a headlamp strapped to her forehead. She wiped a dusting of snow from her jacket and boots, then gave me a smile. I wanted to smile back and say, "Good morning," but smiling hurt my jaw, so I just nodded, remembering to keep Noble Silence.

Soon a young man wearing a thick down jacket and ski cap entered the room. In slow motion, he removed his cap, jacket, and boots. He was thin and dressed in jeans and a heavy flannel shirt, with unruly shoulder-length dark hair and dark-framed glasses. Inside the glass case, I found Pete, a resident. He passed me as though I didn't exist, walked toward the stove, briefly warmed his hands, and disappeared around the corner toward the meditation hall. Polly followed him with slow, exaggerated steps.

Charles and I were now alone on the porch. Engrossed in his book, he seemed unaware of my presence. I glanced at the clock in the dining hall. Fifteen more minutes to go before meditation started. I approached the woodstove and held out my hands. The tiniest bit of heat radiated through my frozen fingertips. *Why isn't anyone tending this stove on such a frigid morning?*

"Good morning," a cheery voice chimed.

I turned around. Careful not to break the rules again, I hesitated to respond. But there was something compelling in the tone of Charles's voice; something so playful, warm, and inviting I simply couldn't resist speaking to him. Besides, no one was around.

"Good morning," I said.

"Are you here for the retreat?"

I noted the ocean-blue color of his eyes. "Yes, I am. I just happened to come early."

He nodded and went back to his book.

"I thought we weren't supposed to talk," I said in a hushed voice.

"We're not." He chuckled, his eyes creasing at the corners. "But I've never been very good at following the rules."

I liked him right away. Suppressing giggles, I blurted out, "Neither have I!"

Halfway down the corridor on my way to the meditation hall, I stopped short. Several feet ahead of me, the figure of a tall, slim monk stood in the doorway of the library. He removed an orange knit cap from his shaved oval head, and was about to enter the corridor. I recognized Bhante Upali from his headshot. According to the *Guidelines,* when crossing paths with a monk, you were instructed to stop and let the monk proceed ahead of you. I waited until the monk's skeletal figure entered the corridor ahead of me, and watched him walk with slow, solemn, barefoot steps toward the great hall.

With equally slow steps, I followed several yards behind Bhante Upali. The monk walked lightly but purposefully down the center aisle of the majestic candlelit hall. He paused beside the aisle cushion in the first row on the men's side and remained standing, tall and straight, gazing up at the golden Buddha statue. When I reached my cushion in the third row on the women's side, I remained standing as he did. I watched him gently drop to his knees and gracefully prostrate himself toward the altar three times. His every movement and entire being exuded the manner of a true contemplative. In awe, I followed his lead, feeling just as awkward and uncomfortable bowing three times to the Buddha as I had the night before.

I couldn't tear my eyes away from Bhante Upali. An aura of deep spirituality and reverence surrounded him. His devotion was palpable in the way he seated himself on his cushion, arranged his legs, adjusted his robes. He sat perfectly still, his back straight, ears in line with his shoulders, hands folded in his lap, thumbs touching.

I meticulously copied his posture, then closed my eyes. But it wasn't long before I opened them again to peek at the digital clock. *Oh God, only fifteen minutes have passed!* I could have sworn I'd been sitting on that hard cushion for half an hour. A chill shot up my spine. *Damn it! I forgot to grab a blanket from the box!*

I tried not to fidget, but my knees, ankles, and buttocks were growing more uncomfortable by the minute. Instead of meditating, I kept checking the clock or staring at the stained-glass design in the window directly behind the Buddha. The image was a large green leaf with a pointed tip. Although I could identify most common trees by their leaves, I'd never seen this leaf before. Could it be a Bodhi leaf? A Buddhist symbol for enlightenment?

A long time later, the muffled tones of the gong outside being struck three times echoed inside the hall. Grateful, I uncrossed my legs. Bhante B's soft voice mumbled something in a foreign language. I could barely hear the translation that followed. Something about "wisdom" and "concentration." Everyone rose to their knees and bowed three times to the Buddha statue. Then we all remained still and silent during the monks' slow, single-file procession out of the hall.

After breakfast I headed to the library and browsed the section containing contemporary Buddhist publications. Many of the authors were Jewish. The names Kornfield, Epstein, Saltzman, Goldstein, Levine, Boorstein, and Flickstein all jumped out at me from the shelves. It made me wonder: *Is there something in our Judaic religious background that somehow failed us, causing us to look toward the East*

for spiritual fulfillment?

Charles entered the library, plucked a book from the shelf, and sat down at a long table. I went over and sat beside him. "Excuse me, Charles, can I ask you a question?"

He turned to face me. "Certainly."

"I was just wondering . . . would it be possible for me to borrow a book to read in my room during the retreat? I was hoping to learn more about the Buddha's teachings and make notes during the retreat, but according to the *Guidelines,* that's not allowed." My eyes probed his. "I mean, I just thought I'd ask. You know, in case the rules might have changed."

He gave me a sly grin and closed his book. "Technically, reading and writing are discouraged during retreats. But many people do, so it's not a problem as long as you're discreet."

"Oh. So you're saying it's okay to bend the rules a bit?"

"Why not? Sometimes bending the rules is exactly what's needed around here in order to move forward. If you feel it will enhance your retreat experience, borrow whatever books you like, and have at it!" He smiled.

Compared to the many fleeting, obligatory smiles I'd seen flashed both inside and outside the monastery, Charles's smile was different: It was real. And it was refreshing.

"Wow. That's great news, Charles. Thank you!" Now I didn't have to worry about breaking another rule. I had permission!

"Borrow any book you'd like. Just sign your name in the register and write down the title of the book and the date. Just remember to return the book to the library at the end of the retreat."

"Oh, of course I will. I'll return it before then. I have to leave early. I really don't want to miss the last day of the retreat, but I have to work."

"What type of work do you do?"

"I'm a vegetarian cook. I run my own business. I have regular customers I cook for each week. Some have special dietary needs."

"Sounds like a wonderful way to earn your living. What prompted you to start your own business?"

"Oh, it's a long story." I wanted to tell him that although I had a college degree, I had no interest in climbing the corporate ladder. I wanted to tell him that I abhorred the idea of slaving my days away in some dull, fluorescent-lit, soul-sucking office cubicle working for a company that cared more about profits than it cared about me. I wanted to tell him that I'd always valued my freedom, that I'd decided to pursue meaningful, enjoyable work of my own choosing and was willing to make the sacrifices and accept the tradeoffs that usually came with surviving on one's own terms. But instead, I said, "Well, it's nice being your own boss. And I really do enjoy feeding people healthy, tasty food."

"Running your own business can be difficult and challenging. You must be quite a capable woman."

Blood rushed to my cheeks. At home, all I received were criticisms and complaints, never compliments. I didn't know what to say. After a decade of loneliness and isolation, maybe I'd finally found a friend. I had no real friends back home, no social circles, and zero support. Mack had seen to that. He'd managed over the years to chase away any person with whom I'd make a close connection.

"You'd better be careful." Charles laughed. "Vegetarian cooks are highly prized around here. If Bhante B or Bhante Upali find out you're a professional vegetarian cook, they might not let you leave!"

For an instant, I wondered what that might be like. Absorbed by his gentle blue eyes, I managed a half-smile despite my aching jaw. *Hmmm, maybe coming on this retreat wasn't such a bad idea after all.*

5

Smoke Alarm

(Day 3)

At 4 a.m. I groaned and turned over in bed, dreading the hour of sitting on my hard cushion before dawn. Once inside the meditation hall, despite my diligent efforts, I could not stop my racing thoughts, daydreams, and fantasies. All that happened during that hour was at various times my legs, knees, or back would hurt, and I'd have to shift positions. Still, there were two bright spots: I wasn't cold because I'd remembered to take a blanket from the box, and the echoing, fading tones of the gong ending the session soothed me like a warm bath on a frigid winter day. Before leaving the great hall, completely comfortable and without thinking, I was on my knees along with everyone else in the hall, bowing three times to the golden Buddha seated high atop the altar.

After breakfast, I helped Polly at a large three-tub sink below shelves of drying racks in the dishwashing room adjacent to the kitchen. Barry entered clutching a broom, followed by Pete. Instead of his usual jeans and flannel shirt, Pete wore a long-sleeved white shirt and baggy white pants, his usual black ski cap covering his head.

"Hey, Pete," Barry said, "show Laurie the new hairdo!"

Pete laughed. "You mean the new hair-*don't*." With a flourish, he removed the ski cap. I gasped. Pete's long, wavy locks were gone! I'd overheard some talk the day before of the ceremony being held for Pete. He'd become a Samanera, or monk in training.

Shocked, I stared at his shiny freshly shaved head. "My God, Pete, I barely recognize you. Do you feel any different?"

He chuckled. "Yeah. I feel bald."

"Better get used to it," Barry kidded.

Polly dipped a soapy plate into the rinse water. "Did you need something from the kitchen, Pete?"

"Oh, yeah. Bhante B asked me to pack up some of his special food to take on his teaching trip to Costa Rica. He said you'd know where we keep the snacks reserved for him. You know, the special ones he really likes."

Bhante B's request seemed odd. I'd read that Buddhist monks were supposed to rein in their desires, ask for nothing, take only what was offered to them, and own only their robes and begging bowls. Yet Bhante B was requesting his specially reserved snacks. I'd also read that Buddhist monks lived the simplest and barest of lives, yet I saw no evidence of that at Bodhi Community. The kitchen cupboards, pantries, refrigerators, and freezers were abundant with foodstuffs. Dozens of bottles of expensive nutritional supplements were available on the breakfast and lunch tables. The library shelves were overflowing with books, magazines, and various periodicals. Each monk had a computer, and their needs and desires were catered to by a constant stream of guests and residents coming to the monastery for different lengths of stay.

It was obvious the monks at Bodhi lived a pretty comfortable life.

And in my mind, they had a big advantage: they didn't have to work for wages, drive in traffic, take care of a family, pay bills, or handle the emotional ups and downs of marriage or romantic relationships like everyone else. Some of the monks even traveled for free all over the world. They were guaranteed a roof over their heads for life, paid health insurance, and food in their tummies, even though it was only two meals a day.

When the kitchen was finally clean and the floor mopped, I put on my hikers, coat, and hat, eager to take a walk and explore my new environment. At home I walked every day, no matter the weather. It was my one and only pleasure. When I sauntered up and down narrow country lanes, my mind relaxed and merged with the natural world and I escaped my misery. At the end of Bodhi's driveway, I turned right onto Winding Creek Road. It was flat—an easy jaunt compared to the steep hills I was used to back home. The road paralleled a wide creek that meandered in gentle curves. Beyond the creek, spacious fields dotted with snow separated a few large farmhouses tucked among the distant tree line. All at once, the flowing creek, rocks, fields, trees, and expansive sky appeared incredibly vibrant, surreal, and inviting as a lover welcoming me into a wonderful new world—a world filled with light, beauty, and enormous possibility.

Fluffy snowflakes tickled my cheeks as they drifted lazily from the gray sky. My lungs inhaled deep breaths of crisp air, and my nostrils recognized the faint smell of wood smoke. Several inches of snow had fallen since my arrival. I was glad I'd stashed my fleece-lined, rubber-bottomed snow boots in the trunk of my car just in case the weather turned really bad, which I'd learned from experience could happen at any moment in the mountains.

Up ahead, a group of about half a dozen horses grazed inside a fenced pasture. Small patches of green were visible where their hooves had scraped the snow away, and a half-eaten round hay bale rested in the middle of the field.

I tiptoed toward the edge of the road. In a soft voice, I greeted a chocolate-colored horse with a tangled mane standing close to the fence. "Well, hello there, my friend. Aren't you a handsome one!" The horse raised his head and stared at me with dark, glassy eyes. I inched closer to the barbed wire fence, hoping to touch his velvet muzzle. Slowly, I raised my hand, but no. He backed away, afraid.

"It's okay," I whispered. "I'll come back tomorrow and we can try again."

Breathing hard, I climbed the wooden steps onto the porch of the main building and brushed the snow from my coat and hat. I'd quickened my pace on the walk back to the monastery, and my skin was damp and sticky beneath my thermal shirt. Before going inside, I plopped onto the bench to catch my breath. The huge brass gong beside the porch railing drew my attention like a magnet. Studying its perfectly round shape suspended on its frame by two thick wires, I relived the soothing effect the gong's long, echoing tones had on me that morning as each vibration faded into nothingness. My thoughts had faded away as well, and my entire being was bathed in peace.

I heaved a long sigh. A mallet with a wooden handle rested on the railing beside the gong. The rubber head of the mallet was twice the size of my fist. I tried to imagine what sorts of sensations I might experience if I were to grasp the handle and strike that big brass gong dead-center. Would the resounding vibrations circulate throughout my entire body? Oh, the thought of it gave me goosebumps!

I sat upright and watched snowflakes floating down from the sky like puffy white specks of cotton. Then my thoughts turned to the one thing I came here to forget—Mack. It was on a snowy winter day like this when I first met him at the local laundromat. I was an adventurous twenty-one-year-old college student living in Boston, and Mack lived in the apartment building across the street. I used to spy on him from my bedroom window each evening when he sat on the stoop of his building holding court, drinking beer with the college kids and railing against the system.

Back then, Mack was the proverbial salmon swimming upstream. He was a maverick, a rebel battling the status quo, mocking the establishment and giving the finger to the elites and wealthy corporations. He was also educated and well-read. He could quote Plato, Dr. Johnson, Hemingway, Shakespeare, and Donne. Not long before I met him, he'd divorced, quit his suit and tie job in the suburbs, and started driving a cab. He claimed he'd dropped out of mainstream society in order to have the freedom to pursue his passion for creative writing. Mack lived on the edges—exciting, alluring places I'd never known—and once I met him, he quickly assumed the role of mentor. I was young, a rebel myself, enthralled by his passionate intensity, raw determination, and artistic creativity. He became my hero, and I fell in love with him. Back then I couldn't wait to read what he'd written. Later on, I typed his stories for him. I made copies and organized his manuscripts. I wrote letters on his behalf, researched literary markets, and sent his manuscripts off to agents and editors. He refused to do such mundane, secretarial work himself.

But after we were married, everything changed. Mack grew increasingly hostile, bitter, and reclusive. He became obsessed with what he called his "life's work," shutting himself away in his room for hours on end either banging feverishly on his big old manual typewriter or listening to white supremacist broadcasts on the shortwave radio. He withdrew from the world and from me, demanding his "privacy," declaring he must "sacrifice all" for his precious writing. Mack lived in his own little world where he was the "undiscovered literary genius" and everyone else was his inferior. And he didn't hesitate to abuse or berate his lowly subordinates with vicious snipes, insults, and caustic remarks. Sadly, I was the closest subordinate to berate. Later, his wrath came to include the entire Jewish race.

Now, almost twenty years had passed since the day I met him in the laundromat, and instead of being my hero, Mack had become my mortal enemy. Instead of insightful, humorous short stories, pages of gibberish were piling up in his room. For several years now, I couldn't avoid asking myself the question: Was Mack truly the reclusive, misunderstood literary genius he claimed to be, or was he simply a cruel, raving, anti-Semitic maniac?

I shivered. Worried I might cry, I hauled myself up off the bench, entered the main building, brewed a cup of lukewarm peppermint tea, and sat opposite the woodstove hoping to soak up any faint heat it might offer. Charles, wearing a thick gray sweater, sat not far away, reading as usual.

Alone on the covered porch, we sat in silence. I finished my tea, set the mug on the windowsill, and blew on my cupped hands. My fingers were so numb I thought they'd fall off. I stood up, peered through the glass front door of the stove, and sighed. There was barely a glow inside the firebox. I turned to Charles. "Do you know anything about how this stove works?"

"Not much," he said.

"Isn't someone supposed to be tending it?"

"Yes, I think so."

"Well, it's freezing in here."

"It certainly is."

Obviously, Charles wasn't going to help me. I wanted to strangle this mysterious stovemaster who, for some insane reason, insisted on keeping the temperature of this building like the inside of a refrigerator! I couldn't stand it anymore. If I wanted heat, I was going to have to stoke the fire myself. I studied the large metal firebox, the knobs and levers above and below the glass front door. There was another door on the side facing the woodpile, and below this door were a few more levers, plus there was a damper in the middle of the flue connecting the stove to the chimney. It looked complex, but I'd tended several farm-house woodstoves quite successfully in the past. Hell, I'd even fired a coal stove one winter. I knew what I was doing. Surely, I could heat this baby up quickly, and no one would ever know.

I glanced toward the front door, then back at Charles. "Well, I'm going to get us some heat." I selected a medium-sized split log from the woodpile, opened the side door, grabbed a poker that was leaning against the wall, poked the bed a few times until it glowed red, placed the log on top, and shut the door. Immediately, gray smoke billowed out the sides of the metal box. *Shit!*

I opened the door again and the smoke stopped. I poked and prod-ded the log, turned a knob, pulled a lever, and then closed the door again. A second later the smoke returned, seeping out the crevices of the stove and filling the room like a toxic cloud. My heart banged against my chest. *What did I do wrong? Damn it!* I was in big trouble now! I turned to Charles for help, but he was gone, his fleeing figure vanishing around the corner at the end of the hall.

My instincts told me to run—leave the scene of the crime. Panicked, I followed Charles and found him in the library. My heart pounded like a jackhammer. I shut the library door, hurried over to the magazine rack, and buried my head in a copy of *Tricycle*. *Shit, shit, shit!* I'd really screwed up this time. Plus, I'd broken another rule. I never should have touched the stove, because I was not assigned the job of stovemaster. I was certain to be reprimanded, maybe even asked to leave, if they found out it had been me.

I tiptoed over to Charles and whispered, "You won't tell anybody I did that, will you, Charles?"

Grinning with delight, he closed his book. "Of course not! Rarely does someone show up here who's willing to shake things up a bit. Don't worry. Your secret's safe with me!"

I heaved a sigh of relief. My hand cupped his shoulder in gratitude. "Thank you, Charles. You're a lifesaver."

6

The Vibrancy of Chant

(Day 4)

At 4:45 a.m., I was perched on the low bench in the semi-darkness of the covered porch sipping a cup of tea that was, to my great delight, piping hot. Darkness filled the windows. The palpable, pre-dawn stillness seeped into my blood and my bones. I welcomed its peaceful presence.

When the clock in the dining hall reached 5:20, I rose, walked down the long corridor, and paused just inside the glass double doors at the entrance to the meditation hall. The soft glow of the solitary candle on the altar infused the lofty hall with mystical tranquility; the expansive presence of the giant Buddha statue radiated benevolence, his subtle smile hinting the possibility of awakening.

Standing motionless beside my cushion, I gazed at the golden Buddha's serene face. Silently, I asked for his guidance. *Dear Buddha, could you please help me discover your special secret for myself?* I dropped to my knees, bowed three times, settled onto my cushion, crossed my legs, closed my eyes, and didn't open them again until the reverberating tones of the gong being struck three times filled the great hall.

The usual vegetarian breakfast buffet consisted of hot and cold cereals, stewed fruit, toast, yogurt, nut butters and jelly, nuts and seeds, and fresh fruit. At home I was a habitual breakfast skipper, but because the monastery served only two meals per day, the last one ending just before noon, I figured I'd better eat a hearty breakfast. Afterwards, I jumped on the dishwashing with Polly. We worked side by side at the three-tubbed sink, while Charles scrubbed the bigger pots at a separate single sink on the opposite wall.

"Well, looks like that's it," Polly said, taking off her rubber gloves. "I'll go get the mop and bucket."

I was surprised. Polly actually spoke to me despite her clear instruction to keep Noble Silence until after puja. Maybe the monastery rules weren't as rigid as I'd imagined.

My hand dove into the water and unplugged the stoppers to drain the sinks. Charles grabbed a broom from the corner and started sweeping the floor. He seemed distant, intent upon his work. Earlier, Polly told me that Charles had been a resident for quite a long time. Why would a handsome, intelligent, distinguished-looking man of his age choose to live and work at a Buddhist monastery at this time of his life? Did he have no family? Was he retired and independently wealthy? Was he considering becoming a monk? *Well,* I thought, *if Polly can speak and break Noble Silence, so can I.*

I dried my hands on a dishtowel and turned around. "So, Charles, how long have you been living here?"

Without looking at me, he said, "Oh, on and off now, about three years."

"Wow. That's a pretty long time."

"Yes, it is."

40

I'd planned to ask him more—about his reasons for coming here, for staying here, and if living here had deepened him spiritually or changed his life in any way, but I sensed he didn't want to talk about the monastery, so I changed the subject.

"And where do you come from, Charles?" I asked. "Where do you call home?"

Perplexed, the motions of the broom stopped abruptly. Then his playful smile emerged. With a raised brow and swift wave of his hand, he said, "Oh, Bimini. The islands."

"Oooh, wow. That sounds exotic."

Half an hour later we were all back in the meditation hall for puja. This devotional service was chanted in Pali, the ancient language of Theravada Buddhism. I followed along silently, staring at the strange-looking words printed in the big book titled *Bodhi Vandana*. Some of the words were repeated so often, they were becoming familiar:

NAMO TASSA BHAGAVATO ARAHATO
SAMMASAMBUDDHASSA

Although I'd read and listened to these ancient, foreign words several times now, I hadn't had the nerve to chant them aloud. When I was younger, I loved to sing. I'd sung in school choirs and musicals, but I'd never chanted before.

My attention was drawn to the small woman dressed in white robes seated on a cushion in the front row. Her name was Machee Nee, a nun visiting from Thailand. Besides Polly, she was the only other woman living at the monastery, occupying a small kuti at the top of the hill. Machee Nee chanted in a clear, resonant voice, the foreign words flowing like swift water from her lips.

On the men's side, Bhante Upali's voice, exactly on pitch, rang out confidently, leading the others. I ached to join the chorus, but inexplicable fear, combined with my sore jaw, prevented me from trying. Bhante Upali's deep, resonant voice filled the hall with magnetic energy. Captivated, I zeroed in on a distinct vibration within the monk's voice. Spontaneously, my lips parted, and I chanted: "Dutiyam pi Buddham saranam gacchami."

Suddenly, it was as though I existed somewhere outside my body hearing my own clear-toned voice project sounds emanating from a mysterious place deep inside me. My head became hollow like a flute, and the ancient words I chanted were the breaths blown into the instrument. Delightful sensations coursed throughout my entire body, and I didn't hold back. Following Bhante Upali's lead, the Pali words now rolled easily off my tongue.

"Panatipata veramani-sikkhapadam samadiyami," I chanted in a strong voice, my eyes glued to the printed page.

When the puja ceremony ended, my head was numb; my mind empty, yet clear and alert; my body light and relaxed, as though relieved of a heavy burden. Outside the windows, the new day announced herself in subtle hues of peach, orange, and gold. Transfixed, I gazed at the golden Buddha with a combination of curiosity, reverence, and gratitude. From that time on, my time at the monastery took on a different quality.

After lunch, I was so cold I had to take action. I'd been keeping an eye on the woodstove, waiting for this nonexistent stovemaster to show up, but the fire remained unattended. Polly had informed me that if I had a question, or wanted to speak to one of the monks privately, the best time to do this was after the meal, while the monks were drying their large begging bowls. She explained that the proper way to approach a monk at this time was to walk slowly toward the platform, kneel, and with palms pressed together, quietly ask my question.

My heart pounded wildly at the thought of approaching Bhante Upali. How could I come to this wise, holy man with my selfish request? But I had to speak up; I was freezing. I waited until Bhante Upali was drying his begging bowl with an orange towel. Then I took several deep breaths, and rose from my cushion. Several feet from the platform, I dropped to my knees in front of the monk. With palms pressed together, I said, "Excuse me, Bhante."

His bulging eyes held me fast. I was surprised by the large size of his ears. They were almost as big and droopy as the ears on some of the Buddha statues placed around the monastery. For a few moments, I couldn't speak.

"Did you want to ask me something?" Bhante Upali's voice was more welcoming than I'd imagined. His tone invited safety, and I relaxed. Unexpectedly comfortable in his presence, I addressed him as though he were a friend.

"Excuse me, Bhante, but it's terribly cold in here, and it doesn't seem as though anyone is tending the woodstove. I have some experience keeping fires going, and if no one else is doing it, I'll gladly volunteer to be stovemaster during the retreat."

The corners of his mouth turned upward in a gentle smile; his oval face expressed amusement. With a raised brow, and a hint of gratitude in his voice, he said, "I wish you would."

Ah, what a relief! Within the luminosity of his gaze, I sensed a deep knowing. At the same time, I recognized the eyes of a shy little boy. His comforting presence touched a hidden part of my soul, and I couldn't turn away. All of a sudden, I was angry about having to skip the last day of the retreat, certain I'd be missing something terribly important.

I followed Bhante Upali to the woodstove, where he explained its operation in detail. He showed me which levers controlled air flow, which were dampers, and how to open and close the flue. Pointing to a colored dial on the wall, he said, "To heat both this room and the dining hall, you'll want to make sure this indicator stays in the red area. But don't let it get beyond the red. That could be dangerous."

"Okay," I said. "I understand."

"Generally, we keep the fire low when we're in the meditation hall. So you'll always want to check and adjust it when we come out."

"Got it."

Bhante Upali cleared his throat. "Now these logs over here," he said, pointing to several large, round logs at the end of the row of stacked firewood, "these we call 'overnighters.' You can put one of these logs into the stove before you retire. Each one should burn six to eight hours."

I moved closer to reassure him. "Don't worry, Bhante. I've fired woodstoves before. Once I get the hang of this one, I'm sure we'll all be quite comfortable."

There was an awkward silence. We stood fairly close, alone on the covered porch, our eyes locked on each other. Bhante Upali's pale cheeks flushed pink as his tall frame jerked backward. "Uh, thank you for volunteering," he said. Then he turned around and headed quickly down the hallway.

Wow. So that's it. I'm the new stovemaster. I cringed, suddenly anxious about the tremendous responsibility I'd just been assigned. For the duration of my stay, it was my job to keep everyone warm. Never mind it was the middle of February, with temperatures below freezing and a thick blanket of snow covering the ground. Still, I'd do my best.

Once I had a good fire burning, I put on my coat, eager for a walk and a visit with my friends the horses. Outside near the office, a heavy-set monk struggled to push a two-wheeled wooden cart piled high with firewood. His orange robes were visible beneath a dirty orange down coat, and a knit orange cap covered his shaved head. It was Bhante

Ganda. I recognized his pale face, jowly cheeks, and thick, rubbery lips from his headshot inside the glass case. When he saw me, he set down his load and addressed me.

"You know, I never had to do all this work when I was living in Sri Lanka. Man, the Sri Lankan people treated us monks like kings! They hung on our every word. They did everything for us. Here at Bodhi, they work you to death. Just to keep warm, I have to haul all my own firewood up this steep hill to my kuti. And my back is killing me! Boy, I can't wait to get out of this place. I've put in five months so far, and I only have two more months to go. Then I'm going back to California. Where it's warm. A friend of mine has a job all lined up for me. I'm going to counsel heroin addicts. That'll be a lot easier than hauling heavy loads of firewood up a snow-covered hill in the mountains of West Virginia in the dead of winter!"

Before I could offer to help him, Bhante Ganda turned his back, lifted the wooden handles, and, huffing and puffing, pushed the cart toward the base of the hill. As I watched him trudge up a narrow path through the woods, I realized that not all monks who dressed in robes were the quiet, contemplative, humble human beings I'd imagined them to be.

When I returned to the covered porch after my walk, an Asian woman was on her knees in front of Bhante Upali, who was seated in one of the wooden chairs reserved for monastics. The woman had short black hair with bangs and wore a long brown skirt. I sat on the low bench, removed my hikers, and eavesdropped.

"I hope this was all right, Bhante," the woman said. "But when I heard the weather report warn of a major snowstorm, I made the decision to come one day early." She spoke in an accented staccato voice. "I hope I am not disturbing anything by my early arrival. I will just put my things in my room, and then tomorrow I will not bother anybody, and perform any needed service to your Vihara."

She bowed, touching her forehead to the carpeted floor three times, then rose to her feet. Still facing the monk, the woman backed away, head bowed, palms pressed together. Draping a woolen shawl around her head and shoulders, she exited the building.

Fifteen minutes later, as I washed my face in the Women's Dorm, the Asian woman entered through the front door carrying a suitcase and shoulder bag. Her face was round and freckled, and her bangs cut very short. She was probably in her late fifties.

"Can I help you with those?" I asked, moving toward her.

"Thank you. Here. You may put these in my room. Number 4. I have two more bags I must bring from the car. My name is Lin. I am from Burma."

"Nice to meet you, Lin." I swung the embroidered bag over my shoulder. "I'm Laurie."

That evening in the meditation hall, Lin took the cushion beside Polly in the second row. The cushion below the altar where Bhante B usually sat was now empty. Pete had driven the elder monk to the airport earlier in the day to catch his flight to Costa Rica.

As the meditation period concluded, Bhante Upali struck a bowl-shaped bell resting on a small cushion on the floor beside him. I remained perfectly still as the bell's clear, pure tones lingered and faded into silence. After the third strike of the bell, Bhante Upali chanted a verse in Pali, followed by the English translation: "All conditioned things are impermanent. When one sees this with the eye of wisdom, one becomes disenchanted with suffering."

That evening I sat on the covered porch opposite the woodstove later than everyone else. I had a good fire going, and was warm and content for the first time since my arrival at the monastery. Snow had started to fall at around dusk. I wondered if the snow would continue overnight, and perhaps turn into a major winter storm as Lin had predicted. Wouldn't that be something.

7

A Promise to Myself

(Day 5)

Wide awake before the alarm sounded, I jumped out of bed, eager to check the condition of my firebox. Lights burned in the kitchen. Through the open door, Machee Nee stood next to the big black six-burner stove. Flames glowed under four tea kettles. *So, she was the one to thank for yesterday morning's hot cup of tea!*

With her sweet smile, Machee Nee acknowledged me standing in the doorway. She had the brightest, most uplifting smile of anyone at the monastery. She was slight of build, with a wide Asian face and large dark eyes. Both her head and eyebrows were shaved. The diminutive nun was constantly performing one task or another. Besides cleaning the beverage area and refilling the hot water urns, she helped put dishes and grocery items away, dusted the statuary and candleholders on the altar and in the dining hall, vacuumed the covered porch, and tidied up different corners of the monastery. She moved with the grace of a deer, and in such a quiet, inconspicuous way that you were unaware she'd been close by except for the brief flash of her white robe disappearing around a corner.

She didn't speak to me, and I figured I'd better not speak to her in order to keep Noble Silence. But her smile was contagious, and I couldn't help smiling too. *Wow, my jaw doesn't hurt nearly as much as it did yesterday.* My smile broadened, and I almost blurted out the big news: *Guess what? I'm the new stovemaster!*

Morning meditation passed relatively easily. My concentration was broken only once, when the first chirpings of the birds commenced their sweet morning serenade. After the gong sounded three times, Bhante Upali turned around on his cushion in the front row to face us.

"Any announcements?" he said. "I know the retreatants will be arriving today. Anyone have a count?"

Polly raised her hand. Kneeling beside her cushion with palms pressed together, she said, "The latest count is forty-three, Bhante. But only thirty-five have confirmed."

Bhante Sabbakittika raised his hand. He was the retreat coordinator, and the youngest monk living at the monastery. With a thick African accent, he reminded everyone that there would be no puja ceremony because there was still so much to do to prepare for the retreat. He asked for volunteers to help him set up and work the registration table. Polly and Pete raised their hands.

"Okay, thank you," the African monk said. "If you will meet with me briefly after breakfast, I will show you what I need you to do."

An energetic mood swept through the monastery. It wasn't overt excitement, but more like subdued, eager anticipation of a baby about to be born. I sensed this mostly among the residents. Perhaps they were hungry for new faces, different interactions, and a break from the daily, often dull monastic routine. Since my arrival, I hadn't noticed any genuine liveliness among the monks; they were reserved in emotion except for Bhante Ganda's raucous complaints. I'd read that Theravada

Buddhist monks are expected to renounce the world, and to do so, they must reign in their desires, remain dispassionate, and detach from worldly pleasures. One slip, one indulged emotion could lead to desire, craving, and attachment, which, according to the Buddha, were the cause of suffering.

We all lined up at the beverage table before breakfast to prepare our drinks. I came to enjoy the mealtime ritual at Bodhi. After everyone is seated on their cushions in the dining hall, the cook opens the kitchen door and rings a bell. Then the head monk leads a formal procession from the platform to the kitchen. Single file, the remaining monks follow behind with slow, mindful steps, clutching their large begging bowls to their chests. Once seated back on the platform with their food, the monks chant a short passage in Pali. The rhythmic cadence of their voices elevated and transformed the usually unconscious act of eating to a sacred event.

But my favorite part of the ceremony was reciting a portion of the Loving-Kindness Discourse in English. There were three short paragraphs that jumped off the xeroxed page, landing directly inside my heart:

As a mother would risk her own life
To protect her only child
Even so towards all living beings
One should cultivate a boundless heart

One should cultivate for all the world
A heart of boundless loving-friendliness,
Above, below, and all around,
Unobstructed, without hatred or resentment.

Whether standing, walking, or sitting;
Lying down or whenever awake,
One should develop this mindfulness;
This is called divinely dwelling here.

Seated on my cushion in the last row, I silently repeated the last three words: *divinely dwelling here.* I wasn't sure what it meant, or where "here" was, but it sounded like a wonderful place to be, and I wished I were there.

After breakfast I added several logs to the fire before heading out for my walk. I wanted the porch and dining hall warm and comfortable for the retreatants when they arrived.

Patches of bright blue sky between puffy white clouds dazzled me. Although four or five inches of snow now covered the forest floor, I could still make out the outlines of paths through the woods. Sauntering down the driveway amid shrubs and branches coated with a layer of fresh snow was like entering a winter woodland fairyland. Although the snowflakes were gone for now, Lin had warned everyone that more snow was on the way.

Halfway down Winding Creek Road I stopped abruptly and closed my eyes, embraced by an unfamiliar calmness of mind I hadn't experienced in years. Grateful, I reveled in this brief, wonderful moment of unforeseen contentedness. The retreat would be underway soon, and I couldn't help wondering if more peaceful moments like these were to come in the days ahead.

When I reached the familiar bend in the road, I spotted the chocolate-colored horse standing in his usual spot beside the fence. I approached him gingerly, my hand outstretched. "Well, hi there,

Chocolate. How are you doing today?" The horse raised his head, then backed away. "Aw, it's okay. Don't be afraid. I won't hurt you."

I stood beside the woodstove, watching them all arrive. They came from everywhere, from every direction, just as I had come. Some of them seemed quite familiar with the surroundings, others seemed totally lost. One of the first to arrive was an elderly woman with gray hair so stiff it appeared frozen. She wore a green polyester pantsuit, and appeared a bit disoriented. Polly had asked me to show new retreatants around, answer their questions, or help them find their kutis. I approached the woman.

"Is this where you register for the retreat?" the woman asked. I detected a slight Southern drawl.

"Yes, you're in the right place." Her name was Margaret, and this was her first time at Bodhi Community. She'd driven all the way from Georgia. We checked the bulletin board together. She was assigned to stay in the Women's Dorm, Room 2. "Oh, you'll be close to me! After you register, I can show you to your room, and help you with your bags."

More and more people arrived—short, tall, old, young, heavyset, thin, Black, White, Asian. It started snowing again. I fed the fire as new faces filled the narrow porch. An older man with a bulbous nose and scraggly white beard entered the building. There was a calm, grounded quality about him that intrigued me. I watched him slowly remove his lumberjack coat, hat, and rubber boots, take a mug from the shelf above the beverage table, place a piece of masking tape on the mug, and write his name. Obviously, he'd been here before.

Everyone milled about, fixing beverages, talking, and moving to and from the registration table set up in the dining hall. Bhante Upali sat on the largest of the wooden chairs reserved for monastics, greeting people. The other monks moved about the rooms, exchanging brief words with retreatants and giving directions, except for the Asian monk with the diamond eyes. I'd hardly seen him since practically bumping into him in the office when I first arrived. His name was Bhante Tagarasikhi, and according to the bulletin board, he was "in seclusion."

With all the new bodies, the porch was growing warm, so I damped down the fire. A thin woman with short dark hair approached me. She had a determined, yet slightly confused expression.

"Hi," she said. "My name's Meryl. Meryl Lamartine." Her tone suggested I ought to know her. Her face was vaguely familiar, but I had no idea who she was.

"Hi, I'm Laurie. I guess you're here for the retreat."

"Oh, yes. I've been here *dozens* of times over the years. My husband and I are on the Board."

"Oooohh." Now I remembered where I'd seen her face. Her headshot was displayed inside the glass case with all the others.

"Do you know if Bhante B left yet for Costa Rica?" Her face was sallow, drawn, and wrinkled around the eyes and mouth. She wore jeans, a turtleneck sweater, and knee-high leather boots.

I grimaced. *If she's such a regular here, why didn't she remove her boots upon entering the building?* "Yes," I said. "Pete took Bhante B to the airport yesterday."

She gave me the once-over, then told me she was from Baltimore. Her husband was a doctor, recently retired, and she was a music teacher.

"Oh, I love music," I said. "What do you teach?"

"Piano. I just do it part time now. I have a group of students who come to my house for lessons."

"Isn't it great to be your own boss and work from home?"

"Oh, yes. I absolutely love it!" She paused. "Is this your first time here?"

"Yes, it is."

"Well, if you have any questions, don't hesitate to ask me. I know this place like the back of my hand. Dick and I have been coming here for, well, it seems like forever. We came regularly even before the meditation hall was built."

She glanced over her shoulder, then back at me. "I'm going to go claim a cushion in the meditation hall before everyone else gets there. I like to sit near the front." She turned and clomped down the hallway in her thick-soled boots. I hoped she had enough sense to remove them before entering the meditation hall.

⌒◦⌒◦⌒

The candlelit hall was filled with new bodies. On the cushion to my right, I had a new neighbor: Meryl the Board member. Bhante Upali sat on the cushion below the altar, facing us instead of his usual spot in the first row. After an hour of silent meditation, he took the striker and rang the brass bell three times. Beside me, Meryl heaved a long sigh.

Bhante Upali welcomed everyone, made a few brief announcements, then turned the microphone over to Bhante Sabbakittika. The young monk rose from his cushion, opened several sheets of folded paper, and cleared his throat.

He introduced himself, the other monks, and residents. "I will try to speak clearly, but please bear with me as English is my second language." He reviewed all the rules; there were many more than I'd imagined.

"The library will be closed during the retreat. Please turn off all beeper watches. Do not wear perfume or cologne, cosmetics, or noisy jewelry. Do not use cell phones." He glanced up from the papers. "The reception is so poor here your cell phone will not work anyway." His comment produced laughter among the group.

"Please observe all signs. Please do not let cats into the building.

54

Please do not speak. Minimal talking with the cook in the kitchen is allowed *only* if your job is to help prepare meals. Noble Silence formally begins tomorrow morning. If you must ask a question, you may quietly approach me after lunch, or you may write a note. Put the note on the bulletin board with the name of the monk or resident you wish to receive it. We also ask that you remain at Bodhi until the end of the retreat. Do not leave the grounds, and when walking on the road, be respectful of other people's property. If you must leave the retreat early, please come and let me know the day and time you will be leaving."

He ended his comments with his broad, characteristic smile and wished us all a "wonderful retreat."

That night in my room, I reviewed the Retreat Schedule I'd received upon registration. Because I was leaving one day early, I'd only miss one meditation session and the Closing Talk. The schedule was as follows:

Tuesday

4:30 – 7 p.m.	Registration
7 p.m.	Meditation

Wednesday through Sunday

4:45 a.m.	Wake up gong
5:10 a.m.	Yoga (Optional)
5:30 – 6:45 a.m.	Meditation
7 – 7:45 a.m.	Breakfast
8 – 8:45 a.m.	Work Period
9 – 11 a.m.	Meditation (sitting/walking)
11:15 – Noon	Lunch
Noon – 2 p.m.	Personal time

2 – 5 p.m.	Meditation
3 – 4 p.m.	Dhamma Discussion, Q&A (Optional)
4 – 5 p.m.	Meditation and Optional Interview
5 – 6 p.m.	Yoga (Optional)
7 – 8 p.m.	Dhamma Talk
8 – 9 p.m.	Meditation
9 p.m. and above	Optional Meditation

Monday

4:45 a.m.	Wake up gong
5:10 a.m.	Yoga (Optional)
5:30 – 6:45 a.m.	Group Meditation
7 – 7:45 a.m.	Breakfast
8 – 9:45 a.m.	Clean up and pack
10 – 11 a.m.	Closing Talk
11:15 a.m. – Noon	Lunch

For the fourth time, I counted up all the hours of meditation on the schedule. *At least seven hours daily, with the option for more! Oh my God, how am I ever going to manage this?* I recalled a story I'd read in a Buddhist magazine about an American spiritual seeker who traveled to India pursuing enlightenment. He entered a monastery, and because he meditated so intensely over a short period of time, he went crazy and had to be hospitalized. *Could that happen to me? What if I freak out after three or four days, and they have to cart me out in a straitjacket?*

I wanted to rest, but anxiety about the interminable hours of meditation and silence battered my brain like crashing booms of thunder, frightening me to my core. I took a pen from my purse, and on the back of the Retreat Schedule I wrote the word "FEAR" in capital letters followed by a large question mark. Then I undressed, got into bed, and pulled the sleeping bag over my head.

A lone tear slipped down my cheek. I swallowed hard and told myself to be brave, to remain positive. I hoped the Buddhists were right. I hoped there really was an end to suffering. Even though the chances of attaining that end during this retreat were slim to none, I told myself I'd have to try. Silently, I repeated the promise I'd made to myself after signing my name on the registration form: For as long as I'm here at this monastery, I will throw myself into this retreat completely, and with every ounce of strength that I have. I'll do whatever they ask me to do. I'll participate in every single activity on the schedule. I won't speak a word. I'll observe every rule, and comply with all of Bhante Upali's instructions. For as long as I'm here, I'll follow the Buddha's path, let nature take her course, and pray for the best.

8

Compost Duty

(Day 6)

Alone on the covered porch at 4:30 a.m., I built up the fire. The retreat had now formally begun, and I tried to prepare myself. The coming days would require a tremendous effort. I sat opposite the stove, a piping hot cup of tea in my hand, and worried. My heartbeat quickened. I'd been experiencing occasional mild panic attacks since my arrival, but discovered that if I closed my eyes and took several slow, deep breaths, the anxiety didn't last long. *My God, what the hell am I so afraid of?*

Others came straggling in, their faces heavy with sleep, hair tousled. Most wore baggy sweatpants and sweatshirts. They staggered from the beverage area to the low benches where they sipped tea or instant coffee. When the clock in the dining hall struck five, about a dozen retreatants ambled into the adjacent room for the optional yoga session. I maintained an on-and-off yoga practice at home, and since I'd promised myself to participate in every single activity on the schedule, I damped down the fire and joined the group, taking a spot in the back near the kitchen.

After a few minutes, Pete entered the room. "I will be leading the morning yoga sessions, which will help us prepare our minds and bodies for meditation."

Silence filled the darkened meditation hall. All eyes were on Bhante Upali, seated tall and straight on the cushion below the candlelit altar. Waiting for instruction, I focused on the monk's pale face; the bony outlines of his sunken cheeks, his protruding eyes. I was surprised when his gaze met mine, and stayed there. *Please, Bhante, just tell me what to do!*

He cleared his throat. "The first thing I'd like everyone to keep in mind is that your experience during this retreat will be heightened if you practice slowing down. In our daily activities, we are constantly moving from one task to another, from the time we awaken in the morning to the time we go to sleep. We rush from our home to our job. Often we're so busy we don't have time to eat, and we stop for a fast-food breakfast or lunch. Then after work we hurry to pick up the kids and take them to soccer practice or ballet lessons, or hurry to the gym to work out, or hurry to the store to pick up something for dinner. We even hurry when we're on vacation, wanting to cram all the sight-seeing and shopping into the short time we've saved up for vacation—a time when we're supposed to be slowing down and relaxing from the usual stresses of our lives. So we never really have the chance to focus on slowing ourselves down. Well, for the next six days, you have that opportunity."

He went on to advise us to walk slowly and mindfully throughout the building, especially in the long corridor to and from the meditation hall. He also instructed us to eat slowly and mindfully. "Lift your fork slowly. Chew your food slowly, being aware of the movements of the jaw and the tongue as the food is being masticated and pushed from side to side inside the mouth and then swallowed. By slowing down in all that you do, you are bringing your practice of heightened awareness to the periods of time in between sitting meditation, and you're cultivating mindfulness. And the more you slow down, the better you are able to tune in to the present moment. And that's really all there is—the present moment."

Okay, I thought. *Step one. Slowing down. That doesn't sound too difficult.*

Next Bhante Upali explained what I'd been longing to hear—how to approach our meditation. I hung on his every word: "Think of meditation as a continuous process of surrender, of letting go. When we sit on our cushions, we become nonjudgmental observers. We start by focusing on our breathing, then when thoughts arise, we simply notice them, gently let them go, and come back to the breathing. You might start by saying to yourself, 'Breathing in, sitting. Breathing out, sitting. Breathing in, letting go of the past and the future. Breathing out, letting go of the past and the future.'"

He made it sound so simple, but I knew from past experience just how difficult meditation actually was. For me, sustaining my attention on my breathing was virtually impossible—like trying to hold water in the palm of my hand and watching the clear liquid seep through the cracks between my fingers.

"So," he continued, "let us begin by taking three slow, deep, complete breaths. On the inhale, breathe in loving-kindness to yourself. A lot of people today have a tendency to blame themselves for things that have happened in their lives. They beat themselves up unnecessarily. It is impossible to make any progress on the spiritual path, and impossible to be kind to others, if you are not first kind to yourself. So, on the in-breath, say to yourself, 'May I be well, happy, and peaceful. May I be free from pain and suffering.' Then, on the out-breath, send that loving-kindness you just sent to yourself to everyone else, and say to yourself, 'May all living beings be well, happy, and peaceful, free from suffering and delusion.' We all find it easy to send loving-kindness to the people we care about, but as your practice deepens, you'll find it easier to send loving-kindness to all sentient beings, including neutral persons, and even your enemies."

I closed my eyes and did as Bhante Upali instructed, although it was impossible for me to send even the tiniest bit of loving-kindness to Mack. During the meditation period, I tried letting go of my thoughts, but they kept returning like a boomerang. Occasionally, I was distracted by rumbling noises which I concluded had to be coming from Meryl's stomach. When I peeked at the digital clock, the great hall was bathed in dawn's rosy glow. A moment later, sweet birdsong filled my ears, making me smile. Soon after, the gong was struck once, twice, three times, followed by Bhante Upali's soft voice: "All conditioned things are impermanent. When one sees this with the eye of wisdom, one becomes disenchanted with suffering."

After the monks exited the hall with slow, mindful steps, I followed the group of retreatants down the long, windowed corridor. Outside, the sleeping forest appeared incredibly vivid, as though a zoom lens had brought the lovely wintry scene into better focus. The outlines of the snow-covered conifers sharply contrasted the blue sky. Clusters of tall bamboo swayed gently, their slender green stalks taking on a life of their own. My gaze shifted to the bronze Buddha statue overlooking the pond. His lotus flower pedestal and crossed legs were no longer visible; a thick layer of snow covered his lap as a white quilt.

Toward the end of lunch, Bhante Sabbakittika rang a bell and rose from his cushion. "Please continue eating your meal. I just have a few announcements to make." He asked for two volunteers to empty the kitchen's compost bucket each day. I'd already signed up for the job of vacuuming the covered porch, but since that job was fairly easy, I raised my hand. A pretty, young girl with long black hair sitting two rows in front of me also raised her hand.

"Okay, you two. Thank you. You will please see Bhante Ganda after lunch. He will show you what to do. Also, tomorrow I will post a sign-up sheet on the bulletin board. Bhante Upali will be available for private fifteen-minute interviews from 4 to 5 p.m. If you would like an interview, write your name on the sheet and please arrive on time for your scheduled interview, which will be conducted in the library."

In the kitchen, I scraped the remains of my meal into the compost bucket. When I turned around, the pretty girl with long black hair was standing right beside me, smiling. Her natural beauty was intoxicating; her appearance exuded an exotic, almost mystical quality. She had slightly Asian features, smooth, olive skin, high cheekbones, dark eyes, and wore a long, flowing white skirt, a white hooded sweatshirt, and a white kerchief on her head. I returned her smile, resisting the urge to speak. Bhante Ganda entered the kitchen from the dishwashing room and approached us. "So, you're the two who will be doing the compost job?"

We nodded.

"Okay. First thing. Make sure there is *no paper* in the bucket." He removed the lid. "We can't have any paper going into the compost bins outside because the wildlife that eat and recycle our compost could eat the paper, strangle, and die. Oh, would you look at this! You tell them and you tell them! How many times do I have to remind Bhante Sabbakittika to announce NOT to throw paper napkins into the compost bucket? And still, no matter how many times he announces it"—Bhante Ganda's fleshy cheeks jiggled as he shook his head—"it never fails. No matter how many times people are told, somebody will *always do it!*"

The pretty girl and I locked eyes, suppressing giggles. We put on our coats and boots, and met Bhante Ganda outside. Another two inches of snow had fallen during the night. We followed the monk as he carried the five-gallon bucket up the hill and past the first kuti on the right. He emphasized it was of vital importance that this job be performed exactly as he showed us.

After demonstrating the bucket-dumping procedure, Bhante Ganda said, "Now, this job has to be done twice a day. After breakfast and after lunch. One of you can do it one day, and the other can do it the next day. Just switch off. That way it won't seem so bad."

We both nodded, our palms pressed together.

"Now, after you dump the compost, you take the bucket to the laundry room and wash it out with the organic soap that's on the top shelf. It's very important you use *only* the organic soap. We don't want to poison the wildlife. Then take the bucket back to the kitchen. I'll do it this time because I'm heading that way." And off he went, slipping down the hill with the empty bucket.

The pretty girl and I walked back to the main building together. I was surprised when she addressed me. She told me her name was Jessica. In a low, passionate voice she said, "I don't know about you, but it would be a lot easier for me to remember to do this job if I knew I was responsible for either breakfast or lunch. I'm afraid I'll get mixed up and forget if it was my day or not!" She laughed, revealing a set of straight, white teeth almost as bright as her kerchief. There was no trace of an accent in her voice, despite her Asian features.

"I agree," I said. "Even back home, I can't always remember what day it is!" My hand covered my mouth. *Oh, no! I just broke Noble Silence!* Then I recalled Bhante Sabbakittika saying "minimal conversation" was allowed at times regarding the performance of a job, so maybe these few words I spoke to Jessica didn't count. "Why don't you do breakfast, and I'll take care of lunch? I usually go outside for a walk after lunch anyway."

Jessica gave me a glowing smile. "Perfect."

Later that evening, while most of the retreatants drank a last beverage on the covered porch before bed, I shut myself in my room, glad to be alone. It had been a long day. The afternoon meditation session seemed to last forever, and I struggled to stay awake during Bhante Upali's evening dhamma talk and the hour of meditation afterward. The weather forecast posted on the bulletin board called for more snow overnight and colder temperatures. I'd had a nice fire burning all day long, and was confident the thick "overnighter" I'd loaded into the stove would burn slowly throughout the night, giving me a lovely hot bed of embers to build on in the morning.

I undressed, crawled into my sleeping bag, and read the back cover of the one book I'd checked out of the library—*Journey to Center: A Meditation Handbook,* by Matt Flickstein. Opening the book at random, I read: "Our fears are never related to the unknown; we cannot be afraid of something that does not yet exist. We are actually afraid of the loss of the known." I squinted. *Yes, loss of the known. Maybe that's what I'm so afraid of.* Even though my life with Mack was terrible, it was familiar, it was known.

I sat up in bed, grabbed the pen and Retreat Schedule, and copied the quotation below the word "FEAR." My eyelids grew heavy. I placed the book on the table along with the Retreat Schedule, which I kept consulting throughout the day even though I'd read it so many times I knew it by heart.

I turned out the light, snuggled into the warm folds of my sleeping bag, and congratulated myself. I'd made it through the entire first day of the retreat without breaking any rules, and without speaking— except for those few words I'd exchanged with Jessica about our job, which didn't count. I'd survived the lengthy hours in the meditation hall despite the fact that my cushion was as hard as stone, and my mind

kept drifting off into daydreams, speculation, and sleepiness. I'd partic-
ipated in every activity on the Schedule, including the optional ones.
I'd walked and eaten slowly and mindfully and performed my assigned
job, plus a second job. I'd managed to keep the fire going all day long so
everyone was warm, and I'd taken my daily walk down Winding Creek
Road during the only personal time on the Schedule. I'd even snatched
a couple of carrots from the kitchen to bring to my friends the horses,
although the chocolate-colored horse still wouldn't let me touch him.

Not bad for my first day, I thought as I drifted off to sleep. *Not bad
at all.*

9

Unearthly Vision

(Day 7)

The deep, resonating sounds of the gong echoed throughout the forest, waking us. I was already dressed, eager to embrace the darkened peace of early morning. Soon I was seated in front of a blazing fire, sipping tea and looking forward to my slow walk down the center aisle of the candlelit hall where I'd relax my mind in quiet meditation until the rising sun gradually brightened the room and sweet birdsong beckoned a new day.

Breakfast passed as usual, followed by another long period of sitting meditation. My knees and back suffered periodic twinges of pain, and I shifted my posture every fifteen minutes or so seeking comfort. Grateful when the gong finally sounded, I uncrossed my legs. Beside me, Meryl heaved her usual long sigh of relief.

Everyone bowed three times to the golden Buddha statue, then the monks made their procession out of the hall, except for Bhante Upali. He disappeared through a door in the back of the meditation hall on the men's side, closing the door behind him. He'd entered this adjacent room on several other occasions, and each time, I couldn't help wondering what was inside that room, and what he might be doing in there. I sensed there was something mysterious hiding inside that room, something important I needed to see. But I didn't dare cross over to the men's side to appease my curiosity. As a woman, I wasn't sure if I'd be breaking another rule by stepping onto "forbidden ground." While everyone filed out of the meditation hall, I remained seated still on my cushion and listened. Yes, something inside that room was definitely calling me, a mythical Siren beckoning me to come and take a look.

At two o'clock, we were all back in the meditation hall for the afternoon session. I was able to sustain my attention on my breathing for about five minutes before my unruly mind wandered off in nonsensical rumination. At three o'clock I rose from my cushion and, along with about a dozen other retreatants, exited the hall to attend the optional dhamma discussion and Q & A in the library.

The chairs were arranged in a circle, with Bhante Upali sitting farthest from the door. I sat beside Jessica. Meryl was there, and Margaret, the older woman with the frozen hair. The other female in the room was a heavyset woman with shoulder-length black hair, high cheekbones, and thick, black eyebrows. A poncho covered her sweatshirt, perhaps to hide her bulk. I knew her name was Dahlia because it was on her mug, but I'd never seen her smile. Not once. Her lips remained constantly pursed, her brow furrowed.

It wasn't unusual to see retreatants who didn't smile. Many took their retreat so seriously they wouldn't even make eye contact. Others, myself included, had no problem with meeting the glance of a fellow retreatant, giving him or her an encouraging nod or gentle smile. To me, it was the right thing to do since we were all in this together. And because my jaw hardly hurt at all, smiling came a lot easier.

Bhante Upali spoke briefly about cultivating mindfulness. He defined mindfulness as "present moment, non-judgmental awareness of things just as they are." He told us that according to the Buddha, the true nature of existence is *dukkha*—the Pali word for suffering. "A better translation for dukkha is unsatisfactoriness. Basically, dukkha means wanting things to be different than they actually are. So, the more we can develop mindfulness in our daily lives and see things as they truly are, the less we will suffer."

After he finished speaking, Bhante Upali suggested we go around the room so each of us could ask a personal question. I prayed he wouldn't start with me; I had no idea what to ask.

The first to speak was a pudgy man of medium build with graying hair and an aquiline nose. He asked Bhante Upali how to deal with pain he'd been experiencing over the past years. He suspected his pain was due to stress and tension. The next person to speak was a young Black man. He wore gray suede pants, a white button-down shirt, and gray sweater-vest. He was from South Carolina and attended a Southern Baptist church, which he found comforting but spiritually challenging. He said he was having difficulty explaining his interest in Buddhism to his fellow churchgoers, and asked how he might reconcile this dilemma and not lose friends.

Beside the Black man, a pale middle-aged man with manicured fingernails spoke next. Thick gold jewelry adorned his neck, wrists, and fingers. The jet-black mound of neatly combed hair on his head was obviously not his own. He asked Bhante Upali in a completely serious tone what Buddhism taught about pursuing an active sex life.

I hadn't been paying attention to any of Bhante Upali's responses to these questions because I was preoccupied with deciding what my own question should be. My mind kept leaping from one possibility to another—this question sounded too serious, that one was too personal, and another one seemed just plain silly. When it was finally my turn, my heart thumped hard and fast against my chest. I tried to ignore the familiar jittery sensations and focus on which words to say, but I still hadn't decided what question to ask. All eyes in the room were fixed on me, and I had to speak.

"Well . . . I was just wondering . . . sometimes when I'm meditating, just for a short time, and only sometimes, I see these different colors sort of floating around in my mind. Is that okay?"

Bhante Upali smiled softly. He stared at me with the kindness of a loving parent, seemingly amused by my question "Well, sure, it's *okay*. But it doesn't mean anything. People see lights or colors, or even hear voices. But you shouldn't dwell upon them. If you do, you'll find yourself trying to hold on to them, or recreate those colors when what you want to be doing is just noticing them when they do arrive, and letting them go when they leave."

His bulging eyes held me fast. *Why does he keep staring at me like that? He doesn't act that way with the other retreatants.* My palms came together at my chest. "Okay. Thank you, Bhante, I'll remember that."

Next, a young Asian man wearing a green knit sweater and black watchman's cap asked, "Bhante, is anger ever justified? I mean, in the case of war, for example. Many people here are angry with our government for going into Iraq and killing innocent people. I find it very difficult not to be angry about that. And if people don't get angry about this type of senseless slaughter, and raise their voice in protest, the position of our government won't change."

"I agree with you!" Meryl blurted. "We have to make our voices heard! Back home, a group of us have started a letter-writing campaign. There are other things everyone can do to tell the government we don't approve of their murderous policies. We can organize rallies, demonstrations, and—"

"Meryl," Bhante Upali interrupted. "You're getting off track. Let me answer the question." Meryl's gaze dropped to the floor.

"You see," the monk continued, "because anger always breeds more anger, it is never justified. So, no. There is no such thing as 'justified' anger. It doesn't get you anywhere."

At the conclusion of the Q & A period, Meryl announced, "Oh, boy, this was great! I don't remember doing this at a retreat before. Whoever came up with this idea was brilliant! I loved the way we all could sit down together and support each other with our thoughts and concerns. When are we going to—"

Bhante Upali held up his hand. "Meryl, *please.* We can talk about this later."

"Oh, okay. But I just wanted to say that I thought this dhamma discussion group was an excellent addition to the retreat experience, and I hope it continues. We ought to bring it up at the next Board meeting."

Bhante Upali dismissed us, and we filed out of the library. I walked down the long corridor behind Jessica, admiring the way her shiny black hair cascaded down her back practically to her waist. I often watched her as she moved about the monastery. It was impossible not to notice her grace, confidence, and beauty. The angle at which she held her head, her beatific expression, and her exotic appearance projected regal elegance. I was glad that whenever our eyes met, we exchanged knowing smiles as though we were longtime best friends.

Back in the meditation hall, I keep peeking at the clock. *Only half an hour to go! Thank goodness!* I tried to follow Bhante Upali's instructions as best I could, hoping to find that "quiet, peaceful place of centeredness," but wasn't having any luck. Meryl's stomach was particularly noisy, and intruding thoughts kept divebombing my brain from out of nowhere like angry birds. That morning Bhante Upali had said, "When thoughts arise just try to see the thoughts as thoughts. Be aware of *thinking, thinking,* then gently let go of those thoughts or ideas, and come back to the sensation of *breathing in, sitting, breathing out, sitting.*"

I couldn't even notice my thoughts as "thoughts" let alone gently let them go. Before I knew it, I was caught up in the storyline, speculations, and emotions connected to those thoughts. And that particular afternoon, the majority of those thoughts revolved around Mack. My hands tightened into fists remembering the argument we had when he insisted that I cut my retreat short.

"But what if the last day is the most important day of the whole retreat?" I cried. "The culmination of everything that went on before? If I have to miss the most important day, what's the sense in even going?"

"Quit your goddamned whining! Christ, you're behaving like a spoiled child! You're allowed one week off, not a day more. I'm sick of your bullshit excuses! You need to come home on Monday, take care of business, and start cooking. Period."

"And what if I don't?"

"Trust me," he said. "You do NOT want to find out." He'd made idle threats before but hadn't acted upon them. At least not yet. "How many times do I have to remind you? You have responsibilities here! You need to come home on Monday, take care of business, and start cooking. If you cancel the cooking two weeks in a row, we'll lose customers and end up in the poorhouse."

"That's absolutely ridiculous! God forbid I should be 'allowed' an extra day away from home to finish the retreat! Never mind that I haven't taken any time off or had a proper vacation in years! And in case you forgot, *I'm* the one working my butt off to keep a roof over our heads! What do you do to help out? Wash a few dishes? Big deal! And we won't lose customers. They'll understand. I know them personally. And if I *do* take a second week off, we won't starve. My God, Mack, we're talking about losing a measly couple hundred dollars!"

My neck throbbed. My blood grew hot. Silently, I repeated, *Breathing in, sitting. Breathing out, sitting.* But no matter how hard

I tried to let them go, my thoughts about Mack stuck like superglue. Anger swelled into fury as I recalled another particularly awful scene. Several months earlier, around 9 a.m. as I lay awake in bed feeling sick, depressed, and terribly alone, Mack burst into my room.

"Get your lethargic ass out of that bed!" he yelled at the top of his lungs. "Do I have to remind you it's delivery day? All that food you cooked and packed up isn't going to deliver itself while you sulk in bed all the damn day! Christ, you have to be the laziest Jewish woman in the world! It's hard to believe you come from a tribe that's obsessed with making money, because you're an absolute failure at it! Now get the hell up!" He lurched toward the mattress, arms raised. I cowered under the covers. With a menacing snarl, he ripped the sheets and blanket off the bed, and I lay there in my nightshirt, my hands covering my face, exposed, vulnerable, and wanting to scratch his eyes out.

I sniffled, rearranged my crossed legs, and tried to refocus my attention. *Breathing in, letting go of the past and the future. Breathing out, letting go of the past and the future.* But it was no use. After a while I gave up, peeked at the clock, and stared out the windows. Big, fluffy snowflakes tumbled from the sky. Mesmerized, I gazed with loving affection at the falling flakes as though seeing snow for the first time. The towering bamboo stalks among the green, brown, and white hues of the forest exclaimed utter perfection. Transfixed by the wintry scene's tranquil beauty, my thoughts released their grip on the past. As I watched flake after flake fall from the sky and disappear, my mind grew still, and my whole being relaxed into sweet spaciousness. I exhaled deeply and closed my eyes. All of a sudden, my consciousness was outside amidst the sleeping forest; its snowy beauty permeating my tissues, melting into my bones, and gradually enveloping me completely.

A few minutes later, a sensation like warm rain washed over me. There was a strong presence very close, just behind me and to my left. I wanted to open my eyes. I wanted to turn my head and shoulders and look behind me, but I couldn't move a muscle, immobilized in a cozy, peaceful cocoon of contented stillness.

The presence behind me was so palpable and so close that it was impossible to ignore. After a few more minutes, the presence revealed herself. I saw her in my mind—an Asian woman dressed in a long white gown. She was kneeling behind me on the space of carpet to the left of my cushion. There she was, plain as day and beautiful, with straight, jet-black hair and dark eyes. Her gown was brilliant—pure white, glowing from within. Her palms were pressed together at her chest, her lips curved upward in a gentle smile that suggested great wisdom and compassion. My heart raced. *What's going on? Am I dreaming?*

I swallowed hard, aching to open my eyes and turn around, but movement was impossible. Yet, deep down, I knew it wasn't necessary for me to turn around to confirm her existence. She was there. I could feel her. Her loving presence penetrated my soul, and my back grew warm from the closeness of her powerful energy. I watched as she raised her right hand, and with delicate, pearl-white fingers, she gently touched my left shoulder. Then she was gone.

My skin tingled. My heart fluttered, and I could barely breathe. *What in the world just happened? Who was this woman? Where did she come from? Did anyone else see her?* My eyes popped open. Fifteen more minutes to go according to the clock. Outside, it was still snowing.

I built up the fire for the night, then went straight to my room and undressed. In bed, I tossed and turned. Thoughts of that otherworldly vision in the meditation hall kept chasing sleep away. *I must have been either dreaming or hallucinating. But why would my mind conjure the image of an Asian woman in a glowing white gown?* Then it hit me. The radiant waitress at Lu's Place! *Could they be connected? No, impossible!*

For a moment I worried I might be losing my mind. The whole

episode in the meditation hall seemed too bizarre to contemplate, so I did the only thing I could think of—I dismissed it. It didn't mean anything. This "vision" or whatever it was had to be a figment of my imagination—a weird effect of too little sleep and too much meditation. I pulled the sleeping bag closer and groaned. Turning over, I prayed for sleep and for the strength to endure another long day of sitting, silence, and countless hours of meditation.

10

The Baby's Face

(Day 8)

Immersed in the peace before dawn, I dropped to my knees in the candlelit meditation hall, bowed three times, settled myself on my cushion, closed my eyes, crossed my legs, and inhaled deeply. *May I be well, peaceful, and happy. May I be free from suffering.* Exhaling, I sent loving-kindness to my mother, my father who had died a year earlier, my sister, her husband, and their two children. But my heart still refused to release any loving-kindness to Mack.

The sound of the gong being struck three times caressed my ears with its warm, lingering tones, followed by Bhante Upali's soft voice: "All conditioned things are impermanent. When one sees this with the eye of wisdom, one becomes disenchanted with suffering." *Where did the time go? Where were all the intruding thoughts of yesterday?* I hadn't even been bothered by the rumblings of Meryl's stomach. Maybe I was making a little progress.

I walked softly down the corridor behind the others, my mind pleasantly still. The light of the new day streamed through the windows as a miracle. Outside, the sight of the bronze Buddha statue overlooking the pond made me chuckle. The snow that had formerly covered his lap now reached as high as his waist.

Absorbed in my own peaceful little world, I built up the fire. While everyone else lined up at the beverage area, I sat on the bench opposite the stove and peered out the window. The sight of nuthatches chasing each other up and down tree trunks delighted me. It was as though nothing else in the world existed at that moment except the joyful watching of those playful birds.

After breakfast we were back in the meditation hall again from nine to eleven. Toward the end of the session, the face of a young child appeared in my mind. She was a pretty little girl, maybe three years old, with olive-colored skin, dark hair, and large, coal-black eyes. The haunting look in those eyes probed my soul, and I had the distinct impression she knew me intimately. Her face and searching eyes remained in my mind for a long while, penetrating me. What did she want? Then, from a faraway place, I heard my own voice ask, "Whose baby is this?" A moment later, a different voice replied, "That's *your* baby." I gulped, stupefied. Then the child's face vanished.

MY baby? Impossible. I'd never given birth. Fear choked me like a noose. I wanted to dismiss the baby's face just as I'd dismissed the vision of the white-robed woman kneeling behind me yesterday. Yet there was something troubling about this little girl—something I couldn't easily dismiss. I had no idea who she was or why she came to me, but she was obviously expecting some sort of acknowledgment from me.

Toward the end of lunch, Lin walked toward the monks' platform and, with palms pressed together, kneeled in front of Bhante Upali. She spoke quietly to him, and I watched his expression change perceptively, then he whispered, "Yes, all right." Lin rose to her feet, bowed, and backed away from the platform.

Bhante Upali's head turned in my direction. When our eyes met, he pointed with his index finger and motioned for me to come toward him. *Oh, shit! What could he want? I must have done something wrong. Did I accidentally break a rule?* I pointed to my chest and mouthed, "Me?" He nodded.

I stood up, approached the platform on shaky legs, and dropped to my knees a few feet in front of him.

"Do you have a reliable vehicle?" he said.

A reliable vehicle? Did he want a ride somewhere? Or maybe this was some sort of trick question, like a Zen koan—an unsolvable riddle. Hoping to come up with the correct answer, I chose my next words carefully. "My car has served me pretty well."

"Is it a four-wheel-drive vehicle?"

"No, Bhante. It's not a late-model car either. But it gets me around."

"Oh." I sensed his genuine concern for me, and my anxiety diminished. There seemed to be an unspoken connection between us. "You're planning to leave the retreat a day early, right?"

"Yes, Bhante."

"Well, I've just been told there's a big snowstorm headed our way, and I thought I should inform you in case there was an important engagement you couldn't miss. The roads will be bad, so you might want to leave earlier than you planned."

Relief flooded my body, and I almost laughed. "A big snowstorm? That's all? Oh, don't worry about me, Bhante. I'm quite experienced when it comes to driving on mountain roads in winter. I'm a country girl."

The monk smiled. The majority of the time his expression was stone serious, but when Bhante Upalli allowed himself to smile, sincere warmth, deep understanding, and the playfulness of a shy little boy flowed from him. "Still," he said, "the roads back here get very bad. Sometimes only a reliable four-wheel-drive vehicle can make it out to the main road. It's supposed to be a major storm event, and if you wait, you may not be able to leave when you planned."

I hesitated, but only for a second. The answer was clear. "Well, if the weather's going to be that bad, I'm not going anywhere. I'll just cancel my cooking job."

Bhante Upali's eyeballs popped further from their sockets. "I like your attitude," he said. "Most people get really freaked out when there's a big snowstorm coming. They start to panic, then they run around, hurrying and scurrying, making plans and arrangements to get out of here as soon as possible." He smiled. "But obviously, not you."

My heart, which had been racing with fear only five minutes earlier, exploded with joy. *He likes my attitude! Oh, thank you, thank you, Bhante Upali!* Those were the sweetest, kindest, most gratifying words anyone had said to me in years.

"Oh, no, Bhante. I don't get freaked out about big snowstorms. Where I live, there's a major snowstorm every other week!" I giggled and leaned closer. "And you know what I've learned about life in the mountains, Bhante?" His upper body inched forward. "When the weather's bad, no matter what you have planned, you just stay put and wait until the storm's over."

I detected a hint of color in his usually pale cheeks. "And to be honest, Bhante, I can't imagine a better place to be stranded during a snowstorm than a monastery like this one."

I vacuumed the covered porch, put on my hikers, dumped the compost bucket, and returned to the main building to fix the fire before heading back outside for my walk. The sign-up sheet for private interviews already had three names listed, and there was space for only one more name. *Well, I promised myself to participate in every single activity offered during the retreat . . .* I grabbed a pen and wrote my name in the 4:45 p.m. slot.

The snow covering the driveway sparkled under bright sunshine. I practically skipped down Winding Creek Road, inhaling fresh mountain air. The road had been plowed, and was hard with compacted snow. When I spotted the horses up ahead, I called, "Well, hello, my friends! How is everybody doing today?" Standing close to the fence, my favorite horse raised his head. I approached him cautiously, my hand outstretched in greeting.

"Hi, Chocolate. You'll never believe all the crazy things that have been happening to me." Slowly, I inched closer. He didn't back away, and for the first time, he let me touch his soft muzzle.

During the afternoon session, instead of meditating, I practiced two hours of clock-watching. I couldn't stop worrying about my upcoming interview with Bhante Upali. What would I say to this wise man who'd dedicated the majority of his life to practicing the Buddha's teachings? Who had renounced all worldly pleasures in order to seek enlightenment? *And what would he say to me?* I was so high-strung you would have thought I was about to meet the Dalai Lama. When the digital clock said 4:30, my anxiety intensified as I rose from my cushion.

Literally shaking, I waited in the hallway until the library door opened. A heavyset bald man with a neatly trimmed red beard, freckles, and wire-rimmed glasses walked out. Dressed in khaki pants and a crewneck sweater, he reminded me of a university professor I once knew.

"Go on in," he said to me. "He's all yours."

I nodded, entered the library, and shut the door behind me. Bhante Upali sat in a folding chair about ten feet away. I sat in the empty chair opposite him, folded my hands on my lap, and remained silent, having no idea what to say to him.

"So, how's your meditation going?" he asked.

"Not bad, I guess."

"Are you having many interfering thoughts?"

"Oh, yeah. I get a lot." I wrung my hands.

Then he started talking about quieting the mind, but I wasn't really listening. Instead, I was debating whether or not to ask him about seeing the baby's face. When he finished speaking, I said, "Well, I did have something pretty strange happen to me during meditation."

"Do you want to share that information?" His eyes were like magnets pulling me in—round, bulging magnets filled with compassionate understanding. My fear melted.

"Uh, yes, I guess so. I mean, I don't see why not. I was just wondering what this might mean. If anything." I told him about the appearance of the baby's face, and what the voices said.

"Do you have any children?" he asked.

"No, Bhante. That's the strange part. But I was pregnant once. A long time ago. It was an accident. I was so young, a sophomore in college. There was no way I could bring a child into the world at that point in my life. So, I . . . I had an abortion."

I expected to see Bhante Upali's expression switch from compassion to reproach, but he remained unfazed, although he did sit up straighter in his chair. "Uh, yes," he said and cleared his throat. "Back then a lot of women were having that done in their college years. You must have suffered terrible guilt as a result of that action."

Did I? Squinting, I searched my memory. "Well, I can't honestly say that I remember feeling a lot of guilt. I mean, I was only nineteen years old. I was still in college. I had my whole life ahead of me. And even though I worked part time, I could barely afford my own living expenses, so there was no way I could raise a child. It wouldn't have been fair to the child. Or to me. I guess I never really gave that decision a second thought. At the time, it just seemed like the right thing to do."

Bhante Upali remained silent. I searched his eyes, sensing the words he spoke next would be extremely important. "Well," he finally said, "you know sometimes during meditation things from our past will rise to the surface of our consciousness. Things like thoughts and feelings we buried long ago because we didn't want to deal with them, or certain truths we never wanted to admit to ourselves. In rare cases these realizations from our past can rise up so quickly and powerfully they can cause great distress and sweep you away like a flood. I saw this happen to a few people while I was in India. But that's not to say these kinds of events happen to everyone who meditates. Those strange occurrences are not the norm. Very few people actually freak out from intensive meditation during a retreat. However, it's not uncommon to see people crying, even sobbing in the meditation hall because those buried thoughts, emotions, and truths, when released into consciousness, can be pretty overwhelming. Even life changing."

I gulped.

He glanced at the clock on the wall. Our time was up. I stood up, not wanting to hear any more. With palms pressed together, I bowed and thanked him for the interview.

"And thank you for sharing that information about the baby with me," he said.

"Oh, well, thank you for listening."

During the evening dhamma talk I could barely keep my eyes open. The subject that night was the Three Characteristics of Existence. Despite my sleepiness and the pain in my neck and shoulders, I did my best to pay attention.

"The Buddha taught that there are three principal characteristics of existence," Bhante Upali began. "*Annica,* or impermanence; *dukkha,* or suffering; and *anatta,* or no-self. According to the Buddha, the lives of all beings are marked by these three qualities. Humans are subject to delusion about these three characteristics, and that delusion results in suffering. But recognizing these qualities to be real and true in our own experience helps us to relax with things the way they are, to see into our own nature, and eventually gain wisdom and reach Nibbana.

"The realization of impermanence—that all things are constantly changing, constantly arising and passing away—is usually the first insight on the path to enlightenment."

I didn't hear much more of Bhante Upali's talk. My tired brain couldn't absorb it all, and my aching body was a huge distraction. The Buddha's discovery that "life is suffering" wasn't a new concept for me. But the characteristic of impermanence intrigued me. There had to be something more profound to understand about impermanence than simply knowing everything changes. And how could that deeper insight lead someone on the path to enlightenment?

Half asleep on my cushion, I was jolted awake by the sound of the brass bell being struck three times. Bonnnnggg . . . Bonnnnggg . . . Bonnnnggg . . . Aloft its fading tones, I was carried on soft clouds to a spacious universe abundant with love. Basking in the peace of the bell's echoing vibrations, Bhante Upali's voice recited: "All conditioned things are impermanent. When one sees this with the eyes of wisdom, one becomes disenchanted with suffering."

My eyes opened. *Wow. Wouldn't that be wonderful!*

I fixed the fire for the night and headed for the Women's Dorm. As soon as I walked into my room and shut the door, I heard another door open, then a soft knock on my door. I opened the door and Lin entered, the edges of her long brown skirt swaying about her ankles as she shut the door behind her.

"Here," she said. "Take this orange. I have too much fruit in my room. If you are hungry, eat. For myself, I must eat something because right now I am taking medication. I cannot swallow these pills on an empty stomach."

"Okay. Thank you, Lin." I placed the orange on the table next to the bed.

"Here, here. Sit down. I can tell you are hurting. Let me help." She took a cushion from the closet and placed it on the floor.

I sat on the edge of the round cushion. Lin kneeled behind me and placed both hands on my torso. She massaged my back, then moved her hands up to my shoulders, then my neck, pressing hard on certain spots.

"Ow. How did you know I was hurting?"

"You've been hurting for a long time, my dear," she said.

My chest tightened. "Yes. Yes, I have. How did you know?"

"I can see it. But you will be all right. You are looking in the right place. This is an excellent Vihara, and Bhante Upali is a very good teacher. You must listen to him. He is very wise. And Kuan Yin will help you. You just relax. I am going to help you get rid of that pain."

Her hands glided up and over my head as she spoke in Burmese. Then her fingers moved down to my shoulders, kneading and rubbing the muscles. "Ah, there it is. I found it. Right there." I grimaced as she dug her knuckles into a tender spot on my upper back.

"It's all right now," she said. "Finished."

I turned around on the cushion to face her. *Why did she come to my room at such a late hour?*

"Sister Laurie, I can tell you are sincere. I can tell you are concentrating very hard and practicing your meditations seriously. That is good. And it will help you. You are not like all the other people who are here this week. I will teach you some things if you like. I used to be a nun, but then I had to leave my Temple because of surgery for cancer. Sister Laurie, what you are doing here is good. And it will help you in your life. Kuan Yin will protect you. She is very close. I will show her to you tomorrow."

I no idea what to make of all she was saying, or why she'd singled me out. Lin took my hands in hers. "Sister Laurie, I know you are having problems with your husband, but soon you will be able to make things better."

Moisture filled my eyes. "But, but how could you possibly know I'm having problems with my marriage?"

She stroked my forehead. "Now, now. Don't be upset. I know you've been suffering for a long time. I know you have come here looking for answers. You're a good girl, and your heart is in the right place. Believe me, I do not speak like this to everyone who comes here for retreat. Only certain ones."

"But why me?"

Gently, she touched my shoulder. "You and I already know each other. Now, don't cry. You must be strong. You must have courage, self-confidence. You must say to yourself, 'I know what I'm doing.' And don't let anyone tell you otherwise."

I sniffled, searching her kind, round face.

"No need to be afraid of anything."

"I'm not afraid," I lied.

"You know what you're doing," Lin said with the authority of a drill sergeant. She placed her hand high on my chest, directly below my collarbone. "Just listen to your heart. The heart inside your own Temple."

My skin tingled where she touched me. Lin removed her hand, pressed her palms together, bowed her head, stood up, and turned to go.

"Lin, wait! What did you mean when you said we already know each other? And who is Kuan Yin?"

She smiled. "You will see."

11

White Marble Woman

(Day 9)

Wide awake at 4 a.m., I was eager to immerse myself in the bewitching pre-dawn stillness. Before coming to Bodhi, I couldn't remember the last time I'd seen the sunrise. Now I couldn't imagine a life without basking in the peace of this exquisite, most precious time of day. As I dressed, a phrase from Bhante Upali's dhamma talk the night before kept ringing inside my head: *The realization of impermanence is usually the first insight on the path to enlightenment.*

I grabbed the pen and wrote the words "IMPERMANENCE" and "INSIGHTS" on the back of the Retreat Schedule. As an afterthought, I wrote the word "FAITH." Then I hurried to the covered porch to check the condition of my fire.

In the middle of morning meditation, my concentration was broken by the sounds of a dog barking in the distance, and my thoughts turned to my sweet, lovable Booter, the dearest living thing in my life. My chest heaved, and I started sobbing uncontrollably. Big salty tears streamed down my face faster than I could wipe them away. *My God, what's wrong with me? Is it because I miss Booter?* Totally embarrassed, I covered my mouth, dulling my cries. Polly turned around and offered me a tissue from the box she kept beside her cushion.

During the 9 to 11 a.m. meditation period, Bhante Upali gave us instruction on walking meditation. He explained that although many people didn't practice it, walking meditation was a very powerful form of meditation. I was grateful for the option, as it gave my sore butt and achy knees a much-needed break. "By slowing down all our movements while walking, and observing them carefully, we tune in to the arising and vanishing from moment to moment. And once we're able to see our thoughts arising, before those thoughts sneak into our minds through the back door, we can choose to act upon them if they are wholesome thoughts, or let them go if they are unwholesome thoughts. So, this practice of walking meditation helps prevent clinging and attachment, which, according to the Buddha, is the cause of suffering. It can also lead us further along the path toward the insight of impermanence."

Row by row we all practiced walking meditation. After my third round, I was back on my cushion, eyes closed, mind empty. Soon afterward, the cook rang the big brass gong outside three times. Each time, as the muffled tones sounded, echoed, and faded away, a part of me seemed to fade away as well.

I built up the fire, then sat on the bench opposite the stove while everyone queued at the beverage area before lunch. My gaze moved from the man with the bulbous nose and scraggly beard, who, I'd discovered, suffered from a rare kidney disease, to Margaret, whose petrified hair had to be a wig, perhaps as a result of chemotherapy. From the young Asian man who wanted to justify his anger and fight the government, to the Southern Baptist man who needed validation from his church-going friends. From the man who suffered physical pain because of stress and tension in his life, to Dahlia, whose face suggested she was permanently pissed off. From Lin, who'd had surgery for cancer and might still have cancer, to lovely Jessica floating through the hallways in her long white skirt. From Meryl, confused, excitable, and noisy as she was, to the man wearing a toupee and gold jewelry who seemed overly concerned about his sex life.

As I observed each of my fellow retreatants, my perception of them shifted. It became crystal clear that I was no different than any of these people. All of us were in the same boat, and we were all here for the same reason: we were lost, hurting, and searching for peace and happiness. And we were all running out of time. All of us someday would die. This insight hit me like a swift kick to my head, momentarily paralyzing me. It was now impossible to feel anything other than love and compassion toward every single person in the room. Even Meryl.

The cooks at Bodhi always put out an elaborate lunch. The high point of the day for everyone at the monastery had to be seeing the various delectable foodstuffs crowding the lunch table. Today's meal looked especially yummy—onion soup, vegetarian lasagna, rice-mushroom casserole, green beans with almonds, a leafy salad, cornbread, and apple dumplings. Charles had prepared the meal. He stood in front of the stove like a proud Papa, refilling large bowls and platters as the long line of retreatants rounded the serving table in the middle of the kitchen. As usual, I was the last person in the lunch line. I sensed Charles watching me as I filled my plate. Once we were alone in the kitchen, juggling a full plate of food in one hand and a bowl of soup, utensils, and napkin in the other hand, I turned to Charles and whispered, "Aren't you going to eat? I never see you in the dining hall."

"I'll eat later."

My gaze fell to his waist. His belt had a few extra holes punched through. "Please, Charles. Fix yourself a plate. It all looks so delicious."

"I will. You go enjoy."

Toward the end of the meal, Bhante Upali asked for everyone's attention. "A snowstorm is predicted to hit us tonight or tomorrow. Right now, Barry is on the tractor clearing the parking lot in case some of you have to be home on Monday for a work or family obligation. If that's the case, you may want to shorten your retreat and leave today. Because if we get as much snow as they're predicting . . ." Bhante Upali chuckled. "Well, there's no telling when you'll be able to get out of this place."

There was a general buzzing and nervous laughter among the group, plus some very worried faces.

"How much snow are they predicting, Bhante?" Meryl exclaimed.

"Well, they're not exactly sure. I don't want to alarm you, or tell anyone to leave. But I'd suggest if there is some obligation you have for Monday or Tuesday, you might want to consider leaving while you still can. These back roads get awfully treacherous in winter, and they're predicting a major winter storm. Of course, anyone who wants to stay, please stay and we'll continue the retreat. There is a phone in the hallway outside the Women's Dorm if anyone needs to contact family members or make arrangements. But please, let's all try very hard not to let this impending snowstorm disturb our practice of mindfulness. If you need to leave, try to proceed quietly so that there's a minimum of disturbance to the people who are staying. And for those of you who stay, we'll keep to the schedule. After the retreat ends on Monday, I'm sure you'll be able to continue your practice of mindfulness while shoveling snow."

"Do you know if the storm is coming from the direction of D.C., Bhante?" the red-bearded professor asked.

"I don't know. Someone will find out and post a more extensive weather report on the bulletin board. Meanwhile, after you finish your lunch, you are welcome to use the phone. And again, please try to retain the awareness you've been practicing here during these past several days."

"Has Winding Creek Road been plowed yet, Bhante?" the man with the toupee asked.

And that was it. My tranquil state of mind was broken as the room became charged with chaos. Soon I expected to see a mad dash to the one phone. Bhante Upali sighed, obviously tired of fielding questions. "Yes," he said, "I think that road has been plowed."

Despite the confused, frightened faces surrounding me, I smiled. There was no confusion, no question, in my mind: I was staying. For me, this snowstorm was a blessing in disguise. Now I could stay and finish the retreat, undeterred by Mack's veiled threats. Thanks to Mother Nature, it was impossible to return home and start cooking. I was snowbound in wild, wonderful West Virginia. Period.

As retreatants headed back to the kitchen with empty plates and bowls, many whispered or talked aloud in semi-hysterical voices. Several people were on the verge of tears. When I entered the kitchen, Polly was in conference with Charles near the stove. There was an air of chattiness about the kitchen, and I couldn't resist joining in. "Charles, that was an excellent meal you prepared today. I want you to know how thoroughly I enjoyed it. What seasonings did you put in that rice casserole?"

His blue eyes came to life. "Oh, just a little bit of dis, dat, and de other ting." We both laughed.

After I dumped the compost bucket outside, vacuumed the covered porch, and added a couple of logs to the fire, I put on my coat, hungry for my daily walk and visit with my friends the horses. But before I could walk out the door, Lin took my arm and pulled me aside.

"You are going outside? Wait, I will come with you. I will show her to you now. Just let me get my shawl."

I followed Lin along a shoveled path beside the main building toward the pond, where we took another path that curved through the woods toward a dense planting of bamboo. We crossed a little wooden bridge suspended over a gushing stream, and soon we were standing before a three-foot-high white marble statue of a woman. The statue stood upon a brown marble vault which I later learned was a columbarium—a place for ashes of the dead.

"See," Lin said. "Kuan Yin is right here. You can come and speak to her. She will listen."

Awestruck by the beauty of this exquisitely sculpted, richly feminine figure, I stood perfectly still, admiring the gentle folds of her long white robe, the glossy smoothness of her exposed neckline, and the polished white curves of her round cheeks. Atop her head, I noted the outlines of a small seated Buddha figure in her crown. She stood on a lotus flower pedestal, and I marveled at the fine detail of her bare feet and tiny toes. Her right hand was raised about chest height with the middle finger and thumb joined together. Her left hand extended across her body, palm outstretched in greeting. I had a powerful urge to place my own hand in hers, and gently squeeze her delicate marble fingers.

"Kuan Yin is full of compassion for all living beings," Lin said. "She is already close to you, Sister Laurie. She has heard your cries, and if you come to her, she will help you and protect you." Lin pressed her palms together at her chest, whispered a verse in Burmese, and bowed her head. My palms also came together as I lowered my head toward the lovely white marble woman.

After my walk and visit with the horses, I headed to the parking lot. I brushed the snow off my car, opened the trunk, grabbed my fleece-lined rubber boots, and hugged them to my chest, grateful I'd thought to bring them along. During the next several days, I was sure I'd put them to good use.

The Southern Baptist man was using the phone in the hallway outside the Women's Dorm. In line behind him, I overheard him say, "Honey, you don't seem to understand. I am in the middle of the woods in the mountains of West Virginia. The only way to get out is on back roads . . . No, I can't . . . Honey, *I don't know* . . . No, cell phones don't work here. Listen, I've got to go now. I think it's starting to snow. I'll call you when I can." He paused. "Honey, *I don't know.*" He motioned to me that he was almost finished with the call.

After he hung up, I dialed home. I was surprised when Mack answered the phone. He hated talking on the phone.

"Lulu! I was wondering when I'd be hearing from you."

"Is it snowing there?"

"Oh, it's been a bitch! Snowing every day. Of course, the driveway's impassable, and I hear more snow is on the way."

"Yes, that's why I'm calling." It felt odd speaking to him. Our conversations of late had become mere formalities, as though we were distant neighbors instead of husband and wife. "They're predicting a huge snowstorm here. We're supposed to get over three feet, plus blowing and drifting. So, obviously, I won't be coming home tomorrow."

There was silence at the other end of the line. "Well, if you knew this was coming, you should have left already. I mean, you have the car, so basically, I'm stranded here. And I'm running low on food. Not only for myself, but for Booter and the cats. You're being totally selfish and irresponsible, as usual."

I didn't say anything.

"So, when do you think you'll be able to get out of there?"

"I don't know, Mack. I just thought I should call and tell you. How's Booter?"

"He's fine. Listen, call me tomorrow and give me a progress report. I've got to go."

He hadn't asked me how I was doing or how the retreat was going. All he seemed to care about was his food supply and getting off the phone. I recognized the emotion of anger arising within me. "Where do you have to *go*? You said you were stranded."

"I'm working. The muses are calling. I don't have time for this bullshit. I only answered the phone because I thought it might be you."

"How thoughtful." I paused. "Listen, Mack, I need you to do something. That is, if you're not too *busy*. I need you to record a message on the answering machine canceling the cooking for next week. You can say the cook is stuck out of town because of the storm."

He groaned as though I'd just stabbed him in the chest. "Honest to Christ, Lu! Your inattention, stupidity, and negligence are going to run this business into the ground!"

☜ⅎ❦∾❧

The gathering in the meditation hall that afternoon was considerably thinned out. About two thirds of the retreatants had left or were preparing to leave. I had trouble concentrating. My mind kept replaying the conversation with Mack. I trembled, suddenly fearful of the life waiting for me back home. *Home.* Did I even have one? Every time I was away from the farmhouse, whether grocery shopping, teaching a cooking class, or making food deliveries, I dreaded returning to my own home. Inside those walls I walked on eggshells, careful not to do or say anything that might trigger Mack's next volcanic eruption of vitriol. But here at the monastery, for the first time in many years, I could actually relax and be myself. And that felt good. Very good.

Half a dozen of us were gathered in the library for the optional dhamma discussion. Bhante Upali glanced around the room. "Before we begin, does anyone have any questions?"

I raised my hand. "Bhante, I really want to continue this practice once I'm back home. But to do that, I feel like I need to put my faith in something. I know the Buddha didn't want us to worship him as a God, but if the Buddha doesn't want us to put our faith in him, where do we put our faith?"

Bhante Upali's gaze drilled a hole in my head. "That's a good question. The Four Noble Truths are like the granddaddy of Buddhism, and are often the part of the Buddha's teaching that initially attract people: The truth that suffering exists, that suffering is caused by desire, craving, and attachment, that there is an *end* to suffering, and that the end of suffering can be realized by following the Noble Eight-fold Path. Most people can relate in some way to these truths, especially the First Noble Truth. And because the majority of us would like to end our suffering, this is what motivates us to begin practicing meditation and learning the dhamma. Later on, when you begin to have insights, your 'faith' so to speak in the Buddha's teachings naturally becomes stronger. But for now, try to contemplate and understand, at some deep level, the essence of the dhamma: The Four Noble Truths."

My palms came together at my chest. "Thank you, Bhante."

"Anyone else have a question?" The room was silent.

I raised my hand again. "Bhante, after meditation you usually chant and recite, 'All conditioned things are impermanent.' Are there any *un*-conditioned things that are *permanent?*"

Bhante Upali cleared his throat. "Nibbana," he said. "Nibbana is the unconditioned—pure awareness. It's always there."

"But I . . . I can't even imagine it," I stammered.

"Think of Nibbana as the light in an old-time film projector. The film—the little square picture frames that spin on the reel—are our perceptions as they come through our six senses of hearing, seeing, smelling, tasting, touching, and thinking. The images on the film that are projected onto the screen are the stories, the melodramas we create in our own minds. The light shining on these images is pure awareness, or pure consciousness. Together they create the 'I consciousness' or sense of self. Once the film is over, and our perceptions are no longer being formed and filtered through the six senses, the illusion of a sense of 'self' disappears, and all that remains is the light—the light of pure consciousness, which is always there."

"But Bhante," I said, "that sounds sort of, well, frightening."

His next words were gentle and reassuring, as though speaking to a lost child. "No, not frightening." He smiled. "Just changed."

<hr />

At the end of the afternoon meditation session, I went directly to the woodstove. The fire was low, and I set to work. So far, I hadn't let the fire go out. Not once. Through the window beyond the bamboo grove, I could make out the blurry white image of Kuan Yin's statue. Was she a goddess? A celestial being? A female Buddha? Had she actually heard my cries, as Lin had said?

Charles exited the kitchen and walked toward me. He leaned close and whispered, "So, you're not leaving us? I thought you had a cooking job."

Staring at the smooth contours of his clean-shaven face, I said, "It's canceled."

His eyes rejoiced. "Wonderful."

Grinning ear to ear, I replied, "Yes, it is."

12

She Is Right Beside You

(Day 10)

At 5:25 a.m. I walked down the center aisle of the candlelit hall, dropped to my knees, and bowed three times to the golden Buddha. Seated cross-legged on my cushion, I closed my eyes, and inhaled: *May I be well, happy, and peaceful. May I be free from anxiety and fear.* On the out-breath, I sent loving-kindness to all living beings. By some miracle, my heart was able to send a tiny bit of loving-kindness to Mack. Afterward, I fell into deep meditation. The next perception to enter my consciousness was the songs of the birds serenading the arrival of a new day replete with infinite possibilities.

Light as vapor and pleasantly empty, I exited the hall and walked down the long corridor, my feet barely touching the floor. Through the windows, big fluffy snowflakes fell from the heavens, no telling when it would stop. Eight inches or so of fresh snow had accumulated since yesterday. My gaze shifted to the pond and I smiled. The height of the outdoor bronze Buddha's snowy blanket was now up to his chest.

I fed the fire, sat on the low bench opposite the stove, and stared out the window at the chickadees at the feeders. Those tiny black and white birds didn't worry about what was coming next, or what went on before. Snowstorms or rainstorms didn't faze them. They didn't question or analyze or doubt themselves; they were simply being present and accepting life as it is. They were hungry, so they ate. As the tiny birds flitted from tree to feeder, I reminded myself to try to be more like the chickadees.

During the mealtime ceremony before breakfast, as I recited the Loving-Kindness Discourse, tears rained down my cheeks. Embarrassed, I sobbed uncontrollably on my cushion in the last row, hiding my face. *My God, where are all these tears coming from?*

We practiced more walking meditation during the 9 to 11 a.m. meditation session. I focused my full attention on the movements of my legs, breaking each slow step apart in my mind—lift, forward, touch, shift weight, lift, forward, touch, shift weight. I observed each small movement arise and vanish, arise and vanish. At one point I almost laughed out loud when I realized that I'd completely lost track of time. It could have been five o'clock in the morning or ten o'clock at night. I had no idea. I was suspended somewhere in between time, and I found this quite pleasant. But the most wonderful part about not knowing whether it was day or night, morning or evening, summer or winter or fall, was that *it didn't matter.* "Not knowing" didn't bother me in the least; in fact, it was a delightful place to be.

When it was time for lunch, Charles had, as usual, prepared a magnificent meal: vegetable soup with pasta, eggplant parmesan, tofu curry, roasted squash, and a fruit salad. Although I loaded my plate with helpings of everything, when I returned to my cushion with my food, I discovered I'd lost my usual appetite. *What in the world is going on?* Something strange was definitely happening to me, but I hadn't a clue what it was.

After lunch I fed the fire, vacuumed the covered porch, put on my snow boots, dumped the compost bucket, and headed straight for Kuan Yin's statue. I had to tramp through snow up to my knees in order to reach her. Thick snowflakes filled the tracks behind me. With cautious steps, I approached the columbarium and stood before the white marble woman. *Was she placed here to watch over the ashes of the dead?*

Snowflakes melted on my cheeks and eyelashes. I brushed the snow from the statue's tiny feet, her robe, and her headdress. Longing to touch the lovely marble sculpture, I removed my glove and placed three fingers into her outstretched palm. As I squeezed her delicate stone fingers, my heart exploded with love. Then my hand rose to the neckline of her robe, my fingers resting on the spot just below her collarbone. Soon my palms came together at the same spot on my own chest, and I bowed to this beautiful celestial woman, whoever she was.

"Please, dear Kuan Yin," I whispered, looking up at her. "Please give me strength and courage. And please watch over me." It was all I could think of to say. I bowed once more, and followed what remained of my tracks back to the main building.

The sign-up sheet for that afternoon's private interviews with Bhante Upali contained one open slot, from 3:15 to 3:30. I wrote my name on the sheet.

There was still time before the afternoon meditation session began. Maybe I should call Mack. In my present state of mind, my usual animosity toward him had diminished. Lin's prophetic words regarding our marital troubles came to mind: "Soon you will be able to make things better." Maybe if I showed Mack some loving-kindness, his angry heart would soften. After all, he wasn't a total monster. He was just another one of us lost souls struggling to find happiness. I'd made numerous attempts over the years to save our marriage, but maybe I hadn't been going about it the right way. Maybe I could do better. Maybe now *we* could do better.

"Lu! I thought this might be you. Sorry I was a bit abrupt the last time you called, but I was right in the middle of creating my latest masterpiece. Honest to Christ, I never fail to be blown away by my own literary brilliance. But alas, to quote Pound, 'I am a man on whom the sun has gone down.' I'm sure the goddamned friggin' idiots of the world won't discover my genius until long after I'm dead! So, anyway, what's up at the monastery? Have you reached Nirvana yet?" He chuckled.

"Well, no. But I've certainly been meditating a lot. And I think I might be making a little progress." I paused. "You know, Mack, I'm actually glad about the snowstorm. It gives me the opportunity to stay here a bit longer."

"Oh, *really?*"

I detected annoyance in his voice. "Yes, really."

After a brief pause, his tone brightened. "Well, well, I'm glad to hear it! And who was the one who told you that going to that monastery would do you good? That it was exactly what you needed?"

I sighed. "You, Mack."

"That's right. I always know what's good for you."

I sighed. "Listen, Mack, I'm calling because I want you to know that I've sort of hooked onto something here. I'm not sure what it is, some kind of different energy. I mean, all this meditation and getting up super early in the morning has had a good effect on me. So, I have to ask for your help."

"What kind of help?" he growled.

I sighed. "Look, Mack, I don't want to fight with you anymore. Right now, I really need your support, understanding, and cooperation so I can continue this practice at home."

"Is that all?" he chuckled. "Sure, sure. I'm all for it! Get up at 3 a.m. and meditate five hours a day if you like. That won't bother me a damn bit as long as you're in your own room and being quiet. Christ, I don't care if you sit in there and masturbate for five hours a day as long as I'm not disturbed! But seriously, Lu. You need to reign yourself in. How many times have I told you that you need to get up early every single day no matter what, and put yourself on a strict schedule? This is exactly the kind of self-discipline that's been lacking in your frivolous, meaningless existence. Christ, I've been trying to get your lazy Jewish ass out of that bed at 5 a.m. for years! I don't know why you insist on sleeping your life away. Honestly, Lu, you've turned into a slug. Your days have no structure, no purpose."

His words were like bullets ripping my flesh. "Mack, *please!* Eight or eight thirty isn't *that* late to be getting out of bed. And I do *plenty* during the day!" I saw my anger rising. I saw myself being drawn into an argument—the same old pattern. Somehow, by seeing it so clearly, I was able to let the anger go. I took a deep breath and tried again. "Look, Mack, whatever time I get up in the morning isn't the point. Besides, that's history. I want to start something new. I want to continue what I've started here because it's making me feel good, but I need your help. I can't keep fighting with you, Mack. It's killing me. It's killing both of us. Something's got to change."

I waited for a response, but he was silent. "Mack, I just want you to know that I'm willing to try, one last time, to make things better between us. But you've got to at least meet me halfway." I paused. "Mack, did you hear me? I called to ask for your help, and to tell you that because of this retreat I'm willing to make an effort to start a new and better life with you."

"No, Lu," he finally said. "Not with me. With yourself."

Now it was my turn to be silent. *With myself? What the hell was THAT supposed to mean?*

"So, when do you think you'll be coming home?"

My mind went blank. "I, uh, I really have no idea. And to be honest,

I'm in no rush."

"Well, you'd better be in a rush! Don't forget you have a husband stranded up here on this godforsaken windswept hill in the middle of nowhere with no car and a dwindling supply of food!"

"I'm sure you'll survive."

"The drifts at the crest of the driveway are five feet high!"

"Wow. You're kidding."

"I wish I were. It's been a bitch up here, Lu. Just to feed the pets is an ordeal. Every time I go outside, I have to shovel a new path to the barn to feed the cats, and another path to Booter's doghouse because the old paths are blown shut."

"I guess the driveway's impassable."

"I've never seen it so bad. I didn't bother calling anyone to plow. I'm sure it'll cost a fortune. I figured I'd wait until you were coming home. But if you don't know when that will be, I'm in big trouble."

"Oh, come on, Mack. Don't be so dramatic. I'm sure Larry will give you a ride to the grocery store. He's a good neighbor, and his truck has four-wheel drive. All you have to do is walk down the hill and meet him at the road."

I was fidgety during the afternoon meditation session, disheartened by Mack's words, "Not with me. With yourself." I'd asked for his support. I'd opened my heart and practically begged him to join me in forging a new life together. But instead of saying he wanted to try and he'd make an effort too, it was obvious Mack's response was a direct rejection of me. He was still pushing me away, and it hurt.

At three o'clock I rose from my cushion and quietly left the meditation hall. In the minutes before my scheduled interview with Bhante Upali, I paced the length of the covered porch, silently repeating the questions I wanted to ask my teacher. But as soon as I sat on the folding chair opposite the skeletal monk in the library, I couldn't remember a single question I'd wanted to ask. We sat there for several minutes, looking at each other.

"Did you have a question?" he asked.

"Uh, well . . ." My chest tightened. Practically in tears, I leaned forward and an avalanche of words came tumbling out. "I don't know what's happening to me, Bhante! I've been getting such weird sensations lately. I'm wide awake extremely early in the mornings, which is so unusual for me. I'm completely alert and energized at that hour even though I've had only four or five hours of sleep. I've lost my normal appetite. I'm seeing people in a completely different way. I've had visions during meditation. And I keep feeling this intense fear pop up. My heart starts racing like I'm on speed or something, but I have no idea what I'm afraid of. And now I seem to be moved to tears at the drop of a hat." I paused, trying to contain the flood of emotion over-whelming me. "Bhante, what's *happening* to me?"

"You said you've begun seeing people in a completely different way. How so?"

"Well, I guess at this one point it became clear to me that no one was any better or any worse than anyone else. I realized, in a deep and pro-found way, that we're all the same. We all share the same condition—the human condition. We all suffer our share of pain, grief, and misfortune; we all have our own demons to contend with, and for that reason, the only way to relate to anyone is with loving-kindness and compassion."

The corners of Bhante Upali's lips turned up in a gentle smile. I waited for him to speak, but he remained silent.

"Bhante, what's causing the fear, the tears, the heart palpitations? What does it all mean?"

He cleared his throat. "Nothing's real. Whatever you're feeling isn't real. When it happens, just notice it."

Just notice it? I didn't understand. I wanted an answer. I wanted an explanation. "Just notice it? That's all? Nothing else?"

"Nothing else. Just remember it isn't real. Nothing's real. Everything is vibration."

He motioned to the clock. My appointment was over. I stood up, my heart heavy with disappointment. I pressed my palms together, bowed my head, thanked him for the interview, and left the library even more uncomfortable and confused than when I'd arrived. *Everything is vibration? What was THAT supposed to mean?*

Back in the meditation hall I did my best to watch my breathing coming in and going out, arising and vanishing. Gradually, my breaths slowed, and part of me seemed to float away on soft clouds. It was then that I became a sitting spectator. There were no thoughts—no other awareness in my mind besides simply *sitting and watching*. The brass bell sounded three times, and as the tonal vibrations faded away into nothingness, the meditation session ended. My attention was drawn to the closed door on the men's side of the hall—the door that led to the mysterious adjacent room. Yes, something inside that room was definitely calling me.

Before going to bed, I knocked on Lin's door. She opened it immediately. "Can I talk to you?" I asked.

"Yes, yes. Come in, Sister Laurie. Sit down, here."

I sat on the edge of the bed. "I went to see Kuan Yin today. But I'm not sure what I'm supposed to say to her."

"Speak to her from your heart. She hears everyone and has a great amount of compassion for your distress. Some people leave offerings of fruit or flowers beside her, but that is not necessary. She will be with you if you call to her. And she will help you."

"Really?"

"Do not worry, Sister Laurie. Everything will be well. Kuan Yin is protecting you. I can see her now."

I trembled. Warmth coursed throughout my body as though I was being embraced by a thousand loving arms. It was similar to the warm sensation I'd experienced in the meditation hall when the white-robed Asian woman appeared kneeling behind my left shoulder. *Oh my God! Could that woman have been Kuan Yin?* "Lin, are you saying Kuan Yin is here right now in this room? You can actually see her?"

"Yes. She is right here. She is right beside you."

Overwhelmed, I stammered, "She, she came to me once before. In the meditation hall. But, but, I didn't believe, I mean, I wasn't sure. But of course, at that time I had no idea . . ."

"You are very fortunate," Lin said.

"Is she on my left side?"

"No. She is on your right."

Disappointed, my head dropped. The white-robed woman in the meditation hall had definitely appeared on my *left* side. *If Kuan Yin wanted me to know her presence was real, why would she switch sides?* "Are you sure, Lin?"

"Yes. She is on your right side. And she says that you will know her again in that place."

"My God, you can actually hear her?"

"Sometimes. She is very close to you, Sister Laurie. She has been for quite some time. And she will help ease your pain."

I wanted to believe Lin. I wanted to believe Kuan Yin could help me. But the rational side of my brain still had doubts. All I could do was wait and see.

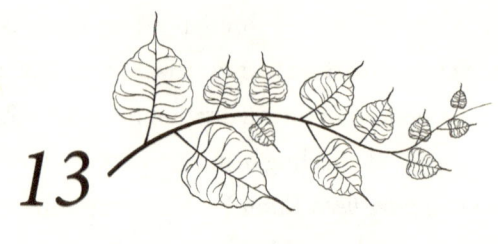

13

Climbing a Mountain

(Day 11)

I sat up in bed, completely alert at 4:07 a.m. Once my feet touched the floor, it became clear I was no longer inside my own body. Instead, my consciousness was somewhere outside myself, watching my body move. I watched my arm rise and open the bedroom door. I witnessed each of my slow steps to the bathroom. I observed my hand reach for the light switch and flip it on, then watched my fingers grasp the toothbrush. As I brushed my teeth, all that existed was the circular motions of arm. There were no interfering thoughts. Actually, there were no thoughts at all. Only watching.

This dreamlike experience continued as I dressed, and I made no attempt to stop it. The woman I recognized as Laurie—someone who usually had a multitude of thoughts, doubts, questions, worries, and fears running through her head at any given moment—had, at least for now, disappeared. And it was unexpectedly pleasant. Instead of trying to analyze, question, or fight this new way of seeing, I decided to welcome it—to embrace it and be with it for as long as it lasted. I'd follow it anywhere it wanted to take me. I'd trust it and stay alert for any clues, signs, or help it might offer along the way. And, to my surprise, I wasn't afraid. I was ready.

Throughout morning meditation, surges of gratitude exploded like bombs inside my heart. Occasionally, tears rolled down my cheeks. Every so often I opened my eyes, gazed at the golden Buddha, and silently thanked him. I also thanked Bhante Upali for his teaching, and I thanked Lin for showing me Kuan Yin. I even thanked the immobilizing snowstorm for stranding me here. Gradually, I fell into deep meditation, and only recognized where I was when the sound of sweet birdsong announced the dawn.

In no hurry to eat breakfast, I remained seated on my cushion after everyone else had exited the hall. Behind me, the door to the mysterious adjacent room on the men's side was open. Now was the perfect time to venture inside and take a look. I tiptoed between the rows of men's cushions. As I entered the glass-enclosed room, my heart leapt with joy. *Oh, wow! It's a greenhouse!* I was a sucker for greenhouses. I'd worked in several because I loved tending plants and watching them grow. Potted houseplants graced the sills of every window of the old farmhouse, and each spring I planted flower and vegetable gardens in beds I'd dug beside the driveway.

Pink orchids in full bloom hung from the low ceiling, and pots of begonias, dracaenas, spider plants, and jades lined the entire length of the little hothouse. There was even a small indoor pond. Toward the far end of the greenhouse were two tall, tree-like plants growing in huge ceramic pots. One tree had leaves resembling the pointed leaf in the stained-glass window in the meditation hall. *Could this actually be a Bodhi tree? The tree the Buddha sat under when he awakened?* The other tree-like plant resembled a jade, except its stems were narrow, with long, serrated leaves covered with plantlets. *How unusual!* Although

I'd been involved with plants my entire life, I'd never come across this particular plant. I inspected it closely. Near the top, hanging large and heavy from the tip of a branch, was a gorgeous, softball-sized cluster of tubular pink and violet blossoms.

Wow! What a rare, exquisite flower! Amazed and excited by the exotic tubular blossoms near the ceiling, I wondered, *Was it this plant that had been calling me to come and see?* Mesmerized by the blossom's unusual beauty, I touched the plant and whispered, "What are you trying to tell me? That maybe with a little luck, I could blossom too?"

At breakfast I managed to eat half a bowl of oatmeal, a couple of almonds, and a bite of toast. Today was the last day of the formal retreat, and according to the schedule, we were supposed to clean up and pack after breakfast, then from nine to ten we were back in the great hall for meditation, followed by Bhante Upali's Closing Talk. There was nothing to pack because I wasn't leaving, so instead I sat opposite the stove with a cup of tea, content to stare out the window at the winter wonderland. The heavens had dumped an additional two-plus feet of snow during the past twelve hours. Beyond the birdfeeders the forest was swallowed by a sea of white, and the small, round wooden kutis in the distance resembled chocolate cupcakes, their roofs frosted with thick white icing.

My gaze shifted to the thick icicles hanging from the roof. I scrutinized each glassy stalactite formation, captivated by the beauty of its sleek surface and hard, icy interior. When the sun appeared through a break in the clouds, the icicles sparkled from the inside, as though filled with shiny diamonds. Awestruck, I gaped at the glittering formations as though they contained the magic of the universe. I focused on the biggest of the icicles, mesmerized by the rhythmic drip, drip, drip of one water droplet after another as it slipped from its slender, frozen tip. It occurred to me that as the weather warmed, the entire icicle, including its lovely sparkling interior, would melt and disappear, and

I noticed sadness arising. But before sadness could take hold in my mind, a soothing voice whispered: *Annica, Annica . . . All conditioned things are impermanent.*

I sensed a close presence and turned around to see an orange-robed figure standing behind me. It was Bhante Targarasikhi, the monk I first encountered on his knees in the office when I arrived. He was from Thailand, and no longer in seclusion. His eyes sparkled almost as brilliantly as the icicles.

"Like diamonds," he said, smiling.

It was the first time I'd heard this monk speak. The comforting tone of his voice and those two little words were perfect—capturing everything I was experiencing at that moment. Our eyes remained locked for a few more seconds, making it clear we now shared a precious secret. He bowed his head, then turned and walked slowly down the hallway, his hands clasped behind his back. My gaze returned to the glittering icicles. Although I had no idea myself, I was certain this quiet monk from Thailand understood exactly what was happening to me.

Before his Closing Talk, Bhante Upali mentioned there would be an Eight Lifetime Precepts ceremony offered in a few months, and he encouraged anyone who was interested in taking these training Precepts to participate. "The Eight Lifetime Precepts serve as a guide to deepen our practice," he said. "They include three Precepts relating to 'Right Speech,' which is part of the Buddha's Noble Eightfold Path. In addition to promising to abstain from false speech, one who takes the Eight Lifetime Precepts promises also to abstain from malicious or harsh speech, and useless speech."

There was no better example of malicious and harsh speech than Mack's cruel language. Because he was a writer, his words were his weapons. He chose each one carefully, sharpening them into blades with the intention of inflicting the deepest wounds. And when he flew into one of his rages, he spewed those words mercilessly, slashing me and anyone else to shreds, especially the Jews. My eyes squeezed shut recalling the nastiness of his speech.

"Your people are the epitome of treachery, bribery, and corruption," he often said. "Greedy, moneygrubbing scum who are out to destroy the Christian, white, heterosexual male." He routinely blamed me for failing to get his work published, and lashed out whenever the mood struck him. "You're nothing but an ignorant, incompetent, disloyal wife! You promised to research literary markets and send out my manuscripts, but it's been years since you've lifted a damn finger to help me! You're a quitter, you're not a partner! Christ, you've been nothing but a hindrance to me and my work ever since I married you!"

I choked back sobs. No wonder I'd become a hollow, depressed, insecure shell of my former self.

After a short meditation, it was time for Bhante Upali's Closing Talk. Silently, I asked him to please address my biggest concern and greatest fear: *Bhante, once I'm back home, how do I continue what I started here?*

"Coming on a retreat is like climbing a mountain," he began. "Just imagine that you lived in a town on the other side of a tall mountain. Maybe you never climbed the mountain because you were lazy. And maybe you had a friend who kept coming over on warm, sunny mornings saying, 'Come on, let's go climb the mountain.' And you'd say, 'Nahh, I'm too tired.' Or you'd come up with some other excuse, and you'd roll over and get forty extra winks. Then finally one day, when your friend comes over and asks you again, you figure, 'Oh, well, I'll do it just to get rid of this guy.' So you force yourself out of bed, and you start climbing the mountain.

"And as soon as you get above the rooflines of the houses, you realize that the air has a fresher quality. And as you keep going higher you notice that the sounds of the dogs barking and the neighbors shouting at each other are much quieter. You stop every hundred yards or so to look around, and the higher you go, the more you see. When you get up quite high, you stop and sit, and it's like seeing a whole new town. You see places you hadn't noticed before. You might say, 'Oh, look, there's a park with shady trees, and it's got swans swimming in the lake.' Or 'Oh, look, there's another route to get to Aunt Judy's house. Instead of following that crowded, pot-holed street, there's another street I could travel more calmly and easily.' And so you see there are other possibilities of how to maneuver around the town. Whereas before you might have just been following your nose, sitting in your car with your hands on the wheel, the radio blaring, traveling the same old routes that you always took even though you might be cursing the traffic or the road construction, complaining about this or that, and just accepting it as your lot. But now, from this vista you can see that you can enjoy your life in the town more because there are other possibilities." He smiled, looking directly at me.

Flooded with hope, I returned his smile. Maybe during this retreat I'd climbed high enough up the mountain to see another possibility, another path leading to a happier life!

"So," he continued, "that was the good news. Now for the not-so-good news. The reality of the situation is that the snow last night was very wet snow. It's almost like wet cement. And on top of all the snow that's already fallen, our tractor is having a difficult time getting through it. Clearing the snow will be a long and tedious process, because right now the tractor is at the top of the hill. So that means snow shovels." There was laughter all around.

As I walked slowly down the long corridor, I gazed out the window toward the pond and giggled. A tall white cap covered the Buddha statue's crown. The level of the snow had risen from his chest up to his face, so all that was visible of him now were his black and white painted eyes.

On the covered porch I loaded the woodstove while the remaining retreatants conversed gaily, congratulating each other as though they'd reached the summit of Mount Everest. A camaraderie had built up among the thinned-out group; we'd survived, we'd made it through long days of silence and meditation. We'd sat on hard cushions for what seemed like eternity, conquering pain and our intruding thoughts and fears, eating only two meals a day. And now we were all here—snowbound together inside this forest monastery way out in the wilds of West Virginia. I stared at the wintry landscape outside and mused, *Now comes the fun part!*

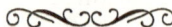

After lunch the great "dig out" began. Living in the mountains of Pennsylvania where snow-filled winters could last from October to May, I was an old hat at shoveling snow. Most of us worked on clearing the parking lot, while Bhante Upali, Barry, Pete, and Bhante Tagarasikhi went up the hill to help with the tractor.

Filled with energy and enthusiasm, I ran from the parking lot up and down the hill several times to check on the progress of the tractor. Not only had I spent a good deal of time around tractors, if there was one thing in my life I was confident about, it was my ability to help vehicles maneuver through thick drifts of snow. Plus, I was determined to keep a close watch on Bhante Upali. Although he was very wise when it came to understanding the dhamma, he'd grown up in sunny California and lived for years in India, so I wasn't sure how much he understood about navigating tractors through deep snow.

By four o'clock the tractor had made it almost halfway down the hill. Evening meditation started at five, and Bhante Upali dismissed us for the day. I went back to my room, put on some dry clothes, and called Mack. I was willing to try one more time to penetrate his hardened heart.

"You wouldn't believe what it's like here," I said to him. "It's incredible, really. Worse than I've ever seen it at home. I hear the whole Mid-Atlantic region is in a state of emergency."

"It's pretty bad here too. But I don't think we got quite as much snow as you did. Of course, it's like Siberia up here on this frozen tundra," he complained. "Booter's doghouse is practically buried, and it took me half an hour just to shovel a path to the barn to feed the cats. Christ, what an ordeal! And thanks to you, I'm doing all this shit by myself! Larry called and offered to come plow me out. I told him I might as well wait until I know when you're coming home. He also offered to give me a ride to the grocery store."

"I knew he would. Larry's a good guy."

"So, will you be coming home tomorrow?"

"Tomorrow?" I laughed. "There's no way."

"That bad, huh?"

"You can't imagine."

"But seriously, Lu, give me an estimate. You ought to have *some* idea when you'll be able to get out of there."

At that point I would have been content to remain at the monastery indefinitely. "I honestly don't know."

"What the hell do you mean, *you don't know?* You're not going to be stuck there forever! I'm sure they have snowplows in West Virginia. Unless of course you have something else up your sleeve. I wouldn't put it past you. You can be a duplicitous Jewish bitch!"

I closed my eyes. Despite the pain inflicted by his words, I was determined not to let his insults lure me into an argument. "Mack, we've been hit by the biggest snowstorm West Virginia has seen in twenty years. We've just started to dig out, the tractor with the front-end bucket gets stuck every five yards, cars are still buried in the parking lot, and there's no telling when the state snowplows will reach our little back road. We're lucky to have working phone lines and electricity."

After a brief silence he hissed, "You knew this was coming. You should have left earlier like you planned."

My teeth clenched. "No," I said. "*Like you planned.*"

"Well, get started on the car. First thing tomorrow morning start digging out the car. Then as soon as it's humanly possible, get your scrawny Jewish ass out of there! Don't forget you have a business to run, mouths to feed, and a responsibility to your husband."

I hated it when Mack told me what to do! I saw my anger rising, but instead of getting irritated, by some miracle I was able to let go of my desire to lash out at him.

"Do you hear me, Lulu?" he barked.

"Yes, Mack," I said calmly. "By the way, Bhante Upali gave a talk today about Right Speech, which is part of the Buddha's Noble Eight-fold Path. Right Speech includes abstaining from harsh and malicious speech."

"What's your point?"

"Well, to be honest, I think the biggest problem in our marriage is the nasty language you use. I mean, I've asked you a million times to stop criticizing and berating me, but you refuse to stop. What's worse is having to listen to your outrageous, Jew-bashing rhetoric and crazy conspiracy theories. I mean, for God's sake, Mack, I'm Jewish, remember? Don't you have any idea how those words affect me? I've begged you to quit subscribing to those White Supremacist newsletters and stop spouting their awful lies. Your language can be so destructive and hateful."

"Right Speech, eh? That's what the monk talked about?"

"Yes! Bhante Upali commented on how easily we can fall into the trap of malicious and harsh speech, and how these are such unwholesome behaviors. If you could just try to—"

"Don't get brainwashed by all that Buddhist claptrap! Just meditate. That's all you need to do. Nothing else. You can't afford to dawdle down there forever playing Buddhist nun. You have a home here, you have responsibilities. Don't you have a cooking class scheduled for Thursday? So, get that car cleaned off tomorrow, and be ready to hit the road. Call me when you know you'll be leaving and I'll tell Larry to plow the driveway."

My words hadn't made a dent. Plus, he expressed zero concern for my well-being, my spiritual growth, or our marriage. Mack could only see what Mack wanted. And right now, he wanted me home.

PART TWO

Snowy Blessings

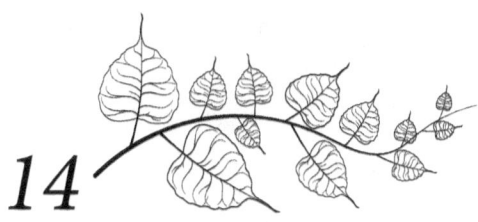

14

Witnessing a Metamorphosis

(Day 12)

I crept out of bed. Jessica was asleep in the bottom bunk opposite mine. I'd invited her to share my room when Bhante Upali suggested that women staying up at Datta House move down to the Women's Dorm. "That way," he'd said, "we can turn down the heat in Datta House and conserve energy."

Jessica lived just outside of D.C. She told me that her father was Japanese and her mother Caucasian. When I'd asked about her clothes, she said, "My spiritual teacher back home told me to wear only white clothes for four months, so I wear white practically all the time. Always when I'm going out. But when I'm home alone, I'll put on another color. Just for a change. It's fun to break the rules sometimes." We laughed together. I understood exactly what she meant.

As I fished the remaining clean clothes from my suitcase, Jessica stirred. "What are you doing?"

"Go back to sleep. I'm sorry I woke you."

"Noooo, I'm getting up too." She wiped her eyes. "What time is it?"

"It's only three thirty. I couldn't sleep."

"What are you going to do?"

"I guess I'll drink a cup of tea, then head to the meditation hall."

"Wait, I'm coming with you."

"Okay, great! We'll meditate together. Sit beside me this morning. You can use Meryl's cushion."

Illumined by candlelight, Jessica's exquisite form radiated beauty, grace, and serenity as she sat with perfect posture on the cushion to my right. We gave each other a reassuring nod, and I closed my eyes, happy I'd made a new friend. Once my mind settled, a warm sensation washed over me. I detected a strong presence nearby. In my mind's eye, I watched my head turn to the right. There was Jessica's image, shining bright, seated on the cushion beside me. I watched her head turn and face me, her sweet expression glowing with unearthly light. Then all at once her face disappeared, and a new face emerged. *Oh my God.* This was the face of the white-robed woman I saw in the meditation hall several days ago—the woman kneeling behind my left shoulder! My brain exploded, sending shockwaves throughout my entire body. *Could this actually be Kuan Yin sitting right beside me?* Astonished, all I could do was sit perfectly still and marvel at this incredible vision, this lovely, luminescent woman beside me, and bask in the warm glow of her presence.

Several minutes later, the woman's face transformed into Jessica again, or this vision of Jessica seated on Meryl's cushion. When her head turned to face me, boundless love and compassion poured from Jessica's dark eyes directly into the center of my heart. Then her mouth formed the most beatific smile I'd ever seen, and that confirmed it. There was no doubt in my mind: Kuan Yin was indeed sitting beside me, *on my right side*, just as Lin had predicted.

I took a deep breath and exhaled slowly. As the shock of witnessing this surreal metamorphosis gradually faded, my mind grew pleasantly still, quiet, spacious. A little while later, the swish of Jessica's skirt down the center aisle broke the silence as she exited the meditation hall. Content and completely comfortable on my cushion, I remained perfectly still, resting in this most sublime place of *sitting and breathing, sitting and breathing*. When I finally opened my eyes to peek at the clock, Machee Nee was seated on her cushion in the front row. The diminutive nun, always the first to arrive for morning meditation, moved so quietly and inconspicuously that I hadn't even known she'd entered the hall.

I rose from my cushion and exited through the double doors. As though in a trance, I walked down the long corridor, enchanted by the snow-covered landscape outside. A change had taken place within me, recircuiting my brain chemistry and flooding my heart with love and gratitude. As one foot moved slowly in front of the other, I had no idea where I was going, but my feet propelled me straight to the library.

Two people sat opposite each other at the center table—Charles, reading a thick book, and Jessica, leaning over a magazine. When I entered the room, Jessica raised her head and gave me her beautiful white smile.

I smiled so hard I thought my mouth would break. I wanted to speak, but words seemed inadequate.

Jessica stood up. "Wonderful," was all she said.

After breakfast I fed the fire, then laced up my boots to join the shovel brigade. In the distance, the tractor's loud engine pierced the sleeping forest, and I hurried outside. There it was! The big orange machine rolled down the hill with Bhante Upali at the wheel. Hoorah! The tractor made a couple of passes in front of the main building, scooping up snow in the bucket and widening the narrow, shoveled paths. I laughed at the sight of this skinny Buddhist monk seated atop the tractor like one of the good old country boys back home. When he turned off the engine, I approached the machine. In a playful mood, I couldn't resist teasing Bhante Upali.

"Not bad for a city boy. You must have been a farmer in a previous life."

He suppressed a smirk.

"What do you need me to do, Bhante? Where do you need help?" I'd proven to him I could work; he could count on me to move the snow and get things done.

He climbed off the tractor. "Why don't you join the others in the parking lot? I think there's one shovel left in the shed." He started for the main building, then turned around. "You know, now that we've finally got the tractor down the hill, it could be a lot of help to us. But I'm afraid there's very little gas left in the tank. And we don't have any extra fuel stored in the garage."

Was he asking for my advice? "Perhaps one of your neighbors has an extra can of diesel fuel. One of us could walk over. Do you know anyone on this road who farms?"

"No, no! We don't want to go bothering any of the neighbors. We don't have a very good relationship with our neighbors. They all think we're strange, you know, because we wear robes and shave our heads. Actually, we've had a few bad experiences with some of them. It's best to stay away. As soon as they plow Winding Creek Road, I'll take the pickup and go buy some gas. It has four-wheel drive."

What? The monks not on good terms with their neighbors? That news not only scraped my nerves like sandpaper, but also starkly contrasted the Buddhist teachings I'd been learning. "Well, if you'll excuse me, Bhante, the only reason I suggested it was because one of the very first lessons I learned when I moved to the country was that in a time of need, you can count on your neighbors. Country folk are always ready and willing to pitch in and lend a helping hand. No matter what. They're some of the best people I've ever met."

"Let's focus on digging out the cars. Perhaps the snowplows will be by later today."

By the time I arrived in the parking lot, two more cars had been unearthed from their snowy tombs. Now that the retreat was over, instead of solemn, silent retreatants, we'd all become happy children playing together at summer camp. Polly and Jessica and I kidded about sculpting a large Buddha snowman. Meryl joked about wishing she'd brought her cross-country skis. Even the monks, wearing puffy orange down jackets over their robes, loosened up and interacted with us differently. Bhante Tagarasikhi worked like a smiling machine, singing in a happy voice, urging everyone on, and Bhante Sabbakittika kept our spirits up, telling everyone what a great job we were doing.

The only problem in clearing the parking lot was where to put all the snow we were removing. The system was to make piles of snow beside each vehicle, then Bhante Upali cruised over on the tractor, scooped snow from the pile, and carted it away. The plan worked well. Plus, I could tell Bhante Upali was having a blast driving the big machine and calling out instructions like a little boy playing with the new toy truck he got for Christmas.

But the system came to a halt when the tractor rolled back into the parking lot for another load and Bhante Upali turned off the engine. I thought he was going to say he'd run out of fuel, but instead he said, "There's no more room outside the parking lot to dump the snow without covering up what we've already cleared. We'll have to make a pile somewhere in here."

"But where, Bhante?" Polly asked, leaning on her shovel. "If we dump the snow in here, we won't be able to get the cars out."

Bhante Upali looked at me. I didn't say anything.

"One car will have to be sacrificed," he said.

I didn't hesitate. "Sacrifice mine!" I walked over to where my car was buried. "Here. This is my car."

Bhante Upali started the engine. As the tractor lurched forward, a peculiar satisfaction settled deep into my bones. When the bucket dumped its first load of snow on top of my car's buried roof, I laughed so hard Polly stared at me as though I'd gone mad.

At four o'clock I walked up the driveway with Pete, Polly, and Meryl. We talked together for a while in front of the office. Through the dense forest, I picked out a woman shoveling snow in front of a cabin about two hundred yards away. "Does anyone know that woman?" I asked. "She must be the monastery's closest neighbor."

"She's been out there about two hours," Pete said. "And she's made quite a bit of progress."

"I know that woman," Meryl said. "She lives alone and works in town in some factory. Her husband left her a few years ago. Story goes he was an alcoholic and used to beat her. Now she's found religion and wants to convert everyone. The monastery's had some trouble with those people in the past. It's come up at a few Board meetings."

"What kind of trouble?" I asked.

"When her husband still lived there, he'd shoot bullets over Bhante Upali's head," Polly said.

"He claimed he was only practicing his hunting skills," Pete added. "And I heard there was also some trouble with one of their kids throwing rocks at the monks."

"Well, even so, I hope that woman's okay," I said. "Maybe one of us should go over and see if she needs any help."

"Maybe," Polly said. "But she's been pretty hostile to people living here."

"Neighbors need to pull together at times like these," I said. "One of us could at least go over and see if she has enough food. I mean, God knows we have plenty of food."

"Why don't you go over?" Pete said. "She might respond favorably to you. You have a kind, friendly face."

"You can borrow my snowshoes," Polly said. "They'll make the trek over to her place a lot easier."

After evening meditation, Bhante Upali made a few announcements and congratulated everyone on their cooperation and hard work in the parking lot. "Tomorrow we should be able to finish digging out the cars." He smiled at me. "Well, except maybe for one. As long as the gas in the tractor holds out, I'll work on clearing the rest of the snow from the parking lot to the road. That way, as soon as Winding Creek Road is plowed, anyone who wants to can leave. Oh, and there seems to be a rumor circulating that someone is going to go check on the woman who lives next door."

I raised my hand. "That would be me, Bhante. I'm going to walk over tomorrow. I want to make sure she's all right. Maybe some of us could even help shovel her driveway."

"You know we've had some trouble with those neighbors in the past."

"I know, Bhante," I said. "And I'll be careful. Don't worry."

Pete raised his hand and addressed me. "I've actually talked to that woman a couple of times, and she's been okay with me. I can go with you if you want."

"That's a good idea," Bhante Upali said. "You go with her, Pete."

⚬⚬⚬⚬⚬⚬

That evening, Jessica, Lin, Meryl, her doctor husband, and I sat on the covered porch drinking tea while Bhante Upali told stories about his travels in India and around the world.

"You know," the monk said, "in certain parts of India the sanitation system is virtually nonexistent, and people just relieve themselves on the beach or on the riverbanks. In this one area where I was staying, there were all these wild pigs that sort of roamed around. Now, these were very big wild pigs, with long, sharp teeth. And every morning when you'd go to the beach to relieve yourself, these huge pigs would be waiting to make a meal for themselves." Bhante Upali started to chuckle. Jessica and I covered our mouths.

"It was sort of funny, but sort of scary sometimes," Bhante Upali continued. "I remember one morning not long after I'd first arrived in this particular area. I was squatting on the beach, and all of a sudden I look up and see this angry mob of ravenous wild pigs snorting and squealing and running right at me!" Bhante Upali couldn't contain his laughter. "And so there I was, literally caught with my pants down, obviously in the middle of something, with this pack of wild pigs coming at me like gangbusters!"

We all burst out laughing. Bhante Upali was laughing so hard tears rolled down his cheeks. He barely managed to add, "Talk about scaring the you-know-what out of you!"

I was laughing so convulsively I thought I might wet myself. Oh, it was wonderful to be laughing again after all those tearful, miserable years! That sweet kiss of laughter showed me just how much of life I'd been missing. I could only hope and pray I'd find my way back to the land of the living once I returned home.

15

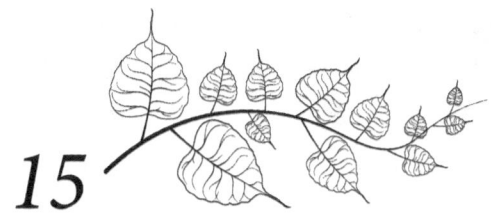

Teeny and the Red Sled

(Day 13)

After breakfast I hurried to the Women's Dorm and knocked on Lin's door. When it opened, I uttered those four inconceivable words: "She appeared to me!"

"Who? Kuan Yin?"

"Yes! Yes, I'm sure it was her!" I said, practically breathless. "She was in the meditation hall with me yesterday morning. She was sitting right next to me, on my right side, just like you said. And this time she took Jessica's form!"

"Jessica is the girl staying in your room?"

"Yes!" I stared at Lin, unsure if I would laugh or cry. "First Jessica began to glow. Then Jessica's face changed into this beautiful woman's face—the same woman in the long white gown I saw before. She was beaming, and she had long black hair, sort of like Jessica's." My chest heaved. "Oh, Lin! Why is this happening? What does it all mean?"

Lin took my hand. "Do not tell anyone about this. They will not understand. They will not believe you. You've been blessed, Sister Laurie. Kuan Yin has come to help you, to guide you, and you must keep this to yourself for now. I know you share many thoughts with your husband, but you must not tell him about this when you return home. If you do, it will cause problems. Maybe you can tell him later. But not now." She paused. "Don't even mention it to Bhante Upali."

"Okay. But I've already shared some pretty personal information with him. And he's been so kind to me."

Lin's face hardened. "Remember, Sister Laurie, it is the *teaching* that we must pay attention to, not the *teacher*."

I nodded.

The snowshoes were awkward at first, but I quickly got used to them. I thanked Pete for volunteering to come with me, and we took off through the woods and deep snow toward the neighbor's cabin. It was slow going, but I was determined; I was on a mission to help this stranded woman. Unlike Bhante Upali, I had zero concerns that I'd be approaching a potentially hostile stranger. Plus, I desperately wanted the monastery to be on good terms with its neighbors. Maybe my small effort would be a step in that direction.

The cabin's sharply slanted roof was covered by thick snow. Smoke billowed from the chimney. I knocked on the door, fumbled with the straps of the snowshoes, and kicked them off, hoping to increase my chances of being invited inside. The shrill barking of a dog quieted when the woman opened the door.

"Hi," Pete said to her.

Shocked, the woman stared blankly at Pete, then raised her arms to him as though he were an angel descended from heaven. "Oh, oh, I don't believe it! Thank you for coming!" She gave Pete a hug. I thought this was a good sign.

"We wanted to see how you were doing," Pete said.

"Oh, I'm all right. Good as anyone would be doin' in this mess."

"We saw you shoveling yesterday," I said. "There are quite a few of us over at the monastery right now. I'm sure we could get a group to come over and help clear your driveway."

"Well," she said, "I was hopin' to get out tomorrow. That is if they've plowed the road." She was short, plump, with broad shoulders, dressed in a stained pink sweatshirt, faded jeans, and fuzzy purple slippers. Her graying hair was combed straight back and tied in a ponytail.

Her eyes narrowed. "I know him, but where do *you* come from?"

"I live in a small town in Pennsylvania."

"What part?"

"Somerset County."

Her face screwed up. "That near Greensburg?"

"It's not far from Greensburg. In fact, I drive through Greensburg once a week to make food deliveries for my business."

"I got my mother in a nursing home in Greensburg," she said. "I go visit her 'bout once every three weeks."

"What a coincidence," I said.

The little dog behind her began yapping. "Now hush, Teeny!"

The small brown and white terrier kept on barking, wagging his tail. "That's funny," I said. "I have a cat named Teeny. Well, actually her name is Tina, but I call her Teeny." I laughed. "Sometimes I call her Teeny Weeny because she's so small."

That piqued her interest. "We both have pets with the same name!"

I smiled. "Yes, we do." I glanced behind her. "Wow, your place looks nice and cozy. I'd love to have a cabin in the woods like this."

"Oh, I'd invite y'all in, but it's a real mess now. I bin workin' some double shifts lately and haven't had time to clean."

"Who ever has time to clean?" I laughed. "I'm Laurie. What's your name?"

"Sharon."

"Nice to meet you, Sharon."

She turned to Pete with moist eyes. "You came all the way over here to check on me? But how'd you get here?"

"We came through the woods," Pete said. "We wanted to see if you needed anything."

"Oh, I'm fine," she said with a sniffle. "That was really sweet of you. I 'preciate it."

The little dog started yelping. "Oh, he's a cutie," I said. "Hi, Teeny."

"It's just him and me here now. And Teeny's gettin' up in years. He don't move around like he used to, but he's still my baby."

Behind her, about a dozen large canvas paintings hung on a high wall. "Wow, look at all those pretty paintings," I said.

"Oh, I'd really like to invite y'all in, but—"

"We don't mind a little clutter, do we, Pete?"

Pete laughed. "You should see my kuti!"

"I'd love to take a look at your paintings, that is, if we're not intruding."

"Intruding? No, no. I don't get many visitors. Well, if y'all don't mind the mess, come on inside and warm yourselves."

The cabin consisted of one large room downstairs with a small kitchen. Stairs led to a loft bedroom. A big wood burner dominated the living space, surrounded by an old rocker and a recliner with tattered upholstery.

"Where did you get all this artwork?" I asked, admiring the colorful canvases decorating the high wall.

"Those're mine," Sharon said.

"You painted them?" Pete asked.

"Yes, I'm an artist. See, I'm working on these cards now." She went over to a round table piled high with stacks of folded white paper. "They'll make nice wedding invitations."

"I didn't know you were an artist," Pete said. He plucked a card from the table. "Wow, this is really good." He handed me the card with purple roses painted in soft brushstrokes.

"Oh, I been foolin' with art my whole life," Sharon said. "But when I found Jesus, I started painting almost all the time. It's like he speaks to me and tells me what to paint. People come to me and ask me to do a painting for them 'cause they know the Lord speaks to me. They know he'll tell me what kind of picture to paint for a certain individual. Each picture I paint has a special message for that individual from our Lord Jesus Christ."

I handed the card to Sharon. "You do beautiful work."

"Purple's my favorite color."

"I'm a big purple fan myself. But I think blue's my favorite color."

She scrutinized me. "Your face," she said.

"Uh, what about my face?"

"I can *tell* somethin' about you."

"You can?"

"Yep."

I glanced at Pete, then back at Sharon. "What can you tell?"

"God is shining his light on you."

"He is?"

"Oh, yeah! I'm *feelin'* somethin' from you! I'll have to give you a verse from Scripture before you leave. God puts a particular Scripture in my head for different people I meet. And this piece of Scripture will have great meaning for you. Have you embraced Jesus as your savior?"

"Uh, well, no. Actually, I'm Jewish."

Her face lit up. "You're one of God's special ones! Your people are the chosen people!"

"Well, I'm not so sure about that."

"But it's true! Jesus was Jewish, and he wanted his people to follow him, to see the light of truth. Yes, the Jewish people are very special. But, unless you become a believer and accept Jesus as your savior, you won't survive the apocalypse and you won't go to heaven."

"I'll take my chances," I said with a chuckle.

"What in Lord's name are you *doin'* at that Buddhist place? That ain't no place for someone like you. You need to commit your soul to Jesus. He's the only salvation. Listen to me, hon. Jesus can *help* you. He'll take care of you. But you must put your faith in him completely."

"Well, I, uh . . . Pete, help me out here."

Sharon turned to Pete sitting in the rocking chair with Teeny in his lap. "The only hope we have is to put our faith in our beloved son Jesus who died on the cross so that we could be saved! Don't believe all the crazy things those funny-lookin' bald-headed guys over there tell you. God didn't want man, who was created in his image, to shave off all his hair. That's unnatural!"

I couldn't resist. "Pete. Take off your hat and show her."

Smiling, Pete pulled off his black ski cap, revealing a quarter inch stubble of black hair.

"Oh, no! You didn't! Now why'd you go and do somethin' crazy like that for? A nice young man like you!"

"I don't know," Pete said. "Seemed like the right thing to do at the time."

"Aw, honey, you got the whole rest of your life ahead of you! Why you gonna throw it all away and hole up in some looney bin like that?"

"Right now, I'm just *thinking* about becoming a monk," Pete said. "I haven't made any firm decisions yet."

I moved toward the center of the room to get a better look at the paintings on the wall. "Oh, my. Look at that beautiful painting up there at the top."

"Which one?" Sharon asked, coming closer.

"The blue one." It was a winter landscape painted in only two colors: blue and white. In the center was a sapphire lake framed on the right and left by a shore of aquamarine trees and indigo shrubs dotted with white snow. The horizon was painted azure, and snow-capped cornflower-blue mountains with their white peaks were reflected in the deep-blue lake. The lines of the landscape were somewhat blurred, in the style of the Impressionists.

"Really, Sharon. I love it. It's absolutely stunning."

"It's yours! I'll give it to you!"

"Oh, no. I couldn't take your painting."

"I give paintings away all the time. I must have painted this one for you. Please take it."

I couldn't tear my gaze away from the calm yet intoxicating blue winter landscape. Thrilled by the prospect of viewing it every day in my own home, I thanked Sharon and accepted the gift.

"Now, how about you?" I said to her. "Is there anything we can do for you? Do you have enough food?"

"Oh, I got plenty of food." She motioned toward the woodstove. "Jes' need to get some firewood in is all. Right before you showed up, I was about to get my boots on and go outside to the woodpile. I'm down to my last coupla logs."

"We'll be glad to bring some wood in for you. Won't we, Pete?"

"Now, you guys don't have to do that. I can fetch my own wood."

"I'm sure you can," I said. "But please, let us do it for you today. Take a break. You've been working hard lately."

"I shoveled almost four hours yesterday. Course I took breaks. When you're by yourself, seems like you gotta work harder."

"Where's your woodpile?" Pete asked.

Sharon wrapped a thick shawl around her shoulders, and we all went outside. On the porch, she pointed around the corner. "Round to the left. I got it covered with a big tarp. It's awful kind of you guys to help." She motioned to a long piece of plastic leaning against the railing. "Take this sled along. It'll be easier. Jes' load the wood onto the sled and drag her along behind you. That's how I do it."

I studied the red plastic sled. No, there was no mistake. "I don't believe it!" I said to Sharon. "I have the *exact same* sled at my house.

I've been using it a lot this winter to lug groceries up the hill to my farmhouse when the car can't make it up the driveway."

"We got the same sled!" Sharon laughed. "And we both got a Teeny!"

After Pete and I stacked several days' worth of firewood beside Sharon's stove, Pete looked at his watch. "About time for us to be heading back. Lunch is in fifteen minutes. And since we only get two meals a day, I don't want to miss it."

But I wasn't ready to leave. "It won't kill you to miss a meal, Pete."

He opened his jacket. "Look at me. I'm wasting away!"

I laughed. "Oh, go ahead. I want to stay a while longer." I turned to Sharon. "That is, if it's okay with you."

Pete headed back to the monastery. I sat in the rocker by the stove, Sharon in the recliner, and we talked about her mother in the nursing home. Then she tried again to convince me to accept Jesus as my savior, insisting this was the only way to find peace and happiness. I found it odd that there were people living only two hundred yards away who believed that following the Buddha's teachings was the only path to peace and happiness. *If we all want the same thing, why can't we all get along?*

Sharon leaned forward. Her face crinkled. "I can *tell* somethin' about you. You're not like the others. God has picked you out. I see His light shining all around you. Really, you're glowing. God has great things in store for you."

"He does?"

"Oh, yes, honey. Good things are in your future. Lots of good things. I can see it. I can *feel* it."

I laughed. "Wow, that would be a nice change."

"It's going to happen. Wait . . ." She sat upright in the chair, eyes closed. Teeny, asleep at her feet, raised his head. "God's giving me your

Scripture: Isiah 43: 18-19. God says this Scripture is for your meditation." She stood up, fetched her Bible and glasses, opened the holy book to the correct page, and read: "Remember ye not the former things. Neither consider the things of old. Behold, I will do a new thing: now shall it spring forth, shall ye not know it?" Sharon glanced over her reading glasses. "I can see that you already *do* know it." She continued reading. "I will even make a way in the wilderness, and rivers in the desert."

Moisture filled my eyes. Of all the verses in the Bible, how did Sharon happen to pick this one? I'd come to the monastery seeking what? A way to break free from the "things of old"? Now would a "new thing spring forth"? Would I really find my "way in the wilderness"?

We said goodbye on the porch. I gave Sharon a hug and thanked her again for the painting. Even though I hadn't embraced Jesus, I sensed the two of us were kindred spirits. We were both hard workers, struggling to survive on our own, no thanks to abusive husbands. I strapped the snowshoes to my feet, stepped awkwardly off the porch with the blue painting wrapped in a plastic garbage bag tucked under my right shoulder. My left hand clutched a two-gallon can of diesel fuel. On a whim, I'd asked Sharon if she had any gas for the tractor. After rummaging around in her shed, she found the rusty can filled with fuel. Oh, I couldn't wait to see Bhante Upali's face when I showed up with this precious gift from his closest neighbor.

The going was tough on the trek back through the woods. I had to stop several times to rest and catch my breath. As I sat upon a large rock, a gentle breeze aroused the still forest. Among the soughing of the trees, a tremendous kinship with my surroundings overwhelmed me, and then the woman I recognized as Laurie disappeared. Suddenly merged with the natural world, I was an intrinsic part of every living and non-living thing within my sight. My bones shared the same molecules as the rocks; my flesh was the bark of trees. My veins were the roots beneath the earth, my blood the flowing water of the stream. My breath was the vapor of the clouds, and my eyes were the vision of the vast sky. Overjoyed by this amazing discovery, I jumped to my feet, and with renewed energy, picked up my load and journeyed onward through deep snow toward the monastery. When I finally emerged from the forest, my joy had mounted to sheer elation with the realization that I was nothing, and yet I was part of everything.

Numb with bliss, I climbed the porch stairs and set down the painting and gas can. I sat on the bench and stared in the direction of Sharon's cabin hidden beyond the magical forest. Yes, I accomplished my mission, and more. Starry-eyed, my gazed shifted to the big brass gong. *Oh, how I'd love to grab that mallet and strike it. Strike it hard!*

The front door opened and Charles stepped outside. "You weren't in the lunch line. There's plenty of food left. Come get a plate."

Grinning, I looked up at his tall figure covered by a stained apron. Eating was the furthest thing from my mind. "No thanks," I said in a faraway voice.

"Are you all right?"

My smile grew broader. "Yes, I'm fine. Never been better."

He looked at the large plastic garbage bag and gas can at my feet. "Everybody was wondering where you were."

I sensed he was waiting for an explanation. Instead, I just stared happily into his eyes, and he seemed to understand. "Yes," he said with a chuckle. "Many strange and wondrous things have been known to happen here during retreats."

Later that evening as we lay in our sleeping bags, Jessica and I chatted away like schoolgirls at a sleepover party. There were lots of giggles, stories about past boyfriends, recreational drugs, and sexual escapades.

"Oh, and I've got to tell you what happened while you were over at the neighbor's house!" Jessica squealed. "Bhante Upali decided to explore Winding Creek Road. He wanted to see if it was possible to reach the nearest gas station. He put chains on the big pickup truck, and asked for volunteers to pile into the truck bed for added weight."

"And you volunteered?"

"How could I miss out on that? But after one look at the condition of the road, we all knew there was no way we were going to make it anywhere. I was sitting right beside Bhante Upali in the front seat, and boy oh boy, we were slipping and sliding all over the place. I thought we'd end up in a ditch! Bhante Upali was squeezing the steering wheel so hard, his knuckles were bright white, and a couple of times his face turned as white as his knuckles!"

We both laughed.

"Even though it was pretty scary, I think down deep Bhante Upali was having fun behind the wheel," Jessica said.

"Well, good for him! I'm sure that little excursion was a lot more exciting than his usual somber monastic routine."

"He even said 'shit' a couple of times."

"No. You're kidding!"

"I'm not! I heard him say it. He definitely said 'shit.' And more than once."

I laughed and snuggled deeper into the folds of my sleeping bag. "Oh, I love it! I wish I could have been there to hear him say it!"

"I'm pretty sure I was the only one who heard him." She yawned loudly and was quiet for a while. Then she said, "You know, when I first got here, I was literally in awe of the monks. I mean, I revered them, like they were supernatural beings. But I've come to realize that no matter how many hours they meditate, or how strongly they try to reign in their desires, renounce the world, and keep their emotions in check, whether they like it or not, monks are still human."

I giggled. "You're right. Being human is definitely something they can't renounce!"

16

The Exodus

(Day 14)

It wasn't until after breakfast as I poked the hot embers inside the fire-box that I faced the difficult decision. Last night the snowplows had reached Winding Creek Road, and I was forced to make a choice. The man with the bulbous nose and scraggly beard sat in front of the wood-stove, waiting for the heat to kick in. I'd learned his name was Arthur. "Are you leaving today?" I asked him.

"Yes," he said. "Goin' back home. And you?"

I grabbed a split log from the woodpile. "I'm not sure. But I'd better decide soon because I'm scheduled to teach a vegetarian cooking class tonight." I heaved the log into the stove and shut the door. "If I start digging my car out now, I could leave before lunch and make it back home in time to prep for class, but—"

"But *what?*"

"Oh, I don't know. I just keep getting this feeling I need to stay a little longer."

"Stay then." The light in his gray eyes comforted me, and I sat beside him on the bench.

"I guess I could call the venue and cancel the cooking class. I'm sure my students would understand. Especially given this storm."

"What does your heart tell you to do?"

I heaved a long sigh, shaking my head. "Well, this may sound crazy, but some really strange things have been happening to me over the past week or so. At times I'll feel this deep, calm awareness and clarity. Other times I'm beyond myself with joy. But then out of the blue, I'm crying like a baby. It's so weird."

"What do you think is going on?"

"I have no idea! I've asked Bhante Upali about it, but he didn't really give me an answer. I've tried not to analyze it. I keep telling myself, just go along for the ride, be open to it, be present, and see where this whole thing is taking you." My gaze fell to my slippers. "But I'm afraid that—"

He placed his hand on my shoulder. "What are you afraid of, my dear?"

I raised my head. *What **am** I afraid of?* "You know, I'm not really sure. Maybe I'm afraid of going back home."

"Is that all?"

His affection for me held me still. "Well, maybe I'm also afraid of leaving the monastery too soon."

"So, you feel you need to stay here longer?"

"I'm not sure how to explain it. I feel like there's something building, something growing deep inside me, sort of like a flower bud getting ready to open. And I'm afraid that if I leave today, all the effort I've put in during my time here will have been for nothing. The flower will die on the vine, and I'll never find out where this journey is taking me."

Arthur nodded. "If it were happening to me, I'd stay in a heartbeat. No question about it. Most of us who have been attending retreats for many years *dream* of experiencing something similar to what you're going through. I've been meditating for thirty years, waiting and

137

hoping to have an experience like yours. It may happen only once in a lifetime. If you're lucky."

"Wow. So, you'd stay?"

"Absolutely."

I focused on the flickering flames inside the firebox.

"Really, what's wrong with me?" I finally said with a laugh. "A cooking class can easily be rescheduled. But what's happening to me now is, well, it's—"

"It's a lot more significant than showing people how to cook tofu lasagna!" Arthur said, and we laughed together.

The fire crackled inside the stove. We were silent for a while, watching the flames twist and curl.

"You know," Arthur said, "it's obvious something's been affecting you."

"It is?"

"Sure. Your face has changed. I think we've all noticed it."

I sat bolt upright, recalling that incredible moment in the meditation hall when Jessica's face changed into Kuan Yin's face. "What do you mean my face has changed? Changed how?"

"Well, how do I put it? Your face has, well, it's softened. At the beginning of the retreat there was a rigidity to your face. I noticed it especially around your mouth. But not now." He smiled.

Has anything else about me changed besides my face? I turned toward the window. Outside, a flurry of activity surrounded the birdfeeders. Ah, there was the cardinal—bright red and puffy against the white backdrop of snow. During the long winter months back home, no matter how sad or depressed I might be, the sight of the male cardinal perched on my feeder never failed to lift my spirits and give me hope for the future.

"Hmmm, so my face has changed," I said, still staring at the cardinal.

"You almost look like a different person."

Am I becoming a different person? As the cardinal flew off into the woods, I made my decision. "Nope," I said flatly. "I'm not leaving today. I definitely need to stay here a little while longer."

☙❧

I telephoned the Arts Center and cancelled my cooking class. Now all I had to do was break the news to Mack.

"Lu!" Mack said. "I figured you'd be calling today."

"Hello, Mack. Did you get out and get your groceries?"

"Yes, yes."

"Well, what's it like up on the hill?"

"You know exactly what it's like! Siberia! Snow everywhere. Frigid temperatures. Howling winds. Drifts five feet high." He sounded irritated, but that was nothing new.

"Are the main roads plowed?"

"The main roads are fine, but I've had a bitch of a time managing up here on this frozen hilltop. Your roads must be plowed by now, so you're calling to tell me you're coming home, correct? You know you have a cooking class scheduled for tonight."

"Yes, I know. But I've canceled it."

"Why'd you go and do a stupid thing like that? Are you insane? You still have time to make it."

"I've decided to stay here another day or two."

"For Christ's sake, Lu! This was supposed to be a retreat, not an extended vacation! You've really crossed the line this time! You must come home immediately! What about the business?"

"What about it?"

"Because of your bullheaded selfishness, we've now lost two weeks' worth of income!"

My eyes closed. "I know, Mack. And I've needed those two weeks off. Look, I'm just canceling one cooking class. It's not the end of the

139

world. I can easily reschedule it. I'll probably be home by Sunday. Then on Monday I'll start filling food orders again for my regular customers."

"What do you mean *probably*? What about your obligations here at home? Have you totally abandoned them? Have you forgotten about me and the pets? Think what you're doing! Oh, you're going to regret this, Lu! I swear you will!"

I couldn't speak.

"What the hell has happened to you? Do you want to become a nun or something?"

"No, Mack," I whispered. "I don't want to become a nun. You don't understand."

"Well, explain it to me."

"Maybe I would if I thought you really cared."

"Of course I care! I'm the only one in the world who gives a damn about you! The only one who has your best interests at heart. Now tell me what in Christ's name is going on at that monastery that's so god-damned important you can't bear to tear yourself away?"

My lips pursed.

"Well?"

"I honestly don't know what's going on. I just want to stay here a little longer, that's all. I feel like something's happening to me."

There was a long pause. "Something positive or negative?"

"Positive," I said. "Definitely positive."

Another long silence. "Well, that was the whole reason for you going down there in the first place, right?"

"Yes, that's right."

"Well, then. Maybe when you finally *do* get home, you won't be such a morbid, lazy, loud-mouthed Jewish pain in my ass."

After lunch the exodus began. There was a bustle of activity: cars driving up and down the narrow, snowy lane from the parking lot to the main building; arms, shoulders, and backs carrying suitcases, travel bags, backpacks, and sleeping bags. People were taking pictures, hugging, and exchanging addresses and phone numbers. I hadn't brought a camera, but Lin had hers, and she was snapping away. I moved from one person to another with light, bouncy steps, saying goodbye, wishing everyone a safe trip home, wishing them luck with their practice. Lin gave me a big hug before getting behind the wheel of her car. She promised to send me copies of the pictures she took, and reminded me not to tell Mack about Kuan Yin. "He won't understand. Maybe someday in the future will be the right time to confide in him, but not now."

"Okay," I promised.

I helped Jessica carry her bags to the parking lot. We stood off in a corner by ourselves, smiling at each other. "I'll miss you," I said. "Wow, I haven't smiled this much in years! It's funny, I could barely smile at all when I first got here."

"It's great to see you smile like that. I've seen a real change in your face over the past week."

"Oh my God, you too? What kind of change?"

"Your face is, well, it's loosening," she said. "When I first saw you, you looked like you *wanted* to smile, but couldn't. Right then I related to you because a lot of times my jaw gets so tight, and it hurts. I think I must clench my teeth at night."

"I think I do that, too. When I arrived, my jaw was killing me."

"I think the clenching is due to stress and tension. I'll tell you what helped me. Last year I was under so much stress I almost had a nervous breakdown. My mom was diagnosed with MS, and my dad and my boyfriend were both giving me a hard time, expecting me to do *everything* for them. I had no money, I couldn't find work, oh, I was a mess! Sometimes I'd actually spend whole days in bed. I didn't want to take anti-depressants, I had no money for counselors, but I had to do *something*. So, one afternoon I called this crisis hotline and I talked to a counselor who told me to start taking hot baths as often as I could. So, I did."

"Oh, I love hot baths!" Yes, I had an intimate relationship with hot baths. There was an ancient claw-foot bathtub in my old farmhouse, and I'd become addicted to soaking my body inside that huge tub filled with steamy hot water. Besides my on-and-off yoga practice, hot baths had become the number one relaxation technique in my life, replacing my former habit of stress reduction—drinking alcohol. I used to love sipping a glass or two of wine in the evenings. When we were first married, Mack and I drank wine every night before dinner. But about seven years ago, because Mack had concluded alcohol consumption interfered with his early-morning writing schedule, he quit drinking. Claiming alcohol was the devil for both of us, he forbade me to bring any wine, beer, or liquor into the house. There were times I missed it terribly.

"I made a ritual of those baths," Jessica continued. "I'd light candles and incense and soak for about twenty minutes with the lights off. And it worked!"

"I'll definitely have to try that. I've never bathed by candlelight before. Oh, Jessica, I'm so glad I met you! You're such a beautiful girl, both inside and out! You have to promise you'll keep in touch with me."

"I will. I'll write to you."

"You better!"

"And you'd better write back!"

We embraced, then she said, "Oh, it's soooo good to see you smiling!"

Now that everyone was gone, the monastery seemed like a ghost town. In the hour before evening meditation, I dashed into the kitchen, grabbed some carrots, and went outside for a walk. The road had been plowed just wide enough for two vehicles to pass comfortably in opposite directions, and the piles of snow on both sides of the road were like mini white mountains.

A sign nailed to a thick oak tree caught my attention. Moving closer, I made out the words painted in thick black letters: "WE NEED PLOWED." To the right of the tree, buried beneath the snow, was the faint outline of a narrow lane. Through the trees, a small house came into view in the distance, smoke billowing from the chimney. *These people need help. Maybe Bhante Upali could come over later on the tractor.*

I picked up my pace. When I reached the familiar bend in the road, there were the horses, alive and well, hanging out in their usual spot. Half the pasture had been cleared of snow, and in the middle sat a fresh round hay bale. I threw my arms wide open to my friends.

"Hi, guys! Hi, Chocolate!" I called. "I guess you made it through the storm all right. Oh, wait till you see what I've got for you!" I pulled the carrots from my coat pocket. "I told you I'd bring you something special, didn't I?"

After evening meditation, as I was fixing the fire for the night, Bhante Upali entered the covered porch and sat down on one of the chairs reserved for monastics. His shaved head glowed under the fluorescent light; his pale face was tense, his body stiff. We were alone on the porch. I selected a rather large overnighter log, and as I heaved it into the stove, he cleared his throat and said, "We shouldn't need as much of a fire in the next few days. According to the weather report it's supposed to get a little warmer."

"Uh, okay."

"And there's supposed to be some rain coming in," he added in a monotone.

I shut the door and opened the dampers so the log would catch. Bhante Upali's unease was palpable. "With the rain and warmer weather coming, all the snow will melt, and instead of shoveling, we'll have to build an ark," I said, being silly to try to see if Bhante Upali would lighten up and come out of his serious monk mode. I detected the faint hint of a smile on his face, so I sat on the bench opposite him.

"Bhante, can I ask you a question?"

"You may."

"Well, you've probably heard me crying sometimes during meditation, or in the dining hall. I just start sobbing, and I feel so embarrassed about it, but I can't help it. I've been really emotional lately. Why am I crying so much?"

He leaned forward in his chair. "We all have so much accumulated suffering and trauma from the past locked up inside our subconscious minds. When we meditate for extended periods of time, this suffering can be released from our subconscious, causing us to cry uncontrollably. Don't be upset over it. I've seen it happen many times before."

"So, it's not a bad thing?"

"No." He smiled as though he were happy for me. "It's *purification*."

I nodded, relieved. I wanted to thank him for his wisdom and kind words. I wanted to embrace him, but I didn't dare, remembering Theravada monks were forbidden to touch women. He jumped out of his chair like a jackrabbit, seemingly sensing my affection. "It's getting late. So, I'll wish you a good sleep." He started down the hallway.

"Oh, Bhante, before you go, could I make a request?"

He turned around. "Uh, you can, but I don't have to grant it."

"Yes, I know. But one of our neighbors has a sign at the end of their driveway that says 'WE NEED PLOWED.' I thought maybe someone could go over with the tractor now that you've filled up the gas tank."

He rolled his eyes.

"Bhante, I know how you feel about your neighbors, but these people need help! Aren't we supposed to cultivate a heart of boundless loving-friendliness?"

He just nodded, then disappeared around the corner.

17

Fear of Attachment

(Day 15)

Early-morning meditation passed gently, sweetly. I opened my eyes occasionally, anticipating the dawn spreading her glowing invitation to the new day, eager to hear my beloved birds serenade the rising sun and awaken the sleeping forest.

After bowing three times to the golden Buddha, Bhante Upali rose from his knees and pointed to the rug beneath his feet. "Someone should pick up these petals," he said, "and clean up those flowers in the vases on the altar."

I raised my hand. "I will, Bhante."

In the dishwashing room, I scrubbed the lovely blue and white Oriental vase with hot soapy water, refilled it with fresh water, gave the remaining living flowers a fresh cut, and was arranging the mums in a simple design when Barry entered the kitchen.

"That looks a lot better than what I did," he said.

"Oh, I've worked in flower shops, but I'm no designer. Are you the one who takes care of the flowers on the altar, Barry?"

"Yeah. I like flowers. Whenever I go into town, I get some for the altar. Sometimes they last almost two weeks."

"It's pretty easy to make a one-sided arrangement like this. Tell you what, when I come back to the monastery, I'll bring some fresh flowers, and we can arrange them together."

"Sounds great."

Oh my God! What did I just say? I couldn't bring myself to leave the monastery, and already I was talking about coming back! There was another, shorter retreat scheduled for next month. I hoped it wasn't already full.

Back in the Women's Dorm, Polly and Machee Nee were sitting on the empty bed in room number two. I thought I heard crying. Polly called, "Oh, come on in. Let's have all the women together. Machee Nee is a little upset. But I think she's beginning to feel better now."

The young nun's tear-stained face concerned me. "What's wrong?"

"I think she's been working too hard," Polly said. "Ganda has really been giving her a hard time lately. Giving her too many jobs."

"Nooo," Machee Nee said, her shoulders shaking. "It not just Bhante Ganda. I do not mind doing whatever job need to be done."

"Plus, she's been helping in the kitchen a lot more," Polly added. "She doesn't have to."

Machee Nee kept rubbing her bloodshot eyes. "I don't believe I crying. I do not cry in ten years! Why I crying now?"

"I'm sure this transition to a new place and a new country has been a difficult adjustment for you," I said.

"Yes. The culture, the people here very different. And in Thailand, I live with only just nuns. No monks there."

"So, we've decided to cut back her hours in the kitchen," Polly said to me. "And we're going to talk to Bhante Ganda about reassigning her days off. That should be very helpful." She turned back to Machee Nee. "And if you don't feel comfortable talking to Bhante Ganda yourself, I'll be glad to talk to him on your behalf."

"Okay," Machee Nee said, sniffling. "But I do not mind working in the kitchen."

"We'll get this matter straightened out. Don't worry." Polly touched Machee Nee's shoulder, stood up, sank her hands deep into the pockets of her white trousers, and left the room.

I sat on the bed beside Machee Nee. "Is there something bothering you that you'd like to talk about?"

"Too many things bothering me," she said. "Polly, she think the problem Bhante Ganda. Yes, it is true he assign me many jobs, more than the others. He even give me his own job to do, but this I do not mind. The problem is *myself*." She sobbed. "Oh, why I crying?"

"It's okay," I said. "Sometimes it's good to cry. It's . . . it's purification." I took her hand. "I'm sure it hasn't been easy for you here. I mean, being the only nun among so many monks."

"When I first arrive here, I feel like stranger. Nobody talk to me, nobody tell me what I need for wintertime. Nobody even give me razors to shave my head. I do not know what to do. I am not allowed to ask for anything, and I cannot leave here myself." Her chin dropped to her chest. "Sometimes, I feel like prisoner."

My heart went out to her. I could definitely relate to feeling like a prisoner. "Look, I'm happy to get you whatever you might need. If you make a list, once I'm back home, I can mail you a care package."

"It not just that bothering me. At home, all the nuns, we work together. Nothing says you need only do this job, and she do that job. No. We just look and see what need to be done, and we do it. We *help* each other." Her face scrunched. "Here, everyone assigned *their own job*. So, when I ask for help to do a certain job, everybody here say, 'No, sorry, that is not my job.'"

We were quiet, then I asked, "What did you mean when you said the problem is yourself? You're an incredible woman, Machee Nee. An inspiration! You work harder than all the monks, you're in the meditation hall earlier than anyone else, you're always helpful, smiling, in a good mood."

She explained through her tears. "It very difficult for me to leave Thailand. I decide to come here to be of service and spread the dhamma, to learn from Bhante B, and to break any attachment I may have to my home. But I am not happy here. And I worry maybe I still have attachment, and this cause my suffering. I promise Bhante B to stay for one year. It been only seven month, and every day I think only of home. I miss it very much. I think about my kuti in the forest. It very pleasant there. I meditate, but not like here on strict schedule. I do yoga, I travel sometimes for teaching. And I get email from my friends in Thailand asking me when I coming back."

"If you're not happy here, maybe it's time for you to return home. I'm sure Bhante B would understand."

"Maybe," she said. "But I worry that—" Her shoulders started shaking again. Fresh tears streamed down her face. "I worry that I *attach* too much to my home!"

I thought carefully before speaking. "Machee Nee, you succeeded in breaking any attachment you may have had to your home when you decided to come here. If you were truly attached to your home, you never would have left. Look, seven months is a long time to live in a totally different country and culture. Especially when you're surrounded by a group of men who have authority over you."

Her sobs quieted. She nodded.

"Maybe it's just time to say goodbye and thank you to Bodhi Community, and return to your hermitage in Thailand. Do you have money for air fare?"

"Yes, the doctor's wife, she buy me round trip ticket."

After lunch, as I walked down Winding Creek Road with carrots stuffed into my coat pocket, the sounds of a large engine in the distance made me quicken my pace. When I came upon the sign nailed to the oak tree, I was relieved. The snow-covered lane beside it had been penetrated. About twenty yards down the lane, I spotted the monastery's tractor moving clumsily in the snow, with Bhante Upali at the wheel. Barry was with him, leaning on a shovel beside the tractor. A man and a woman stood a few yards away.

But the path Bhante Upali had cut in the snow was ragged, shallow, and virtually impassable even for a four-wheel-drive vehicle. I set off down the lane, determined to remedy the situation. As the tractor lurched awkwardly in the deep snow, I stood behind the man and woman for a few moments before saying hello. "Hi, I'm Laurie. I'm visiting over at the monastery."

The woman turned around. "I'm Shelly." She was wearing jeans, a down coat, her brown hair tied in a ponytail. "This is my husband, Dave."

A burly, bearded man with emerald eyes, wearing a thick flannel shirt, suspenders, and a baseball cap, turned around and shook my hand.

"I guess you two live back here," I said. "I saw your sign yesterday."

"Yes," Shelly said. "And our five kids."

"Five kids? Wow, you certainly have your hands full."

"He's got three from a previous marriage, an' I got two. We just moved here a coupla months ago."

"Do you need any food or groceries?" I asked.

"Aw, no," Shelly insisted. "We're fine. We still got some milk. And we got canned goods."

I glanced behind me. "You'll never get out with the driveway in that condition."

"I told him I'd be glad to do my own plowing," Dave said, "but he wouldn't let me—the skinny, bald-headed guy."

"Dave knows how to operate that machine," Shelly chimed in. "He won't hurt it none. And if something did happen to that machine, you know, an accident or something, we'd sure pay for it."

"I know you would," I said.

Shelly motioned toward Bhante Upali high on the tractor. "I mean, we really 'preciate him comin' over like that, but it looks like he's havin' some trouble."

I laughed. "I think you're right!"

"He won't say nothin' to us except that he has to leave soon to go to this meeting. I told him if he'd just let Dave borrow the tractor for a while, he'd bring it back over to the monastery this evening."

"And what did he say to that?"

"He didn't answer. Maybe you could talk to him."

"Let me see what I can do."

When I reached the tractor, Barry motioned to Bhante Upali, who shut off the engine and turned around in the seat. "What are you doing here?" he asked me.

"I was just taking a walk."

"You came to check up on me," he said with a smirk.

"No! Honestly, Bhante, I was just out for a walk and heard the tractor. I was curious to see what was going on."

He turned his head away.

"So," I said, "what's your plan?"

"My plan?"

"Yes. What are you going to do now? I mean, you're not going to try to finish plowing this driveway now, are you? At the rate you're going, it'd take forever. Plus, you'd have to go over the front part again because it's really impassable."

He hung his head.

"Bhante, I know you have to go to a meeting soon. Why don't you let this man finish the plowing? His name is Dave, and he knows how to operate heavy equipment. He promised he'd return the tractor this evening."

Bhante Upali grimaced. "I don't know. You have to be careful with people out here. Many of them don't like us."

I gave him a long, penetrating stare. "You can *trust* him, Bhante. He's a good man. I can tell."

Bhante Upali was silent for a full minute. Then he sighed, climbed off the tractor, and motioned for Dave to come forward. Before we left, Bhante Upali showed Dave all the different levers and knobs that controlled the movements of the tractor and bucket.

"Yes, sir," Dave responded. "I know how it works. I'll be careful."

Bhante Upali, Barry, and I walked back to the monastery in silence. As we approached the parking lot, Bhante Upali said, "I hope he brings that tractor back."

"He will, Bhante," I said. "Have a little faith."

"We've tried in the past to get along with our neighbors. Once we let some people come and cut down some dead trees for firewood, and we told them specifically which trees they were allowed to cut, and which trees they were *not* allowed to cut. Not only did they cut more than they were allowed, but they left a pile of beer cans in the woods."

"Well, yes," I sighed, "some people are like that."

As we climbed the steps to the main building, Bhante Upali sneezed. His cheeks and nose were bright red, and I worried he might be catching a cold. "Would you like me to fix you a hot beverage, Bhante?" I asked. "How about some hot tea with lemon and honey?"

"Well," he said sheepishly, his little boy face coming out of hiding. "Actually, there is a beverage I'm quite fond of."

"What's that?"

"It's hot cocoa with brown sugar."

"Brown sugar?"

"I like the taste of it. It imparts a certain flavor."

"Sugar's not good for you. And brown sugar's just white refined sugar colored with molasses."

"I know," he said. "But I enjoy it, so please don't spoil my illusion." We both smiled.

"All right. How much brown sugar? One teaspoon or two?"

While the monks and residents attended their weekly meeting in the library, I went into the greenhouse. Bhante Upali had asked me to tidy it up. I gathered and discarded dead and dying leaves, watered dry plants, pruned unruly branches, rearranged pots, and swept the floor. Before leaving, I stood before the tall mystery plant and admired the large, gorgeous pink and purple flower cluster. The blossom was breathtaking—at the height of splendor. *What is this curious plant? And how could these slender stalks and narrow green leaves produce such a huge, exquisite blossom?* My gaze fell to the base of the plant. Lo and behold! Baby plantlets had sprouted on the soil's surface. *Oh, how I'd love to snatch a few of these little babies and take them home with me!*

Next, I tended the rest of the large potted plants in the main building, some of which were in terrible shape. I was on a crusade to heal each of the monastery's withered potted plants, ignoring the signs above them stating:

PLEASE DO NOT WATER PLANTS. SOMEONE HAS BEEN
ASSIGNED THIS JOB. WITH METTA

Later that evening, as I relaxed on the covered porch warming myself in front of the woodstove, Barry and Bhante Upali walked out of the kitchen and headed toward the front door. Huddled together, they peered out the window. Although they spoke in low voices, I overheard Bhante Upali ask Barry, "Can you tell? Is that it?"

"I'm not sure, Bhante," Barry said, squinting. "It's too dark to see that far away."

"I'll go check." Bhante Upali put on his high rubber boots, orange cap, and orange jacket and went outside.

I joined Barry near the front door. "Where'd he go?"

"To see if the tractor's in the parking lot."

I chuckled, shaking my head. "It's there. I'd bet my entire life savings on it."

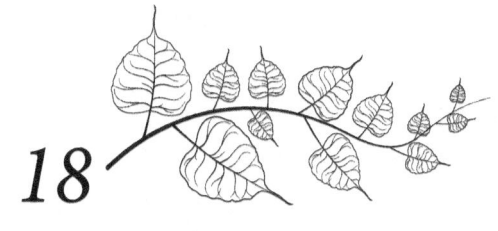

18

Unexpected Rapture

(Day 16)

I'd fallen in love with the serene hours before dawn. Alone on the covered porch in front of the fire, I reveled in the still, potent energy of a day about to be born. Later, sitting motionless on my cushion in the meditation hall, legs crossed in the full lotus pose, a profound tranquility seeped into my pores as sweet, intoxicating vapor. When the hall brightened with the nascent light of the budding day amid the chorus of birdsong, I was consumed by the deepest and most heartfelt sense of peace I'd ever known. *Is this why I stayed?*

After breakfast, when Charles entered the dishwashing room, I pulled the plugs to drain the sinks and asked, "Do you need any help preparing lunch?"

"No, no. You go enjoy yourself. I'm fine, thank you." He tied an apron around his waist.

I stared at him sideways. "I've been here for over two weeks. I'm a vegetarian cook by profession, and so far, I haven't cooked a single thing in this kitchen. Something doesn't make sense." Charles chuckled, and I inched closer to him. "You know the work will go faster if we do it together."

He hoisted a large frying pan from the drying rack. "Well, if you insist, come along and have at it!"

"Great! I can make the salad. I don't mean to brag, but salads are sort of my specialty." We entered the kitchen, and I opened the cooler. "My goodness! Look at all this beautiful produce! Bok choy, shiitake mushrooms, purple cauliflower, orange peppers. Can I use any vegetable in here?"

"Use whatever you like," Charles said with a laugh.

"Oh, this is going to be fun! I promise I won't get in your way. Oh, and look at this gorgeous bunch of kale! I just love kale. I grow three different varieties in my garden every year."

"When I was a young boy visiting my grandmother's farm in a little backwoods town in South Carolina, she fed us all sorts of greens from her garden. But, of course, she cooked it with bacon fat. They couldn't afford to be very health conscious back then. My grandfather raised a few hogs, so there was always plenty of bacon, and everything my grandmother cooked was flavored with bacon drippings and salt and pepper."

I giggled. "I doubt a recipe containing bacon fat would be well-received here at the monastery."

"No. Although I've been tempted to sneak a little meat into some of the dishes. Several people who live here are wasting away."

"Charles! You wouldn't!" I laughed.

"Probably not. Although some of the rules around this place are utterly absurd."

"You sound like quite the rebel."

He laughed. "I've been called worse!"

We chopped vegetables in silence. After a while I said, "Didn't you tell me you've lived here for three years?"

"Yes, on and off." He sighed. "But I'll be leaving soon."

"Really?"

"Yes. I've been here long enough." His body stiffened. "Perhaps too long."

"Where did you live before you came here? You said something about islands."

Charles rinsed off a head of broccoli at the sink. "I lived on a sailboat in the Florida Keys for about twenty years."

"Wow! What a life! It must have been quite an adventure."

"Oh, it had its moments."

I sliced mushrooms. "So, how did you end up at a Buddhist monastery in the middle of nowhere?"

"That's a good question!" He laughed. "I suppose by a very circuitous route!"

I laughed, too. Charles had an utterly infectious laugh. He laughed with his whole being, body and soul. Upon hearing it, you were lifted and transported to a place of sunshine, bubbles, and giggles.

Veggies were piling up on my cutting board. "I don't envy you, Charles. It isn't easy for one person to pull a big meal together and have everything ready at the same time."

"And *on* time." He glanced at the clock. "I mustn't forget to ring the gong at eleven." He opened the kitchen door. "Or would *you* like to do it?"

A thrill shot through me. "*Me?* Ring the gong? Am I allowed?"

"Of course! If you'd like to, go out on the porch at eleven o'clock, take the mallet, and strike that gong three times."

"Really? Oh my God! I've wanted to hit that gong so badly!"

"Just strike it good and hard."

"Where do I hit it? Right in the middle?"

"Right smack in the middle!"

Through the open kitchen door, I saw Bhante B enter the building. He was smiling, obviously glad to be home from Costa Rica. Pete was behind him, carrying his bags. Bhante B peered into the kitchen.

"Bhante B!" I exclaimed. "You're back!"

"Yes, I am," he said, still smiling.

"Welcome home! How was your trip?"

With a slightly dazed expression, he said, "Busy!"

"Well, now that you're back, you can rest."

"That's exactly what I intend to do." He took a couple of steps, then stopped. "And what are *you* doing here?"

His question threw me. *What **am** I doing here?* I thought a moment, then I gave Bhante B a big smile and said, "I'm helping Charles fix lunch!"

It was time. I took a slow, deep breath and went out onto the porch. There was the mallet resting on the railing. My fingers gripped the wooden handle. For a few moments, I just stood there feeling the weight of the heavy mallet in my hand as I stared at the large brass gong like a starving woman before a table laden with delectable food. Then I bent over, raised the mallet above my shoulder, and—*Well, Charles said to hit it hard, so* . . . WHAAPPP!

Instantly I was transmuted into pure vibration. It started at my fingers, traveled up my arm, across my chest, down my spine, permeating my entire body. Oh, it was the most marvelous, glorious sensation anyone could wish for! My whole being tingled with the reverberating tones of the gong as the sounds echoed throughout the woods and gradually faded away. Elated, I composed myself and raised the mallet again for the second strike.

After all the lunch dishes were washed and the kitchen floor mopped, I asked Charles if he'd like to accompany me on my walk.

"Of course. It would be my pleasure."

Outside the air was moist, the temperature warmer than it had been during the past weeks. Although the road and fields were blanketed with snow, the sunshine and moderate temperature put me in mind of early spring. Charles walked beside me. His gait was strong, steady, fluid—suggestive of much time spent outdoors in nature.

"Oh, Charles, I've been meaning to ask you—why do you serve such elaborate meals to the monks? I was under the impression that monks ate fairly simple meals. After all, they're supposed to live an ascetic life, right? You could make it a lot easier on yourself by keeping the menu simpler, giving the monks two or three items instead of half a dozen of your delicious gourmet dishes."

"Look at how dull, how barren the monks' lives are here. Except for retreats, there's no stimulation, no small excitement for them whatsoever. In the Mahayana Buddhist tradition, there are certain amounts of sensory stimulation during their rituals and ceremonies. They burn incense, and ring various bells, clappers, and gongs. They decorate the meditation hall with bright colors, their chanting is more melodic, and Tibetan Buddhists even dance. But not here. Not in the Theravada tradition. About the only stimulation a monk gets around here is during a retreat when a pretty woman like you walks through the door."

Embarrassed, my gaze fell to my boots. "Well, you certainly know a lot about Buddhism, Charles."

"I should by now. I've been making a study of it for nearly forty years. So, to answer your question, I've taken it upon myself to provide a small amount of excitement or arousal for the monks each day in the way of meals. Believe me, the meals I feed them are the highlight of their day. They look forward to sampling all the different dishes. They enjoy the variety of flavors, textures, aromas, and seasonings. I believe I'm doing my part to help keep the monks' spirits up. I'm sure you've noticed they're a pretty dull bunch to begin with. Well, except maybe for Bhante Ganda. Just imagine how despondent the monks and residents would become if all the cook ever served was rice and beans!"

We both laughed.

When we reached the monastery's driveway, we stood facing each other. I glanced toward the parking lot. The hood of my car gleamed under the sunshine. Pete, Barry, and Bhante Targarasikhi had exhumed it from its grave of snow in the hours between breakfast and lunch. The thought of getting into that car and driving back home dampened my bright mood. The monks and residents were becoming almost like family. Plus, I was enjoying Charles's pleasant company and conversation. As though he'd read my mind, he said, "Would you like to walk a little further?"

His ocean-blue eyes, so gentle and inviting, made my answer easy. "Yes, that would be nice."

⚬⚭⚮⚯⚬

We said goodbye in front of the main building. Although I'd only met Charles a short time ago, he seemed familiar as an old, dear friend. Energized by our time together, I took a hike through the forest and up the hill. On the way back down, my stride spontaneously lengthened and quickened. Soon my feet were carrying me so swiftly down the hill I thought I might fall over. I'd spent the majority of my stay at the monastery in slow motion, and now I wanted to break into fast forward. My legs propelled me like an engine as I raced down the hill as fast as I could, exhilarated, jubilant, out of control.

There was no question of holding back. I indulged myself in the motion and the speed, taking delight in each bodily sensation: the warm blood coursing through my veins, the cool air inflating my lungs and tousling my hair, the pronounced pumping of my heart, the damp sweat on my forehead. At the bottom of the hill, unsteady on my feet, I raised my arms overhead in triumph, as though I'd crossed the finish line of a marathon. If I hadn't seen Bhante Tagarasikhi coming out of the office, I might have burst into song.

Delightfully out of breath, I climbed the porch steps and went inside to check the fire. No one was around. I sat opposite the woodstove breathing heavily, my head somewhere in the clouds and my heart about to burst open from sheer bliss. The unexpected rapture consuming me was so wonderful I didn't bother asking myself how it came about. It was probably a culmination of sorts, and I gave myself over to it fully, gratefully, savoring every second. *Is this what I've been waiting for? Is this why I stayed?*

And now it was painfully clear: Although I ached to remain at the monastery, I couldn't keep postponing the inevitable. It was time for me to return home. My time here had been astonishing and rewarding; I'd experienced blissful shifts in consciousness, abundant tranquility, and a clarity of mind I'd never imagined possible. Moreover, I'd been blessed with a visit from an otherworldly spirit, and now, inexplicable, sensuous rapture. What more could I ask for? I decided to leave the monastery the next day.

That afternoon, as I helped Polly unpack groceries, I asked her about the retreat scheduled for next month.

"Oh, the Death Awareness retreat. Yes, that's a very powerful retreat. At least it was for me when I attended it two years ago. That was shortly after my partner died."

"Oh, Polly, I'm so sorry."

"Thank you. I was going through a very difficult period at that time. We were together ten years. We were avid hikers and campers. We even hiked the Appalachian Trail together. It took almost eight months. Then she got very sick. She wasn't getting better, and none of the doctors could diagnose the problem. Finally, one of them figured out that she had an extremely rare blood disease."

"Was she in a lot of pain?"

"No. It wasn't as painful as it was debilitating. She couldn't do anything. She didn't even have the energy to dress herself in the mornings."

"I'm sure it was awful to see her like that."

"Yes, it was."

"How long did—"

"Only two months."

"Oh dear, at least she didn't suffer terribly long."

Polly carried the stepladder to the other end of the kitchen, where she set it up below the high cupboards. "I still miss her very much."

"Of course." I paused. "You know, my dad died about a year ago. Thank goodness he didn't suffer very long either. But the hardest part for me to come to terms with wasn't his actual death. It was how it all happened so fast! He wasn't sick or anything. One day he's alive and coughing, the next day he goes into congestive heart failure and he's gone. Boom. Just like that."

"The fragility of life is amazing, isn't it? And yet we seem to take life for granted, that is, until we experience death up close, through the death of a loved one."

"I still can't get over the way it happened. My family lives in California, and I usually go out West to visit them once a year. My dad could have died anytime, but he happened to die during my one visit last year. I mean, what are the odds of that?"

"One in a million?"

I picked up the phone in the hallway leading to the Women's Dorm, and dialed home.

"Lu! I knew you'd be calling today," Mack said.

"Well, I'll be coming home tomorrow. I'm planning to leave here sometime after lunch."

"I'll call Larry. He said he'd plow the driveway as soon as I gave him the word, so you shouldn't have a problem making it up the hill."

There was a long pause.

"So," he said, "how's everything going?"

I was surprised he expressed interest. "What do you mean?"

"I mean, is everything okay, you know, with all your meditation? You said that some positive things were happening."

"They are. And everything's fine. It's just time for me to come home."

"So, everything should *continue* to be fine once you *do* come home, right?"

"As long as I can continue what I've started here. But, of course, that's going to be the difficult part."

"Well, I certainly won't get in your way."

"What does that mean? I was hoping for your help and support."

"It means I won't disturb you. Meditate as much as you want, for as long as you want. It won't bother me a bit as long as you're quiet. And if you don't want to have supper ready by five thirty, just let me know and I'll make my own food."

It was obvious Mack wasn't at all interested in hearing about any positive effects the retreat might have had upon *me*; his only concern was how my newfound practice would affect *him*. "Honestly, Mack, if you could just for once—"

"Listen, I'm very busy. I've got to go. The muses are calling. Get home before dark so you don't interrupt my bedtime schedule, and call me if you're going to be later than four thirty."

Before evening meditation, I went outside to visit Kuan Yin. A fine drizzle was falling. Devotion and gratitude swelled inside my heart as

I stood before the lovely white marble woman and bowed, my palms pressed together at my chest.

"Dear Kuan Yin," I whispered, "I am so grateful to you for all your help, and for revealing yourself to me." I placed my fingers in her outstretched hand. "This whole experience has been so incredible. I still don't understand what's been happening to me or why, and I guess it doesn't matter, but I know you're a huge part of it. I feel somehow changed inside, in a good way. But now I have to go back home, and I don't know how long this feeling will last. So, I have to ask once more for your help." I fought back tears. "Please, please continue to stay close to me, watch over me, and guide me. And please continue to give me strength and courage for whatever comes next in my life." I bowed deeply, told Kuan Yin I'd be back again tomorrow to say goodbye, and went directly to the meditation hall.

⁓⁓⁓

After evening meditation, I sipped cup after cup of tea alone in front of the fire. Bhante Upali's thin figure appeared in the dining hall. He came toward me and sat on the low bench several feet away from me.

"Were you the one who cleaned up the big plant outside the meditation hall?" he asked.

"The fish-tail palm? Yes. That was me."

"That plant needed some attention."

"Well, I tended to it. Poor thing was in terrible shape."

"Oh, and by the way, you were right about the neighbors. That man returned the tractor last night."

I nodded. "I knew he would." We were silent for a few moments, then I said, "Bhante, I'm leaving tomorrow."

"Oh." He paused, uneasy. "What time tomorrow?"

"I don't know. Sometime after lunch." In the few awkward moments that followed, we just sat there, looking at each other. I broke

164

the silence. "Bhante, what sorts of things are discussed at the Death Awareness retreat?"

He cleared his throat. "Bhante B and I co-lead that retreat. Basically, it's about gaining an understanding of the importance of life and the inevitability of death. We discuss how to prepare ourselves for death, how to handle the death of loved ones, and how we can overcome the fear, confusion, and grief surrounding our own death and the death of others. We also use some visual aids. Why?"

"Well, my dad died about a year ago, and I'm still searching for closure and clarity regarding his death. I thought attending that retreat might be beneficial for me. Do you know if it's full?"

His recoiled, as though I might jump out of my chair and bite him. Perhaps he was anxious about the possibility of seeing me again so soon, afraid we'd become too close.

"Uh, I don't know. You'll have to check with the secretary. I think she's supposed to return to work tomorrow."

I implored him. "Bhante, what's been *happening* to me? I want to know."

"Don't be concerned about it."

"But I want to understand. I mean, it feels so good, so wonderful, and I'm beginning to worry that it's all going to go away once I leave."

"Everything goes away."

I sighed. "All things are impermanent?"

"Yes. Don't try to hold on to it."

"But I just thought, maybe if I understood it . . ."

His tone softened. "All that has happened is you've awakened something that was lying dormant in you, perhaps for many years, that's all."

Not knowing what to say, I turned toward the windows. Half-hidden by bamboo branches, Kuan Yin's statue appeared as a white marble blur. "Bhante, who is Kuan Yin? I mean, is she something like a female Buddha?"

"It's not important. You don't need to know that."

"Oh yes, I do need to know that! I'd like to know who she is and why her statue is placed on top of that wall containing people's ashes."

With a wave of his hand, he said, "Oh, it's just a statue representing the female aspect of compassion."

"Is she like a Buddhist goddess?"

"Well, no. There are no such things as goddesses in Buddhism."

"A celestial being?"

"Uh, no. Not really. Look, don't concern yourself about Kuan Yin. She's really not an important part of the practice. Some people donated that statue to the monastery, and we had no choice but to accept it."

"Well, Kuan Yin is an important part of *my* practice," I stated firmly, "and I really don't think she'd be here unless—"

"We really don't need to be discussing this right now." He stood up abruptly, wished me a good evening's rest, and hurried away.

I finished my tea, washed out my mug, and headed to the Women's Dorm. As I crawled into my sleeping bag, I couldn't shake my annoyance with Bhante Upali's refusal to discuss Kuan Yin with me. *Why would he act that way?* Still, I rested solidly my last night at the monastery, the blue painting from Sharon propped on the mattress where Jessica had slept.

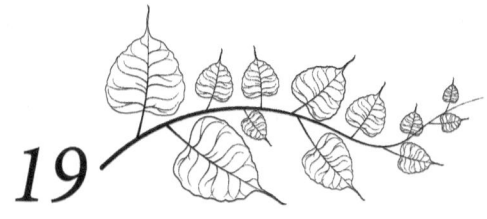

19

Warthogs or Waitresses

(Day 17)

I sat on my cushion during morning meditation, legs crossed, eyes closed. Halfway through the session, from out of nowhere, Trex's face appeared in my mind. Yes, there was my landlord's wizened farmer's face clear as day against a black background. His usual laughing blue eyes were dull, lifeless, so I sent the old man loving-kindness. Trex stayed with me a little while longer, then his face dissolved and faded into nothingness.

Soon afterward, the first chirpings of the birds happily announced the dawn. *Ah, such sweet, beautiful sounds!* I waited for their joyful chorus to continue as it did every morning, craving the next delicious trill, eager to hear the birds' lovely music fill the hall and gladden my soul as usual. Still and quiet on my cushion, ears alert and desirous, heart longing to rejoice in the birds' glorious morning serenade and hold on to it forever, I waited. And waited. But there were no more sounds from the forest. Only silence.

*Oh, no! My beloved birdsongs are **gone!*** I noticed sadness arising, but before it took hold, instead of sorrow, instead of annoyance or anger or grief, the emotion that followed was the most sublime, the most wonderful happiness I'd ever known. A smile crept across my face as my heart burst open with joy. Ah, yes, annica! All conditioned things are impermanent. In a barely audible voice I whispered, "When one sees this with the eyes of wisdom, one becomes disenchanted with suffering."

The gong sounded once, twice, three times. Overwhelmed with awe and gratitude, my palms came together at my chest. I bowed my head, rose to my knees, and lowered my forehead to the floor. This was it. This was the moment I'd been waiting for. This was why I'd chosen to stay at the monastery after everyone else had gone home: to experience the peace of this most precious gift, this precious insight into the nature of impermanence. Oh, thank you, thank you!

After lunch I helped Polly wash dishes, then headed for the greenhouse. I found a bag of soil, a trowel, and several small plastic flower pots in a cupboard. Carefully, I removed half a dozen baby plantlets that had sprouted at the base of the mystery plant with the exotic blossom. I transplanted the seedlings and gave the babies a drink. I didn't think anyone would mind if I took a few home with me. I'd leave the rest of the baby transplants in the greenhouse as a surprise for Bhante Upali.

Back in my room, I stared with apprehension at my suitcase and tightly rolled sleeping bag. Everything was ready for my departure except for me. I didn't want to leave this magical place. Here I'd discovered a degree of serenity I never dreamed possible. And for the first time in my life, I felt completely comfortable with myself without feeling like myself at all. The only thing left to do was say a formal goodbye to Kuan Yin. Deep down, I was certain this beautiful ethereal woman, whoever she was, had played a large role in my newfound peace of mind. Glancing at the orange Lin had given me on the table beneath the window, I had an idea. I stuffed the orange into the pocket of my sweatshirt, hurried to the kitchen, and grabbed two more oranges from the cooler.

"What are you doing with those oranges?" Polly asked. She and Machee Nee were huddled in the kitchen, leafing through a thick cookbook.

"Lin told me sometimes people make offerings of fruit or flowers to Kuan Yin. I have an orange for each of us. I thought we three women could make an offering together."

"It's not allowed," Polly said. "No food can be formally offered after twelve noon."

"I don't care if its allowed or not," I said. "I'm going to put an orange at Kuan Yin's statue. It's important to me."

"But the rules forbid any food to be taken or formally offered after midday," Polly said, exasperated. "You know, some people around here don't understand this. Did you see Bhante Tagarasikhi come into the kitchen the other afternoon around three o'clock and pour himself a glass of milk? Well, he's not allowed to do that! He can drink tea or coffee or hot chocolate. But not milk."

"I'm sure Bhante Tagarasikhi knows exactly what he's allowed and not allowed to do," I said. "And rules or no rules, I honestly don't think I'm doing anything wrong or harmful by placing a few oranges at Kuan Yin's statue after twelve noon."

"But you could have done it any time before lunch!"

"But I didn't, did I?"

Machee Nee giggled.

"Sorry, Polly, but I'm breaking the rules. I know in my heart I have to make this offering before I leave. And I'm inviting you and Machee Nee to join me." I held out an orange to her.

Polly glared at me. We were at a stand-off. Grudgingly, she snatched the orange from my hand. I gave Machee Nee the other orange and she raised it in the air. "Yes," she said. "We break the rules!"

∽∾∿∾∽

After our short ceremony before Kuan Yin's statue, I went back to my room, picked up my suitcase, sleeping bag, and Sharon's painting, slung my purse over my shoulder, and headed to the covered porch. Charles sat on the low bench opposite the beverage area, drinking from a large mug. When I entered from the dining hall, he stood up.

"Oh, before you go, Bhante Upali asked me to speak to you."

"He did?"

"Yes. He said you had some questions about Kuan Yin."

I gasped. "Do you know much about her?"

"Oh, Kuan Yin and I are longtime acquaintances," Charles said. "Would you like to sit down?"

"Yes. Sure." I set down my load and propped the painting on the bench beside me. "This is great, Charles. Thank you."

"Can I get you something to drink?"

"Oh, no thanks. I'm okay."

"If you don't mind, I think I'll make myself another cup of coffee." He stood up.

"You drink a lot of coffee, don't you?"

"Gallons," he said with a laugh.

"But how can you stand that instant coffee? I mean, it tastes so manufactured."

"I suppose I've grown used to it from my years on the sailboat. But sometimes I get a craving for a nice, dark, full-bodied freshly brewed cup of coffee."

"You mean the *real* thing," I said.

"Precisely. Ain't nothin' like the real thing!" He smiled.

Charles sat down beside me with his coffee, and I touched his arm. "Please tell me all about Kuan Yin. Yesterday when I asked Bhante

170

Upali about her, he blew me off."

"That's because Theravada Buddhism doesn't recognize Kuan Yin the way other traditions do. Her statue is like a thorn in his side. A group of Vietnamese Buddhists gave the monastery that statue as a gift. Bhante B doesn't like the statue being here either, but he thought the best diplomacy was to accept the gift."

"Who is she? Is she like a female Buddha?"

"She's a Bodhisattva. In the Mahayana Buddhist tradition, she's considered to be the embodiment of compassion. Her name means 'one who hears the cries of the world.'"

"Hmmm. That makes sense. But what's a Bodhisattva?"

"Bodhisattvas have actualized the paramitas, or perfections. They have attained perfect wisdom and Buddhahood, but have chosen to postpone their entrance into Nirvana until every sentient being is released from suffering. In Kuan Yin's case, out of her great love and compassion for humanity, she chooses to remain on earth, guiding beings on the path until every living creature attains enlightenment. It's also said a Bodhisattva can appear here on earth in various forms."

The air grew thick. For a moment I was back in the meditation hall watching Jessica's glowing face disappear and reappear. Barely breathing, I asked, "You mean Bodhisattvas can appear to us in any form? Any *human* form?"

"Human, animal, insect. Whatever form it takes to bring that particular being to another level of understanding, or to free that person from ignorance or delusion. Bodhisattvas could be bag ladies or butterflies. They can be warthogs or waitresses."

"Waitresses?!"

"Why not?"

Oh my God. That wasn't a hallucination back at Lu's Place. It was Kuan Yin! She was with me even before I arrived at the monastery! I swallowed hard. "So, you're saying Kuan Yin is a Bodhisattva who can

171

hear your cries, can appear to you in any form, and she can help you?"

"Basically, yes. And she's always linked with the aspect of compassion, and is generally regarded as a refuge and protector. In pictures and sculptures, she's usually recognized by the small Buddha in her crown or headdress. Actually, there's a marvelous painting of her dressed in a flowing white robe standing on a dragon in the middle of a stormy sea."

"Oh, I'd love to see that painting. I bet she's beautiful."

"Breathtaking. If I can get hold of a copy, I promise I'll send it to you."

"Oh, I'd appreciate that so much! Why is she standing on a dragon?"

"Well, the dragon is a symbol for high spirituality, wisdom, and divine powers of transformation. There's a story connected to this painting. It's said Kuan Yin can save a person from danger if you call upon her. The artist who painted this image of Kuan Yin was a sailor. He was out on his boat when a terrible storm hit. The man was certain he was going to die, and when he called Kuan Yin's name, it's said she appeared to him and guided his damaged boat home. Later, convinced Kuan Yin had saved his life, in gratitude to the Bodhisattva, the sailor painted Kuan Yin's image as it had appeared to him on that stormy night."

"Wow. So, if you call her name, she can save you?"

"So the story goes."

"And she can appear in any form . . ." I whispered. My mouth went dry. It all made sense. Lin was right. I was blessed. *Thank God I picked up the monastery's brochure at the coffee shop, or I might never have come.* I stood up and approached the beverage area on wobbly legs.

"Are you all right?" Charles asked.

"Yes, I'm fine. Just getting some water." I sat down beside him again, my mind blazing with questions. "What did you say before? You and Kuan Yin were acquaintances?"

He nodded, grinning. "We're old friends."

"Would you say she's helped you reach, how did you put it? A new level of understanding?"

"Most definitely."

I cleared my throat. "This might sound a little strange, but do you believe that Kuan Yin can actually appear to us, either as herself or whatever form is appropriate?"

With a wave of his hand, he said, "Why not?"

His answer, the playful expression on his handsome, clean-shaven face, and the fact that he was an acquaintance of Kuan Yin excited me. But because he planned to leave the monastery soon, I might never see him again. I jumped to my feet, took a piece of paper and a pen from the table beside the bulletin board, and began writing.

"Here, I'm going to give you my address." I blushed, then added, "That way, if you happen to find a copy of that painting of Kuan Yin on the dragon, maybe you could send it to me?"

"I'd be glad to."

His warm smile emboldened me. "And write to me if you like. Let me know where you are and how you're doing." I handed him the paper.

We both sipped from our mugs. "So," I said, "where will you go after you leave the monastery?"

"I don't know. I may just strap on a backpack, hit the Appalachian Trail, and start walking."

"You're not serious, are you?"

With a raised brow, he repeated, "Why not?"

I checked the clock in the dining hall and sighed. "It's getting late. I better be going."

"Let me help you with your bags."

"Oh, thanks. There's just one more little thing I have to grab from the greenhouse."

I returned to the covered porch carrying my three little pots of baby plants. Charles took a thick book from the windowsill and handed it to me. "Here. Take this home with you. I thought you might find it interesting and helpful."

I read the title: *The Seeker's Glossary of Buddhism.* "Wow. Thank you, Charles. I'm sure this book will help keep me on track once I'm home. At least for a while anyway."

We walked down the gravel driveway in silence. The sun was bright, warming my cheeks. Charles carried my suitcase in one hand and the sleeping bag in the other, the blue painting tucked under his arm. Although all I carried was my purse, the book, and my flower pots, a heavy, almost suffocating sadness weighed me down. When we reached the entrance to the parking lot, I turned to Charles and said, "I really enjoyed our walk yesterday."

"So did I. I only hope I didn't bore you with my incessant chatter. I realized afterward how much I monopolized the conversation."

"That's not true! Besides, I kept asking you questions. You're so knowledgeable about Buddhism." I paused. "And about many other important things as well." My car was the only vehicle left in the lot. I shivered as we approached it.

"Are you cold?" Charles asked.

"Not really. I think I'm just a little nervous about going back home. It's not a very pleasant place to be these days. My marriage is, well, it's complicated."

"No need to explain. I've been there myself. I know how dark and miserable relationships can get sometimes."

Behind him through the trees, the white blur of Kuan Yin's statue gave me courage, and the words came flying out of my mouth like angry bees whose nest had been disturbed. "Oh, Charles, my husband can be terribly cruel. I haven't told anyone how painful my life has become because of him. My God, if I repeated some of that man's nasty insults and criticisms, people would think I'm a lunatic for staying and putting up with his bullshit! It's so awful I can't even bring myself to talk to my family about it." I began to tremble. "Oh, the whole thing's just so ridiculous!"

Charles set down the items he carried beside the car. His hand rose to my shoulder. "Perhaps this time away from each other has made him miss and appreciate you."

I laughed. "No way! He enjoys being alone. He prefers it. And he's such a misogynist. Really. He *hates* women. He can't stand men either. Actually, I think he hates the entire human race!" I wanted to add, *and especially the Jews*, but was too embarrassed. "I'm sorry, Charles. I didn't mean to bother you with my troubles. It's just that I've been so alone, so isolated for such a long time that—"

"No need to apologize." We stood there facing each other. Looking into his eyes was like searching the vast depths of a blue ocean. Somewhere hidden near the bottom lay a buried treasure. I moved closer to him, anticipating the next words he uttered. I had a sense they could somehow change everything.

"I can tell you one thing," he finally said. "Whatever good qualities I have at this point in my life, I attribute them, without a doubt, to the few women I've been close to. I've been fortunate. I've had some excellent teachers. I've come to see women as teachers. Men have taught me nothing. They're too stupid."

I chuckled.

"Honestly, I'm convinced that women are the superior sex. Any fool should know that if he has a good woman in his life, he has everything."

The heaviness that had plagued me all the way down the long driveway evaporated, and my heart glowed with the warmth of his kindness. I kept telling myself to open the car door, but my arms wouldn't move. Charles grasped both my shoulders.

"Now you drive carefully, and get home safely."

"Okay." My throat tightened.

"Be strong," he said. "And be good to yourself."

"I will." I fought back tears. We embraced. I clutched his jacket. "And thank you for the book. Thank you for everything." I opened the door and got into the car. Charles loaded my suitcase, sleeping bag, and the blue painting onto the back seat. I rolled down the window. "I might be back for the Death Awareness retreat. Do you think you'll still be here?"

"I'm not sure. Bhante Upali is trying to convince me to stay and cook for one more retreat. But I haven't decided yet."

"Well, write to me and let me know where you are."

He nodded. I started the engine. As I turned onto Winding Creek Road, the tears I'd been restraining erupted in a torrential flood, and I made no effort to stop them. A maelstrom of unidentifiable thoughts and emotions whizzed around my brain in an indistin-guishable, circular blur. With hands locked on the steering wheel, eyes fixed on the road ahead, I just drove, listening to the mournful cadence of my own sobs until they finally wore themselves out.

PART THREE

Return to Darkness

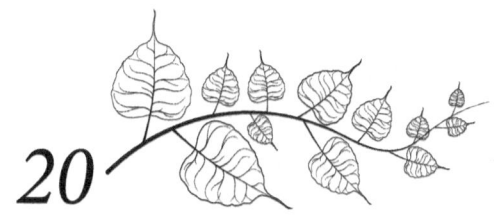

20

Faith and Flowers

It rained practically the entire four-hour drive. Halfway home, I found myself on a residential Cumberland, Maryland street driving through pouring rain in what I thought was the wrong direction. *Did I miss the entrance ramp to Route 220?* I continued driving another ten minutes, then I gave up and pulled over, admitting to myself I was lost. *Shit!* Swollen raindrops pelted the windshield. A chill shot up my spine. My mind leaped into the future, imagining my greatest fear and worst nightmare: Once home, my meditation practice would decline, the joyful woman I'd just found would fade and disappear, Mack would continue ripping me apart and railing against the Jews, and my miserable life would return in full force.

I groaned and peered through the driver's side window. Through the fog, I made out a flower shop on the first floor of a two-story brick building—as good a place as any to ask for directions. As I came through the front door of the shop, the sound of bells tinkled overhead. Several houseplants were scattered about the small, cluttered room. Dried and silk flower arrangements sat on shelves along the back wall.

A young, blonde woman wearing faded jeans and a stained sweatshirt appeared from behind a curtain that separated the shop from another room. She headed toward a long counter and said hello. Behind the counter, a cooler was filled with vases of fresh flowers. I almost tripped on a child's plastic tricycle as I approached her.

"Oh, I'm sorry 'bout that!" the woman said. "She walks away and leaves that bike everywhere. I'm busy in the back room and can't always watch her."

"That's okay." I spied a vase of white roses in the cooler. "Wow, look at the size of those roses. They're as big as my fist!"

Just then a little girl, three or four years old, darted through the curtain and into the shop. She jumped on the plastic tricycle and gazed up at me with dark eyes. My legs buckled. The likeness was uncanny. This was the same face, the same searching eyes and dark hair of the baby who'd appeared to me in the meditation hall. My hand grasped the edge of the counter for support.

After a few moments I found my voice. "Hello, sweetheart. You're a very pretty little girl."

"What do you say to the lady?" her mother asked the child.

The little girl remained silent. Then she started pedaling her bike round and round the small shop.

"Sometimes she don't know how to behave," the woman said to me.

"Oh, she's fine," I said, a bit choked up. "Actually, she's perfect."

My attention was drawn to a houseplant on a windowsill near the front of the shop. *No, it can't be!* I moved closer and inspected the narrow, serrated leaves. "I don't believe this," I whispered. Yet here it was, growing in a glazed blue ceramic pot: the mystery plant from the monastery. Blinking, I shook my head. I even pinched myself.

I sensed a close presence and looked down at my feet. There was the little girl sitting on her bike, her curious eyes drilling a hole in my heart. Inside my mind, the voice that had spoken to me in the meditation hall repeated those same three perplexing words, "That's *your* baby." *What in the world is going on?* I smiled at the little girl. Dressed in a pink terrycloth sweatsuit and pink sneakers, the little girl was adorable, and for a few moments I wished she actually *was* my own baby.

The little girl pedaled over to the counter and hid behind her mother. I followed. "Excuse me," I said to the woman, "but do you know the name of that plant over there on the shelf? The one in the blue pot. I've worked around plants my whole life, and I'd never seen a plant like that until last week. And now, I've seen *two* of them. Isn't that strange!"

"That plant has lots of names, but we call it a pregnancy plant," the woman said.

I doubled over.

"Are you all right, ma'am?"

"I think I need to sit down."

She hurried over to me with a folding chair.

On the verge of tears, I collapsed into the chair. Suddenly, I was back in the library with Bhante Upali, explaining what I had done the one and only time I was pregnant.

"You want a glass of water?" the woman asked.

"No, no, I'm all right. Thank you. It's just that, well, that particular plant has special meaning for me. How much is it?"

"Oh, I'm sorry, ma'am, but that plant's not for sale. A good friend of mine gave me that plant. It's kinda special to me, too. See, I thought for a long time that I could never get pregnant. My husband and I tried for years. We wanted a child so bad! I'd almost given up hope, and then one day the doctor told me I was pregnant with little Faith here. About a month before that wonderful news, my best friend gave me that plant for luck."

I gulped. "Your little girl's name is Faith?"

"Yes. We named her Faith 'cause we never gave up hoping I'd get pregnant."

My head and hands quivered, my eyes squeezed shut. *This is too much. The baby's face. The pregnancy plant. And now, Faith. How can all this be happening? What does it mean?* Completely overwhelmed by these extraordinary coincidences, my head dropped into my hands and I started sobbing.

"What is it, ma'am? What's the matter?" the woman said, rubbing my back. "Honest to God, you're gonna make me cry right along with you!"

"I'm sorry." I sniffled. "Please don't think I'm crazy. I don't mean to cry. It's just that I've just had an emotionally charged couple of weeks jam-packed with some pretty bizarre experiences. And for some strange reason, I'm being reminded of several of those experiences right here in your shop."

"Look," the woman said, "I can give you some of that plant's babies if you want. It keeps having all these babies all the time. That's probably why they call it the pregnancy plant. I have a tray of babies started up in the back room. I transplanted them a few weeks ago and they're doin' real well. Just put 'em near a window and treat 'em just like a jade plant."

"Thanks, but actually, I already have a few of that plant's babies." I wiped my eyes with the back of my hand and stood up. "I'd better go. I'm running late as it is. My husband expected me home by now."

"Maybe having some fresh flowers in the house would make you feel better," the woman said.

I glanced at the white roses inside the cooler and couldn't resist. *Maybe I should give a few to Mack as a gesture of goodwill.* "You know, I think you're right. How about wrapping up three of those gorgeous white roses?"

"Do you want baby's breath with that?"

"Sure, that would be nice." Behind the counter several dozen colorful magnets were displayed on a wide metal sheet against the wall. There were animal magnets, flower magnets, tree magnets, and . . . *No. It can't be.* To the right of an elephant magnet was a miniature blue and white flower vase magnet—an exact replica of the Oriental vases adorning either side of the altar in the meditation hall. I blinked. But at this point, I wasn't surprised. "And I'll take that little flower vase magnet too," I said, pointing. As I reached for my wallet, I laughed at myself. "Oh, I almost forgot! I need directions. That's the reason I came in here in the first place. I'm lost. I need to get onto Route 220."

"Oh, that's easy!" the woman said. "Just keep goin' straight down this road you're on and you'll bump right into it." She plucked the flower vase magnet from the wall, wrapped it in tissue paper, and handed it to me.

"Really? Just keep going straight on this road? That's all?"

"Yep. Easy as pie. Just stay on this road. You can't miss it."

"So, I wasn't lost," I whispered. My fingers squeezed the little blue and white vase wrapped in tissue. *All I have to do is stay on this road . . .*

⚬⚭⚬⚮⚬

At last, I was back in the mountains I loved, driving along familiar country roads. The rain had stopped, but darkness had settled in. Almost home, only one thing remained to be conquered: my driveway. Fortunately, I had tons of experience propelling my two-wheel-drive vehicle up that steep, slippery slope in winter. Sometimes I made it, sometimes I didn't. The key, I'd discovered, was to get a running start.

As I turned off the main road into the driveway, I hit the gas. Larry had cleared a narrow lane with the plow, but my goodness! The mounds of snow piled on either side of the drive were almost as tall as I was! *If I can just manage to keep the car from skidding into the snow-banks, I should make it.*

The tires started spinning about a third of the way up, and I was losing speed. If I eased off the gas, I'd be a goner. I'd lose momentum, get stuck, and, like several times in the past, I'd have to put the car in reverse and carefully ease the car all the way back down to the bottom of the hill and either try again or park the car at Trex's house and walk up. But even though the tires were spinning, I wasn't about to give up.

As luck would have it, the car inched forward, slowly gaining ground. "Come on, come on!" I jerked forward in the seat. With the crest of the hill in sight, I took a risk, punched the gas pedal to the floor, and the car sailed up and over the windswept crest. I parked the car at the barn. In the distance, my little ramshackle farmhouse with peeling white paint gleamed beneath the security light, shining like the pot of gold at the end of the rainbow. Even though it was practically engulfed by snowdrifts, that little farmhouse never looked so dear to me. I parked at the barn, jumped out of the car, and raised my fist in triumph. "Yes! I made it!"

Booter, my big black bear of a dog, stuck his head out of his house. "I made it, Booter!" I shouted. The dog bounded through the drifts toward me. Kneeling in the snow, I gave him a big hug. "I'm home, Booter! Were you a good boy? Did you miss me?"

"Lulu, is that you?" Mack's voice called from the front porch.

"Yes. Yes, I made it up the hill!"

"You're late. It's already dark. I told you to be home by four thirty."

"I got held up."

"Come inside. I'll get your bags in later."

I grabbed the roses wrapped in tissue from the back seat. With Booter by my side, I stood for a long while staring up at the clear night sky. The bright stars, like an intricate lighted roadmap to the heavens, welcomed me home. The vastness and splendor of that starry sky, combined with the quiet stillness of the surrounding fields, reminded me how lucky and blessed I was to live in what some people called "God's country." Overwhelmed with gratitude, I placed the flowers on the hood of the car, pressed my palms together at my chest, and bowed to the vivid points of light above me.

Mack sat the kitchen table drinking a cup of tea. He didn't get up when I entered the room. I surveyed the large country kitchen. It looked changed—the linoleum seemed faded, the green countertops and oak kitchen cabinets smaller than usual, and the glare from the overhead light gave the glossy white walls an almost greasy appearance. Mack also appeared different—hardened and brittle.

"Here," I said, holding up the bouquet. "I brought you something."

He stood up and blinked several times. "Lu, what's happened to you?"

"What do you mean?"

"You look great!" He gave me a bear hug and stepped back, staring at me with his protruding, multicolored eyes. His sunken cheeks were unshaven as usual. His receding hairline above deep creases in his forehead made him look much older than his age. "Seriously, Lu. You really do look good. I'd much rather see this face than that ugly mournful mug of yours I've been forced to look at every day."

I took off my coat and hung it on the rack. "I'll put those flowers in some water."

"Wait a minute," Mack said. "Honestly, Lu. Your face. It's different. In fact, everything about you seems different."

My hand touched my cheek. "Different how?"

"You're . . . you're glowing."

I went into the living room and inspected my face in the mirror hanging above the buffet table. I couldn't see that I was glowing, but my face did appear to have a softer quality than before I'd left.

Mack followed me into the living room. "Seriously, Lu, what happened to you? Did you get a glimpse of Nirvana? Have you attained enlightenment?" He cackled.

I remembered Lin's wise counsel: *Don't tell anyone about Kuan Yin. Especially not your husband.* Staring into his mocking eyes, I said,

"Nothing happened." Then I went back into the kitchen, opened a cupboard, and removed a flower vase. Mack followed me.

"What do you mean, nothing happened? Something obviously happened. You admitted to me on the phone that something had happened or *was* happening. I think I have a right to know."

Talking was the last thing I wanted to do, yet I knew that if I didn't give Mack some sort of answer or explanation, he'd follow me all over the house and continue to harass me for the rest of the night.

I filled the vase with water and turned to face him. "Look, Mack, I don't know what happened. I don't know that *anything* happened. Besides, whatever I think *may* have happened is impossible to explain. Besides, you wouldn't understand."

"Try me."

"It can't be explained in words. It's an experiential thing. Now please, I'm exhausted, and I really don't have the energy to talk right now. All I want to do is soak in a hot bathtub and climb into bed."

His eyes filled with malice. His facial muscles tightened. I thought he might erupt in hostilities, but instead he said, "Suit yourself." Then he bolted up the stairs, went into his room, and slammed the door.

As my old clawfoot bathtub filled with hot water, I lit several candles and a stick of incense, then placed them on the bathroom windowsill. Then I undressed and, out of curiosity, stepped onto the bathroom scale. My God, I'd lost eight pounds! Eight pounds in two weeks! I turned off the overhead light and lowered myself into the steaming tub.

As my body luxuriated in deliciously hot water by candlelight, the scent of sandalwood carried me to a place of peace. I sank deeper into the tub, submerging my shoulders and neck. In doing so, my knees and thighs poked above the water's surface, exposing large purplish marks on my kneecaps and thighs. I gawked at the bruises in shock.

My God, where did **those** *come from?* Then it dawned on me: I'd just spent the majority of the past two weeks dropping to my knees and sitting in the full lotus posture with my ankle bones pressed sharply against my thighs. I leaned forward, inspected my damaged legs, and instead of being upset or annoyed, I chuckled. These glaring battle wounds were a small price to pay for the tremendous victory I'd won during my stay at the monastery.

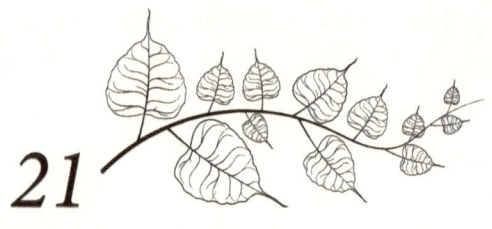

21

Overdue Remorse

When I came downstairs before dawn the next morning, Mack was in the kitchen pouring himself a cup of coffee. Last night I'd knocked on his door and informed him I'd be keeping Noble Silence all morning as was the custom at the monastery. Later, it occurred to me that my silence was no different than our usual morning routine when Mack forbade me to speak to him until his lunch break. Without looking at me, he climbed the stairs with a steaming mug in his hand. I flinched as his bedroom door slammed shut. Five minutes later, the familiar banging of typewriter keys filled the house.

I brewed a cup of green tea, climbed the stairs, shut the door to my own little bedroom, sat at my desk, and stared out the window. The first rays of dawn were breaking behind the darkened mountain range. Soon the impressive peaks would be visible, shining tall and majestic under the white winter sun, stretching along the horizon as far as I could see, and disappearing into forever. I sipped hot tea, determined to maintain my meditation practice and preserve the peace I'd discovered during my stay at the monastery. But it wouldn't be easy now that

I was living and working in the real world filled with distractions and stresses. Still, I'd commit to at least half an hour of meditation in the morning and evening, and try my best to follow the Buddha's path.

I opened the book Charles had given me and turned to the listing for the Buddha's Noble Eightfold Path. I read: "The Noble Eightfold Path is the Middle Path which the Perfect One rediscovered and expounded, which gives rise to vision and knowledge, which leads to peace, wisdom, enlightenment, and Nibbana. Right Understanding. Right Intention. Right Speech. Right Action. Right Livelihood. Right Effort. Right Mindfulness. Right Concentration."

I couldn't imagine practicing all eight simultaneously. Instead, I'd try to focus on one or two at a time and start with "Right Effort" and "Right Speech." At least I could check "Right Livelihood" off the list since my job involved feeding people healthy meals and teaching natural foods cooking classes.

I turned to the index and looked up Kuan Yin. Under her name it said "See Avalokitesvara." That page said:

"Avalokitesvara. Syn: Kuan Yin. The Avalokitesvara (twenty-fifth) chapter of the Lotus Sutra states: If living beings much given to carnal passion keep in mind and revere the Bodhisattva 'Regarder of the Cries of the World,' they will be set free from their passion. If those much given to irascibility (hatred and anger) keep in mind and revere the Bodhisattva 'Regarder of the Cries of the World,' they will be set free from their irascibility. If those much given to delusion keep in mind and revere the Bodhisattva 'Regarder of the Cries of the World,' they will be set free of their delusion."

On a notepad I wrote, Lotus Sutra, Chapter 25, then closed the *Seeker's Glossary. Hmmm. How can I "keep in mind and revere" Kuan Yin now that I'm home?* I had no statue of her to bow to, no image to remind me of her. I supposed I could start by reciting her name. Quietly, I practiced saying the new name I'd learned for her: "Avalokitesvara,

Avalokitesvara." I liked the way it rolled off my tongue.

I swallowed the last bit of tea, unrolled my yoga mat, and settled myself onto a thick pillow I used as a meditation cushion. Since I had no altar, I couldn't bow three times to anything, so I crossed my legs, closed my eyes, and inhaled deeply. *May I be well, happy, and peaceful; may I and all living beings be free from suffering and delusion.*

Mack was in the kitchen eating breakfast. I walked past him, slipped on my coat, and stepped outside onto the porch. With the pale light of dawn upon the surrounding fields, I witnessed the full effect of the winter snowstorm. The drifts to the left and right of the house were like mini White Cliffs of Dover, and Booter's doghouse resembled an oversized igloo.

Beyond the doghouse, the old barn with the metal roof loomed large. I thought about Trex. We'd been renting his dilapidated farm-house—the house he was born in—for the past seven years. He lived all alone at the bottom of my steep driveway in the crumbling stone house which was slowly falling apart just like he was. I visited him daily and had come to love him as a grandfather. When I went to the market, Trex had a standing order for orange juice, canned peaches, and cough drops, which he practically lived on. He was an eighty-five-year-old bachelor who'd farmed most of his life. Every spring, despite his arthritis, weak heart, weak lungs, and failing kidney, he managed to get the old tractor started, haul himself up onto the seat, plow his fields, and sow his grain. Oh, it was impossible to keep a man like Trex down. I'd become convinced that like dinosaurs, strong, hard-working, good-natured, uncomplaining men like Trex no longer roamed the earth.

I recalled the cool spring day when I first met him in front of the barn. Desperate to find housing after the first farmhouse I'd rented had been sold, I'd answered his ad in the newspaper and had come to view the rental. Vacant for years, the small farmhouse sitting atop a steep hill and surrounded on all sides by fields needed extensive repair. The floors were cracked, and the kitchen had no cabinets or countertops. After the house tour, Trex and I stood together on the front porch. Spellbound by the majestic mountain views in every direction and convinced I absolutely had to live there, I said to Trex, "I'll make you a deal. I'll pay for the installation of new flooring and kitchen cabinets in exchange for reduced monthly rent and a five-year lease. And I promise to keep the house neat and clean." Trex was all in. That day we bonded like silent partners saving his childhood home from ruin.

A chill swept over me and I went back into the house. "I'll walk down the hill and give Trex his newspaper this morning," I said to Mack. "I want to check on him."

"You don't need to do that."

"Why not? You already did?"

"No. I, uh, well, Lu, I wasn't going to tell you this until later today. Trex is in the hospital."

My world went dark. Unconsciously, my palms came together at my chest, remembering the vision I had of Trex's face back at the monastery. *Did he appear to me because he was sick?* I imagined the worst: Trex lying in some cold hospital bed, in pain and alone, waiting to die. I collapsed onto the kitchen chair and broke out sobbing.

"What are you blubbering about?" Mack snapped. "Where's all your goddamned calmness and detachment now? You come home acting like you're some blissfully enlightened, vastly superior human being, pretending you're beyond the mundane world, beyond giving in to your sloppy feminine emotions. And look at you now! You're a wreck! As soon as there's the slightest glitch in the picture, you fall to pieces! Yesterday I was beginning to think you might have made some progress out there in West Virginia, but obviously you haven't. You're still the miserable, wailing emotional wreck you were when you left here!"

I stared at him through wet eyes. To my surprise, his caustic words had no effect on me, like snowflakes that quickly melted upon touching my ears. I also hadn't the slightest urge to lash out, retaliate, or explain myself as I usually did when he attacked me. I plucked a tissue from the box on the kitchen table, blew my nose, and said, "Please tell me what happened to Trex."

"He fell and broke his arm. He's in pretty bad shape. He's very weak and his lungs are full of fluid."

"When did this happen?"

"A couple of days ago. When I went down in the morning to give him his newspaper, I found him on the floor."

"So, you called the paramedics?"

"Of course I called the paramedics! For Christ's sake! Do you think I'm such a monster that I'd leave an old man with a broken arm to die on his kitchen floor?" Hostility oozed from Mack's bulging eyes. His hollow cheeks were flushed, his jaw twisted with rage.

Where did all his anger come from? But I knew the answer. He raged about it countless times over the years. "They cut my balls off!" he always said. "They silenced me, the bastards! I was their star reporter! I was a big fish in that little town! People knew my name. People respected me. The whole town couldn't wait to read my latest piece of journalism exposing those miserable, corrupt politicians, govern- ment officials, even the priest. But I was a threat to their power, so the Jewish cabal that owned the town and controlled the media got rid of me. Those slimy Hebrew cock-sucking bastards! After they ordered the newspaper to fire me, I said, 'Fuck you' and started my own newspaper. But those filthy moneygrubbing kikes pressured my advertisers and put me out of business!"

I plucked another tissue from the box. "So, after the paramedics left, did you call Robert?" Trex's closest living relative was his nephew,

Robert, who lived twenty miles away.

"Hell, no! I won't speak to that jerk! He can take that sanctimonious religious bullshit of his and shove it up his ass! Christ, I can't *tolerate* his kind! If he's so goddamned loving, sympathetic, and full of Christian spirit, why wasn't *he* the one over here every day checking on his uncle?"

I headed for the stairs. "Oh, so that's it?" Mack snarled. "Now you're leaving? You think you can just walk away and blow me off? Oh, no! You're not going to treat *me* like that! You Jews are a haughty, contemptuous bunch! You come in here, all high and mighty with your phony spiritual bullshit, yapping about Noble Silence, but you can't even manage to keep your trap shut, you loud-mouthed Jew! And not only do you spoil my breakfast with your wailing, now that you've done your damage, you think you can just dismiss me like I'm some kind of servant! Imagine, the likes of *you* dismissing *me!* Christ! You're not even worthy of carrying my jockstrap!"

The pain in his twisted face was palpable. But instead of hatred toward him, compassion entered my heart. "You poor man," I said in a gentle voice. "You must be suffering terribly."

His jaw slackened; his eyes widened in confusion. Then he shook his head and roared, "Oh, shut up, you dumb Jew bitch! Why don't you go back to your precious monastery and mind your own goddamned business!" He grabbed his cereal bowl and threw it across the room, where it shattered against the wall. "Nothing's changed! You've just ruined another meal for me! No wonder I suffer from stomach distress!"

My palms came together at my chest.

"And quit making that stupid gesture! You look like a moron! Plus, it's annoying! Why don't you go upstairs and call your boyfriend Robert? Go on! I know that's what you're up to! And while you're talking to him, go ahead and ask the Good Samaritan why your husband was the one to find his uncle lying half dead on the floor!"

I hurried up the stairs, my palms still pressed tightly together.

That afternoon it was back to work. I wrote my grocery list and went shopping. There were more food orders than usual waiting for me on the answering machine. I'd be quite busy during the next several days with all the cooking and clean-up, the 150-mile delivery trip down the mountain to Pittsburgh and back, plus teaching my cooking class Thursday night.

Fortunately, the wintry weather had calmed, replaced by brighter, warmer days. After I unloaded the car, put all the groceries away, and cooked two stockpots of cauliflower-potato soup, I took a break and went out for a walk, eager to breathe the fresh mountain air and hike my dear, familiar paths. I left Booter at home this time. Something told me I needed to be alone.

The air was perfectly still. Snow-covered fields on either side of the driveway sparkled under the sunshine. I crossed the main road and climbed the steep hill of Kline's Mill Road. Gray tree trunks on both sides of the road stood tall, stiff, and barren inside the sleeping forest. A thick, undisturbed layer of snow covered the forest floor as a pristine, white blanket. Come spring, as it did every year, the snow would melt in torrents and rush down the mountainside, the forest would awaken, and the miracle would begin once again, bringing new life to all that grew from the earth.

When I reached the pond at the top of the hill, I stopped to catch my breath and admire the water's smooth, tranquil surface. I'd read that Kuan Yin is deeply tied to water and its miraculous healing capacities. Could she be with me now? "Avalokitesvara, Avalokitesvara," I repeated, my head bowed, palms pressed together. "Thank you so much for watching over me. Please continue to help, protect, and guide me." Then I headed back toward home.

Halfway down the hill, I became keenly aware of the road's hard surface against the soles of my hikers, and the motion of my hips as my legs propelled me forward. A few minutes later, my skin tingled with familiar warmth. I stopped on the side of the road, closed my eyes, and there she was: the baby's face that had appeared to me in the meditation hall. My heartbeat quickened. *Who are you? Why have you come to me again?* Her dark, beseeching eyes ripped a hole in my heart. Clearly, she needed something from me. Something important. *But what?* All of a sudden, from the deepest recesses of my soul, the answer rose to the surface of my consciousness. Shocked and heartbroken, I collapsed into a snowbank and burst out crying.

My hands clutched my stomach as I wailed uncontrollably, tormented with grief, guilt, and remorse. Then the words which had been buried in some long-forgotten place for over twenty years clawed their way up my throat and into my mouth. My lips spat them out as though expelling a deadly poison: "I'm sorry! I'm soooo sorry!" I cried, hot tears dripping down my cheeks. "Please forgive me! I'm so sorry I killed you!"

Later that evening as I sat in the living room reading the book Charles had given me, Mack entered the room. It was seven thirty, the time he usually retired to his bedroom for the night, and the pungent aroma of marijuana floated down the stairwell. "Sorry I lost it this morning, Lu," he said. "I do my best, but sometimes my life just gets to me. I've got nothing. No money, no friends, no family, no security for my old age. Hell, I'm old *already!* This August I'll be sixty fucking years old. Soon I'll be dead. I've given up everything for my work, and for what? Headaches? Stomach problems? Having to put up with you and your neurotic Jewish bullshit? Nobody's been there for me. Nobody's been in my corner encouraging me. I've had to do it all alone. If I'd had one person—just one person who believed in me, who really cared about what I wrote, well, who knows?" He hung his head. "Ah, it's all bullshit. Blah, blah, blah. I ought to just blow my brains out."

His face had aged ten years since last winter. The lines on his forehead were now crevices, his cheekbones prominent because he'd lost weight. Maybe I could practice "Right Effort" and "Right Speech" and find words that might ease his pain. I closed the book. "I know how terribly dark and difficult life can seem at times. God knows I've been there. The Buddha says we all suffer. Every one of us. We grow old, we suffer pain, fear, sickness, grief. But it's not all negative. The Buddha says there's an end to suffering. There's a path. And that path is full of loving-kindness and compassion."

His eyes narrowed.

"Maybe if you tried to open your heart to others, and put something above yourself—"

"I already do that! I've sacrificed everything for my work. Everything! And look where it's got me. I don't have a pot to piss in or a window to throw it out of!"

"Why don't you consider going on a retreat? You never leave the farmhouse. A change of scene might do you good." I smiled. "Retreats can be magical. Wonderful, unexpected things could happen."

His face hardened. "Retreats may work for someone as weak-minded and gullible as you, but it won't work for me. I see through all that crap. I'm too smart to fall for all that Buddhist mumbo-jumbo. I meditate every evening. That's all I need."

I sighed. I wanted to tell him that sitting on the floor and getting high wasn't meditating; it was medi*cating*. But I didn't dare go there. Instead, I said, "Suit yourself. It was just a suggestion."

"Well, you can keep your suggestions and your goddamned prose-lytizing to yourself! Honest to Christ, I don't know why I even bother trying to talk to you about my life. You're no help whatsoever. Utterly useless! I'm going upstairs."

At 2 a.m. I was jolted awake by the sound of loud clanking noises coming from the radiator in my room. *Shit. I bet the furnace is on the fritz again.* Too tired to go downstairs and investigate, I pulled the covers over my head, praying I was wrong.

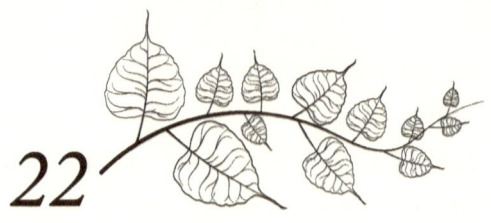

22

More Comfortable in Heaven

Early the next morning while Mack was downstairs pouring coffee into his mug, I broke Noble Silence and asked him if he'd heard the loud clanking noises.

"Yeah. Once or twice while you were gone. I think it's coming from the basement."

"It's probably the furnace acting up. Remember all that trouble we had last winter? I'd better call Rick."

He slammed the coffee pot on the counter. "Oh, that's fucking great! Now you want to call some loud-mouthed moron plumber who thinks he's a goddamned Jewish comedian! What a fucking inconvenience!"

"He's not Jewish, Mack."

"Yes, he is. If you behave like a Jew, you're a Jew. It's a mentality, not a religion. It reveals itself in obnoxious behavior."

My gaze dropped to the kitchen floor. "Mack, will you *please* give the Jewish thing a break? How many times do I have to ask you?"

"And I know *exactly* what will happen. That imbecile is going to show up here in the morning while I'm trying to get some work done.

And you'll be just as noisy and annoying as he is! You encourage this jerk by laughing at his so-called jokes. Every time he shows up, the two of you make a terrible racket down here, completely ruining my writing time."

"Mack, please!"

"You've been a hindrance to my work ever since I met you! You're nothing but an inconvenient pain in my ass that I constantly have to work around. It's a wonder I've been able to get *anything* done with your incessant demands, interruptions, and juvenile need for attention! Add to that your malicious, calculated, Jewish need to control, to boss, to manipulate, to emasculate. Christ! I don't know why I continue to put up with it! The fact that in order to survive I have to put up with the likes of *you* is beyond laughable! It's disgraceful!"

I held my tongue. There were many things I could have said to him. I could have told him that if the furnace wasn't fixed, he'd have to write in a frigid house. I could have reminded him that instead of being a hindrance to his work, I was, at one time, his only and most avid supporter, reading and typing his stories, researching publishing markets, and sending his manuscripts to magazines, agents, and editors. I could have said that the only person in this house with the need to control and manipulate was standing right in front of me. But I didn't say any of these things. Instead, I took a slow, deep breath, closed my eyes, and silently repeated, *Avalokitesvara, Avalokitesvara.*

By noon I had two pots of brown rice pudding and a stockpot of garlicky greens and lentils cooling on the stove. I figured I'd prepare the quinoa salad and pack up all the food I'd made into quart containers after Mack had retired to his room for the evening. The next morning I'd embark on my delivery trip into Pittsburgh.

I glanced at the clock and grabbed my hikers. Mack sat in the wicker chair in the living room reading a white supremacist newsletter. I sat down on the couch. "I'm going to visit Trex," I said, tying my laces.

"You're *what?*"

"I said I'm going to visit Trex."

"In the hospital?"

"No. They've moved him to a nursing home because he's too weak to go home. It's somewhere in Davidsville. For some reason this particular nursing home is the only place Trex would agree to go to. You know how stubborn he can be." I stood up. "The beds were full, but because Trex refused to go anywhere else, Robert was able to pull a few strings and make a special arrangement to get him in."

"Oh, so you've been keeping in touch with your boyfriend, Robert? What a pussy-whipped jerk he's turned out to be! It's a shame. A big, strong, handsome country boy like him being led around by the nose by that obnoxious, neurotic wife of his! Christ! And she isn't even good-looking!"

I stayed silent as I removed my coat from the coat rack.

"If you feel the need to show a little kindness, you *could* start right here at home instead of driving off to some goddamned nursing home in Davidsville. You could fix me a nice supper. Or you could clean the house for a change and give me a break. Really, Lu, you're a terrible housekeeper! I'm always the one cleaning the bathroom, running the vacuum. The hamper's full of dirty laundry, the kitchen floor needs to be scrubbed, and I won't even *mention* that pigsty you call your bedroom. If I weren't around to clean the house, you'd be living in filth. And do you know why? It all stems from laziness. You're basically a lazy twat. You really should take care of your responsibilities at home before you go running off to spread joy and good cheer to people who don't deserve it."

Normally after comments like that, I'd be furious, lashing out at him in self-defense. Instead, I just shook my head, somehow able to get past the emotion of anger and see his attacks on my character clearly for what they were—the mad ravings of a lonely, troubled, frightened man consumed by anger and bitterness. But my patience was wearing thin, and I didn't know how much longer this clarity of mind would last.

The strained expression on his face concerned me. Ever since that horrible scene last Christmas when Mack flipped out and burned some of his manuscripts, there was an air of desperation about him, an un-raveling, as though the vital links holding him together and keeping his head above water had snapped, plunging him into a seething pool of irrational rage and hostility. Also, since Christmas, he'd begun talking about suicide again.

Recognizing there was absolutely nothing I could do for this poor man, I put on my coat. "I'm going to visit Trex," I said softly. "I need to see him."

The nursing home was a huge operation—a village in itself, complete with assisted living apartments, separate housing units for the retired and elderly, a hospital wing, and acres of parking lots and landscaped gardens.

The lobby of the main building was decorated to the hilt: plush rugs covered the polished floors, ornately framed artwork graced the walls, expensive-looking furniture filled the room, and huge vases of fresh flowers adorned tabletops. Nurses hurried past me carrying IV bags or empty trays. Uniformed employees pushed well-dressed, white-haired bodies slumped in wheelchairs. Several of those bodies were attached to various machines that rolled along beside them. Men wearing dark suits and white jackets with clipboards under their arms waited by the elevators as a parade of ancient-looking men and women pushing walkers roamed the lobby. Some of the residents were accompanied by visitors whose expressions suggested they'd rather be someplace else.

At the reception desk, I asked a young woman for help. "I'm looking to visit Mr. Trexler. Mr. Dwight Trexler. I know he's in here somewhere."

"Let me check." She slid her chair over to the computer. "Oh, yes, here he is. Just go straight down this hallway, past the administrative offices, and turn right at the library. That will take you to the hospital wing."

"Thank you."

"The entrance to the DU will be the double doors right in front of you. Just ask the woman at the desk there to let you in. They keep those doors locked."

"What's the DU?"

She seemed surprised I didn't know. "Mr. Trexler's in the Dementia Unit."

I just stared at her in disbelief.

Completely unprepared for what awaited me, I entered a large room with a kitchenette and about a dozen round tables where residents sat slumped in wheelchairs, eating their lunch. The din was incredible—a mélange of voices shouting, wailing, moaning, shrieking all at once, and addressing no one in particular. And on top of all that human clamor, music was piped in through a speaker on the ceiling, giving the place an absurd, carnival-like quality. I stood motionless amidst the cacophony and the smell of urine, petrified by the surreal scene before me.

To my right, a neatly dressed old man with a full head of white hair stood behind his walker, his arms flailing as he pontificated in an obscure language, oblivious to the fact that no one was listening. To my left, a large man with oily hair wearing a hospital gown sat alone, gurgling in a deep voice as he shifted food around on his plate with his fingers. In the far corner, a screaming emaciated woman, her arms strapped to a wheelchair, was being spoon-fed by a nurse.

I scanned every table, searching for Trex. When I finally spotted him, my heart wept. There he was—at a table near the only window, slumped in his wheelchair like the rest of them, staring at the floor. His left arm was bound in a tight sling taped to his chest. He wore a flannel button-down shirt, a blanket covering his legs. A tray of untouched food lay on the table before him. Unconsciously, my hand squeezed the paper bag I'd brought with me so tightly my fist began to hurt. I hurried over to him, glad to see him, yet horrified to see him here.

Standing very close, I said, "Hi, Trex."

Slowly, his head rose and he turned to face me. His usual laughing blue eyes were dull.

After a few moments he said, "Ohhh, Laurie. What are you doing here?"

"I came to see you." I smiled. "I thought you might enjoy a visit."

"Ohhh. Thanks for coming." His voice was weak. "Robert was here yesterday."

"I brought you some orange juice," I said, taking the carton out of the bag. He made no response. The other men seated at Trex's table were watching me with hungry eyes, as though any minute I might take off my clothes. Several of the men were drooling, most wore bibs. There was a lot of food on the table, but no one seemed to be eating.

Just then, a heavyset nurse with a huge bosom came over to the table carrying a chair. "Here," she said, setting the chair down beside Trex. "Why don't you sit down and visit with Mr. Trexler awhile? We're just having our lunch."

"Oh, thank you. I brought him some orange juice. He likes orange juice."

"How 'bout I pour you a glass of orange juice?" the nurse asked Trex. "You hardly touched your lunch."

Trex was silent.

"I usually have to speak to him pretty loudly," I told the nurse. "He's hard of hearing." I scrutinized Trex's ears. "Trex, where are your hearing aids?"

His chin had sunk to his chest.

"Trex!" I repeated. "Where are your hearing aids?"

His whiskered, wrinkled face was pale. His head rose, and in a barely audible voice he said, "Ohhh, I don't know."

"Well," I said, "maybe you'd enjoy a glass of orange juice."

"I'll get you a clean cup," the nurse said, and off she went to the kitchenette.

I sat down in the chair. Waves of anger and sadness crashed inside my chest. Oh, I couldn't bear to see him in this place among the mentally unwell and forgotten! It just wasn't right. It wasn't fair. He didn't deserve this!

I swallowed hard and tried to think of something uplifting to say. "So, Trex, I've missed you. How are you doing?"

He brightened for an instant. Then came his usual response: "I've got one foot in the grave and the other foot on a banana peel."

I smiled. He hadn't lost his sense of humor. This place hadn't broken him. At least not yet.

"Trex," I said seriously, "why did they put you in here?"

His gaze dropped to the sling strapped to his chest. "Broke my arm. Right near my shoulder. It's a bad break. Just snapped in two, the doctor said. Said they can't set it." He looked at me. "I can't move it."

A golf ball–sized lump formed in my throat. "I, I know. But I mean why did they put you in *here*? In this part of the nursing home?"

"It was the only bed available. My nephew Robert got me into this place. It's real nice. Best care in the whole county."

My heart grew heavy with grief and love for him. Staring at his thick farmer's fingers, I asked, "Does your arm hurt?"

"Course it hurts. I've never been in so much pain in my life. Not even when I had my heart attack."

"Are they giving you any pain medicine?"

He gazed out the window. "Ohhh, I don't know."

He seemed so weary—weary of talking, weary of living. I wanted to scream at the top of my lungs. I wanted to get him out of there. I'd have to find a way to take him home. Maybe Robert could arrange for a nurse to come to Trex's house and take care of him, like after his heart attack. I kept staring at his shriveled body, the brown age spots covering his bald head, wishing I could do something, knowing I couldn't do a damn thing.

"Well," I said, "you'll be feeling a lot better once your arm has healed and you're back home." I forced a smile. "And I'll come down the hill and visit you every day."

He faced me with a mix of hopelessness and resignation. "Ohhh," he said, "I won't be going back home."

My eyes grew moist. "You, you don't think so?"

He turned back to the window and shook his head "No," he said flatly. "I won't be going back home."

What did he mean? Of course he'd be coming home. He had to come home! Last year no one expected him to come home after his heart attack, but Trex surprised them all. "But are you *comfortable* here?" As soon as the words left my mouth, I was aware of the stupidity of my question.

As he turned back to me, the corners of his lips turned up. "I'd be more comfortable in heaven."

The gentle light of peace and acceptance brightened his face. I wiped a few tears from my cheek with the back of my hand and stood up. I had to get out of there fast, or I'd lose it.

"Well, Trex," I sniffled. "I'd better be going. I still have some cooking to do when I get home."

"Thanks for coming," he said.

"Oh, you're welcome."

"Come back again."

"I will." Without thinking, I leaned over and kissed his forehead. Then I hurried down the corridor toward the locked doors.

As soon as I got into my car, I started bawling. I cried because Trex was alone and in pain. I cried over the unfairness of a good, sound-minded man like Trex having to spend his last days inside a dementia unit. And I cried because there was absolutely nothing I could do to help him. My fist pounded the dashboard several times, then my forehead dropped to the steering wheel as I wailed, grieving for Trex as though he'd already died.

When I got home, Mack was upstairs in his room, banging away on his typewriter. It was almost four o'clock. I sat in the kitchen wishing I had a bottle of wine to open, wishing to forget the whole sad visit to the nursing home. I thought about Trex and how kind he'd been to me over the years. Shortly after we'd moved in, he gave me permission to plant a vegetable garden in the yard. I spent an entire day digging that huge garden bed and carrying heavy five-gallon buckets filled with dried manure from the barn to the garden site. The next morning, a shiny new wheelbarrow had magically appeared on the front porch. When I asked Trex where the wheelbarrow had come from, he said, "Can't have a working farm without a wheelbarrow."

My thoughts then turned to the kindness of everyone I'd met at the monastery. I'd discovered the Death Awareness retreat was a short retreat, starting on a Friday and ending on a Tuesday. If I attended, I'd have to cancel a week's worth of cooking orders, but I could still make my Thursday night cooking class. Curious, I approached the calendar hanging on the wall beside the phone and flipped the page to the next month. In red letters, I'd written "Dad's Yahrzeit" on the twelfth. *Oh my God!* The one-year anniversary of my father's sudden death coincided exactly with the first day of the Death Awareness retreat. Well, that confirmed it. I had to go back. I picked up the phone and dialed the monastery. The secretary told me the retreat had been full, but some-one had called an hour earlier and canceled, so there was one spot left.

"Please add my name to the list," I told her.

"Your timing couldn't have been more perfect," she said.

The image of Kuan Yin's white marble statue appeared in my mind. "I think I might have had a little help."

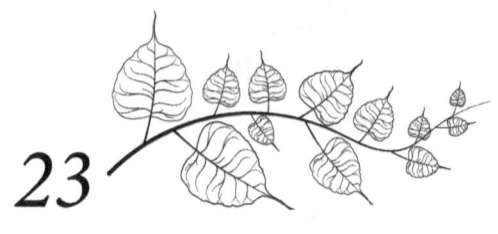

23

Blizzard Conditions

I rose before dawn Friday morning and meditated for a solid hour. Now that my workweek was over, I planned to devote extra time and effort to my practice. On the way home from my delivery trip to Pittsburgh, I'd stopped at a flea market in Greensburg and bought a two-foot-high wooden plant stand for ten dollars. In my bedroom, I'd covered the stand with a cloth napkin, then placed a brass candleholder and white taper candle in the center, and beside it, a glass bud vase of mini carnations. The only other thing I needed to complete my makeshift altar was a Buddha image.

At nine o'clock I called Rick the plumber. In addition to the occasional clanking noises, black smoke now poured out of the chimney. "What should I do, Rick? Oh God, do I have to shut down the furnace?"

"I would," Rick said. "It could be dangerous. I'll come over first thing tomorrow morning. We're booked solid the rest of the day taking care of people without heat. In the meantime, you could build a fire in the old coal burner. Good thing I kept that ancient monster hooked up to the new oil furnace, just in case. I'm so smart, ain't I?"

"Yes, Rick. You're a genius."

"You got wood?"

"We keep a small stack of firewood in the old coal bin in case of emergency," I sighed. "I guess I can keep a fire going until you come tomorrow."

"Oh, so *you're* the fireman? Why don't you get that lazy husband of yours to keep the fire going since he don't go to work? You're too easy on him."

Embarrassed, I said, "Well, he's very busy all day with his writing."

"Writing don't keep you warm," Rick said. "Writing don't put food on the table. Not unless you're famous. And he ain't. But don't you worry, little lady. I'll have your radiators cooking by end of day tomorrow."

"Okay, Rick. Thanks." I hung up the phone and shut off the thermostat. The dank, filthy cellar was dotted with cobwebs and coated with coal dust. Fortunately, there was some kindling to start a fire, and enough wood in the bin to keep us warm until Rick arrived.

<hr>

Mack entered the kitchen as I was chopping broccoli for dinner. He'd been sitting in the living room for the past hour poring over one of his white supremacist newsletters.

"No question about it," he said. "Your race is destroying the world. I was just reading about the Jewish mafia in Russia. Do you know what those slimy, greedy bastards are doing? Not only are they Russia's biggest organized drug dealers, they're also masterminding a huge, multi-national white slave trade."

"Mack, please! Enough about the Jews!" The wind howled through the cracks in the single-pane windows. Outside, snow was falling sideways, and beginning to accumulate. "How can an intelligent man like you believe all this crap? Don't you realize you're being brainwashed?

It's all a bunch of lies and conspiracy theories."

"You couldn't care less about what your tribe is up to! Your people are cunning, I'll grant you that. The Jews utilize their exclusive ownership of the media to inoculate the country with their multi-culturist notions of 'diversity' in order to achieve their goal of destroying the Christian, white, heterosexual male."

My grip on the knife handle tightened. "That's absolute nonsense! You're really getting me upset, so please, just shut up!"

"Oh, and by the way, tell that fat, obnoxious mother of yours not to call here before noon. The sound of your yammering on the phone so early in the day disturbs my concentration," he ranted. "Same goes for that air-headed, self-centered sister of yours."

That was it. He'd gone too far. Enraged, I hurled the knife onto the cutting board and turned around. The peace of mind I'd brought home with me from the monastery was no match for these constant attacks on the Jewish race, and now my own family. I struggled to contain the vicious words forming in my brain. Somehow, I managed not to yell or scream or cry. I just headed directly for my boots beside the front door with one intention: *I have to get out of this house.* A sudden gust of wind rattled the kitchen window as I tied my laces.

"What are you doing? Where are you going?" Mack shouted.

"I'm going to visit Betty Sue." I grabbed my coat from the rack.

"What? In this weather? Are you insane? Those are blizzard conditions out there. The roads are too treacherous. You can't go anywhere."

I headed for the door. "Oh, yes, I can! I'm going to walk. Don't try to stop me!" As soon as I stepped onto the porch, blinding snow hit my face, and frigid wind whipped my cheeks. I zipped my coat up to my chin, pulled the hood up over my head, and shouted, "And, in case you hadn't noticed, I had to turn off the heat and build a fire in the old coal stove to keep us warm. So, whatever you do, DO NOT LET THE FIRE GO OUT!"

I took off toward the barn.

"You get your goddamned ass back in this house this minute!" Mack shouted from the porch. "What do you think you're doing, you miserable cunt! You don't walk out on *me* like that! All right! All right! You'll see! You'll see what you come home to, you dumb, Jew bitch! This time I swear I'm going to do it! I'll blow my brains out! When you come home, you'll have my blood to clean up!"

Emotionally numb and wounded, the wind in my face, I trudged up the steep hill of Kline's Mill Road with every ounce of strength I had. Halfway up, I started to cry. Fat, wet tears stung my frozen cheeks. My head throbbed, my stomach churned, and I could barely see three feet in front of me. I wished I were inside a warm car driving anywhere far away—it didn't matter. Instead, I was lumbering up a steep, slippery, snow-covered mountain road in the middle of a blizzard. All I could do was keep moving, one foot in front of the other, while Mack's ugly words tortured my brain: *You miserable cunt! You dumb Jew bitch!*

I stopped for a breather and lifted my head to the darkened sky. "No, no, no!" I wailed. "I'm not going to put up with it anymore!" I'd go away. I'd live in an unheated one-room shack if I had to. Snow whipped my face. My toes grew numb, and I urged myself to keep moving. Otherwise, I'd be tempted to lie down in a snowbank, and they'd find me cold and stiff the next morning.

At the top of the hill, Betty Sue's house came into view. Right now, her tiny two-story dwelling opposite the pond resembled a dollhouse inside a snow globe. Wet and crying, I knocked at her front door.

"Lord have mercy!" she said, opening the door. "Heavens, come in, darlin'! What in the world are you doin' out on a night like this? Here, come inside before you catch your death of cold!"

Betty Sue was a small, thin seventy-year-old woman with shoulder-length permed hair who dressed in blue jeans and sweaters from the thrift store. She grew up in Texas, where she'd lived for most of her life until she divorced her husband of forty years and moved up north. She was a nervous woman, prone to depression, yet she loved to laugh. She also suffered from Graves' Disease, which made her right eye bulge. She couldn't see well enough to drive, so her girlfriend who lived down the road drove Betty Sue to the grocery store, and to flea markets and auctions. Betty Sue loved finding old collectables at bargain prices. Although she had no savings and lived on social security, each time I visited her, she showed me the latest old chest, picture frame, doll, or lamp she'd found on her last outing. I'd met her on my walks, we became casual friends, and she called me "Laurie Mae."

Seated in her cozy living room, I said, "Mack and I had a big fight. Things aren't good at home. I don't know what to do. I think I've really had it." I sniffled and she handed me a tissue.

"Oh, darlin'! I'm so sorry you're going through this mess! But it will pass. It'll all work itself out." She rocked in the rocking chair. "One way or the other."

"I hope so. I mean, I really don't think I can take much more of his abuse. It's just too painful."

"I remember how bad things got between me and Jessie. Oh, it was awful! He was physically abusive, you know. My only regret is that I waited too long to leave him. If I'd only come to my senses earlier! I was an old woman before I finally had enough courage to get out. But you're still young, darlin'. You still have plenty of time to find someone else, someone who will treat you like the wonderful woman you are."

"I'm forty-three years old. But today I feel like I'm eighty-three. Oh, Betty Sue!" I cried. "I've been so miserable! I haven't told you how terrible it's been. I haven't told anyone. It's too humiliating!" Tears streamed down my face. "Why do we stay? It doesn't make any sense. All we're doing is torturing ourselves."

"I suppose each of us has our own reasons for staying," she said, rocking. "You know, Laurie Mae, I never did care for Mack. There's something about him. I don't know. The first time I met him he just rubbed me the wrong way."

"You're not the first person to say that." I blew my nose into the tissue.

"Now, don't get me wrong. I'm not tellin' you what to do. You've known Mack a good many more years than me. You'll figure this out for yourself. Don't you worry, darlin'."

But I *was* worried. Betty Sue's cat, Whiskers, appeared from around a corner, jumped onto my lap, and I stroked her furry neck.

"But you better start figurin' it out pretty soon," Betty Sue added, "'cause before you know it, one morning you'll wake up and look in the mirror and you'll see an old, wrinkled, seventy-year-old, gray-haired lady who lives with her cat!"

I laughed and wiped my eyes. "Thanks, Betty Sue," I said. "Thanks for being here. I just couldn't stay inside that house one more minute."

"Well, you sure picked a fine night for it!" she said with a laugh. "And you know you're always welcome here, girlfriend. Any time. For any reason."

It was now pitch-black outside and still snowing. I was safe and warm in Betty Sue's living room, and I didn't want to leave. "Mack's probably wondering where I am. But you know what? I don't care. Let him wonder. I have no desire to speak to him. And I really don't want to go home tonight. Would it be all right if I slept on your couch?"

"Of course! You can sleep in my bed if you want to. But if you decide to stay the night, I think you owe Mack a call to let him know that you're safe. I know he worries about you, darlin'."

"Well, I guess you're right." Whiskers jumped off my lap as I stood up. Betty Sue's phone was an old rotary type she bought at an auction. It was so awkward dialing that old phone I had to start over twice.

"Mack, I'm at Betty Sue's house. I just wanted to let you know. It's still snowing and dark outside, so I'm going to stay here overnight."

"Like hell you are! You're not going to walk out on me like that, and then spend the night at some psychotic old lesbian's house! You're behaving like a lunatic! You never should have gone out in this blizzard. You're my wife. You belong here at home with your husband. I'm coming up to meet you right now. Get your boots and coat on, and start walking. I'll meet you halfway, and I'll bring a flashlight."

"But, Mack, I—"

"I'm leaving right now. Get moving!"

"But Mack, Mack—" I slammed down the receiver. "He hung up on me! Oh, God, he's coming up to meet me! Damn it!"

"What are you going to do?"

"Oh, I'd better go. It'll probably just make things worse if I try to stay. And I don't want to get you involved in my problems."

Betty Sue leapt out of the rocking chair, opened a closet, and pulled out a large yellow slicker. "Here," she said, "wear this on top of your coat. It'll keep you dry." She helped dress me in the slicker and then grabbed an umbrella from a stand. "And here, take this too. It'll keep the wind off you. Now be careful out there, girlfriend."

"I will."

"Maybe you and Mack will be able to work out your differences. Maybe there's still something left of your marriage that's worth saving. And then again, maybe there's not. It'll become clear to you. Just listen to your heart."

Just listen to your heart. That's exactly what Lin had said to me the first time we'd talked. She'd touched me high on my chest, just beneath my collarbone, and told me to listen to the heart inside my own temple. Betty Sue pressed my hand. "I just want you to be happy, darlin'."

I gave her a hug and whispered, "So do I."

Through the falling snowflakes, I made out the dim glow of a light.

When I reached Mack, I didn't say a word. I just kept walking down the hill, holding the umbrella with both hands over my right shoulder as a shield against the wind.

"This has to be the dumbest act you've pulled off since I met you," Mack said, shining the flashlight on the road. The anger was gone from his voice. "Christ, only an insane person would go out on foot on a night like this." I kept walking, staring straight ahead.

"I hope you're satisfied making me come out to fetch you as though you were a child. Listen, Lu, I'm not upset. Just disappointed in you. And don't say a word until we get home. Now watch where you're going. It's slippery here."

I wasn't planning to say a word. I didn't care if I never said another word to him ever again. I just focused on my feet navigating the snow-covered road, and my hands clutching the umbrella as I made my way down the steep slope in the dark.

Once inside the house, I went straight up to my room and closed the door. I was freezing, and the room was ice cold. I sat on the edge of my bed, wrapped myself in a blanket, dropped my head into my hands, and cried and cried.

After a while, Mack's loud footsteps on the stairs startled me. He opened my door, entered the room, and sat on the chair at my desk. "Look, I'm sorry, Lu. I'm sorry about what happened tonight. I'm sorry for my role in the whole ugly mess." Too angry to respond, I just glared at him. "Aren't you going to apologize for *your* role in it, too? Why am *I* always the one who has to come to *you?* You may not be able to see it now, but both of us are at fault. Yet I'm always the one who has to come and kiss your ass, offer the olive branch, and apologize so we can put the matter behind us and get on with our lives. But you're such a proud and haughty Jew, you don't always take the olive branch. You don't apologize for *your* behavior and make peace. You seem incapable of seeing that you could be in the wrong. Oh, but I forgot—you Jews *never* do anything wrong, so there's nothing to apologize for, right?"

My eyes narrowed. Beneath the blanket my fingers tightened into fists.

"Lulu, one day you're going to have to grow up and learn how to say you're sorry."

I turned my head away. *What the hell did I have to be sorry about? He was the one who insulted my people and my family!* I shivered and tightened the blanket around my shoulders.

"Well," he said, "if you can't bring yourself to apologize, I'm going to bed. Maybe you'll feel differently in the morning. Good night." He stood up, left my room, and shut the door behind him.

I piled extra blankets on top of my quilt, undressed quickly, pulled on my thermal underwear, and jumped into bed. An hour later I was wide awake, bitterly cold, my feet numb, my body trembling uncontrollably. I honestly thought I might be freezing to death. And if I *was* going to die, now was the time to examine my life, my faults and behaviors, and make amends. Did I really believe I never did anything wrong as Mack had said? Maybe I had a bigger role in the failure of my marriage than I was willing to admit. Maybe I shouldn't have run out of the house in the middle of a blizzard. And maybe I could have offered the olive branch more often after our frequent, tumultuous fights. It was true my heart had hardened toward Mack over the years, and he was quick to point out the malice in my eyes. *But have I actually become the nasty, disrespectful, unforgiving Jewish bitch he claims I am?*

I rubbed my frigid hands together and whispered, "Avalokitesvara, Avalokitesvara. *What should I do?*" Charles said Kuan Yin was full of compassion for all sentient beings, even the ignorant and deluded— even for someone like Mack. I bit my lip. If I was going to die, my last act on earth had to come from a place of kindness and compassion. And if I *wasn't* going to die, perhaps showing some compassion to my husband would dissolve his bitterness, soften his heart, and possibly save my failing marriage.

I had an idea and jumped out of bed, determined to make an effort—Right Effort—one last time. If Mack rejected me now, if he were cruel, there was no doubt in my mind all would be lost between us. Practically numb with cold, I hurried into Mack's room, jumped into the single bed with him, pulled the covers over me, and pressed my shivering body close to him.

"I'm so cold," I whispered. He didn't respond. "I'm sorry to wake you, but I got terribly chilled outside and I swear I think I'm freezing to death."

"All right, all right." He squeezed closer and put his arms around me. "Christ, Lu, you're like ice. And your lips are blue."

"I'm sorry I went running out of here tonight," I said. "I was so upset, I didn't know what else to do. And I'm sorry I've become such a nasty bitch over the years. I know I've done things to hurt you, but I hope you can forgive me. I honestly don't want to cause you pain. And in my own way, I've tried to help you, Mack."

"You have, Lulu. You've done your best."

"Well, thanks for saying that. But, you know, it would be a lot better for both of us if you'd stop ripping on the Jews. Especially my family."

"I don't intend to. I get frustrated and say mean things."

"I know. Look, Mack, I can see you're in a lot of pain, and I understand your anger can get the best of you. But I know down deep you still care for me. Maybe things can still get better between us." My body warmed from his embrace, and I snuggled closer.

"I've seen a change come over you, Lu. And it's a positive change. You're brighter. You're up and out of bed early. You seem focused, peaceful, relaxed. And you don't argue with everything I say anymore. So, whatever you did at that monastery, just keep doing it."

"I'm trying. I really am. But being at home is a lot different than being at the monastery."

"I know you found something special at that monastery. Just take what you found there, and make it work for you here. Then if you feel the need, you can go back once a year and recharge your battery."

"You're right. I *did* find something very special at the monastery."

"I know. I can see it in your eyes. And I know what you found."

"You do?"

"You found a refuge. That's all."

"A refuge?" *Didn't Charles say Kuan Yin was a refuge and protector?*

"That's it. Trust me, Lu. I know all about refuges. That's what my writing has been for me all these years. I go to the refuge every morning and it keeps me sane. Keeps me going."

"Hmmm. A refuge. Maybe that's why I want to go back for this next retreat."

"What next retreat?"

"Oh, there's a Death Awareness retreat in a few weeks and I signed up to attend."

"That's too soon! You just came back! Call them up tomorrow and cancel. Do you think the rent pays itself? We can't afford you being on a permanent vacation!"

"It's no big deal, Mack. It's only for a few days. And I'll be back in time to teach my cooking class."

"You're steering this business down the shit chute! At the rate you're going, we'll be sleeping on the street and waiting in line at the soup kitchen! Christ, Lulu, how could you be so goddamned stupid and irresponsible? You're a terrible businesswoman! If it weren't for me constantly on your ass to get new clients and grow the business, we'd be in deep trouble. You're too scatterbrained and undisciplined to run a business on your own!"

I recoiled. "Are you kidding? I've built a relatively successful business entirely by myself! I'm my own boss, and if I want to take the *whole winter* off, that's what I'll do! And you know what? I'll survive!"

"What's happened to you? Have you gone mad?"

"Not at all. In fact, I've never felt so mentally sound. Attending this Death Awareness retreat is very important to me. Don't you remember my dad died a year ago next month? Or have you conveniently forgotten? You couldn't care less that I'm still processing his sudden death, which, I might add, happened right in front of my eyes! Don't you understand? I *have* to attend this retreat. I can *feel* it."

"All you feel is your pussy getting hot for one of those monks. People die every day. You don't need to go to some Buddhist monastery to figure that out."

Right Effort flew out the window. Incensed, I leaped out of his bed. "You're the cruelest man on earth! And I'm going on that retreat whether you like it or not!"

I raced down the stairs. In the kitchen I placed my hand on the radiator. It was ice cold. I hurried down to the cellar to check the fire. When I opened the filthy furnace door and looked inside, I wanted to rush back upstairs and wrap my fingers around Mack's throat. Instead, I screamed at the top of my lungs, "You fucking dickhead! YOU LET THE FIRE GO OUT!"

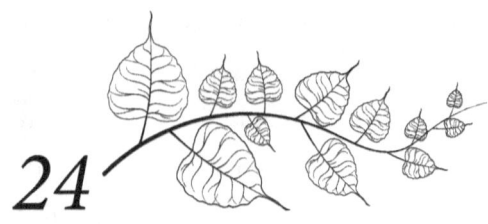

24

Smiles in the Mailbox

As my bedroom warmed, I stood beside the window and watched Rick's truck disappear down the hill. It was almost mid-afternoon, yet the horror of the previous evening's freezing trek to Betty Sue's house and its aftermath still festered like an open wound. Thick, lavender-edged clouds floated like daydreams across the great blue expanse, giving me food for thought. A temporary escape to a neighbor's house was no solution. One day soon I might have to leave my home for good, and with it everything I knew and loved: my dog, my cats, my flower and vegetable gardens, my big old farmhouse kitchen, and this truly idyllic spot on the hill overlooking the mountains. *But do I have the courage to do it?* I wasn't sure. Machee Nee suffered because she was attached to her home and couldn't return. Was I so attached to mine that I couldn't bear to leave it? Or was I staying because I was holding on to something else?

Under the white winter sunshine, the mountain range gleamed with splendor. Its powerful presence, an immortal testament to the grandeur of our world, soothed my aching soul and promised hope. *Was there a dazzling new world waiting for me on the other side of that ridge?*

I ate a late lunch, put on my snow boots, and went outside to fetch the mail. As I tramped through the high drifts at the crest of the hill, I was reminded of plodding through snow up to my thighs in order to reach Kuan Yin's statue. My mind suddenly filled with tender memories of my time at the monastery. I yearned to sit on my hard cushion in the meditation hall as dawn announced herself with sweet birdsong. I missed gazing up at the serene, knowing smile of the giant Buddha statue upon the altar. I longed to be in the presence of the monks with their shaved heads and orange robes, and I craved the sounds and soothing vibrations of the gong being struck three times. But most of all, I missed Kuan Yin. I needed to be close to her, to stand before her beautiful marble image and hold her slender, delicate fingers in my hand.

Halfway down the steep driveway the crumbling stone house at the bottom of the hill came into view, and my thoughts turned to Trex. I wished he were inside, sitting like he always did on the wobbly wooden chair in his dirty kitchen cluttered with stacks of old newspapers. If he were there, I could bring him his mail or a half gallon of orange juice. Or I could sit with him as he recounted the crazy escapades of his youth, and we'd laugh together, his playful blue eyes lighting up the room.

In the mailbox were two letters addressed to me. One was from Lin, and the other, a colorful envelope decorated with a watercolor garden scene, had only "Bodhi Community" as the return address. I opened Lin's letter first. She'd enclosed a brief note along with several photographs she'd taken at the monastery. I examined a photo of me and Jessica standing in front of the altar in the meditation hall. Flabbergasted, my legs buckled. Never in my life had I looked happier. My smile was huge, my eyes brilliant, and my face, in fact my whole countenance, radiated exultation. Wow. The woman in the photo was complete transformation from the frightened, desperate woman with the broken smile whose sad face was reflected in the bathroom mirror at Lu's Place just before my arrival at the monastery.

I placed the photographs back into the envelope. Before opening my second letter, I studied the fluid curves of the handwriting on the envelope. My heart fluttered as I removed the card from the envelope. The face of the card showed a large, multicolored butterfly resting on a thin branch. Enclosed was a shiny, postcard-sized print of a radiant Asian woman dressed in a glowing white gown standing atop a dragon in the midst of a swirling sea. Kuan Yin! The handwritten message was brief:

Dear Laurie,

I hope your trip home was pleasant and uneventful. We all miss your pleasant company. (I miss you.) Hope to see you again very soon.

Bhante Charles

I nearly dropped the card in the snow. With trembling fingers, I stuffed both Lin's and Charles's envelopes deep inside my coat pocket. The rest of the mail I carried back up the hill in my hand.

Mack was in his room banging on his typewriter as usual. I hurried upstairs to my bedroom and shut the door. At my desk, I fished the watercolor envelope from my coat pocket. Charles had kept his promise. I studied the picture of Kuan Yin. There she was, standing on the head of a fierce-looking, red-eyed dragon amid raging ocean waves, her brilliant white veil and robe sparkling like diamonds. She held a blue vase in her left hand. Later, I learned the vase represented the "nectar of wisdom and compassion" which she's said to sprinkle on all who call upon her aid.

I held the butterfly card close to my chest and reread the message Charles had written. When I got to the words "I miss you," my throat tightened. I inserted the card back into the envelope, then buried this precious piece of colored paper beneath a stack of stationery in the bottom drawer of my desk.

Kneeling before my makeshift altar, I leaned the lovely postcard print of Kuan Yin against the bud vase. Perfect! With palms pressed together, I whispered, "Thank you, Charles. Thank you so very much."

Half an hour later there was a knock at my door. When Mack entered, I cried, "Oh my God!"

"What do you think, Lu?"

Dumbfounded, I stared at his bald scalp. "My God, Mack! Why in the world would you want to shave your head?"

"For the hell of it. Who knows? Maybe it'll change a vibe around here. Maybe if I walk around with a shaved head, I'll remind you of those monks you have such an affinity for." He laughed. "Hey, we could turn this place into a monastery. I'll be the Zen master. You'll have to do everything I say, and if you don't, I'll whack you with a stick like they do in Japan. Heh-heh-heh."

"Very funny, Mack."

"Seriously Lu. I'd like to talk to you. Just talk, without any anger or bitterness. And I promise I won't say anything about the Jews."

Is he finally making an effort to save our marriage? Will we be able to have a serious, civil, maybe even productive, conversation without fighting? I doubt it.

Out of kindness, I chose to listen. I'd give him a chance. "All right," I said. "Why don't we go downstairs and sit in the living room?"

I sat on the couch and Mack sat in the wicker chair. I waited for him to start.

"Lulu," he finally said, "I just wanted to ask you . . ."

He struggled to continue. I was surprised by the moisture in his eyes.

"Tell me, Lu, and be honest, what is it about me that you find so abhorrent?"

This was the last question I'd expected to hear. "Wow, Mack. Are you actually doing a bit of soul searching?"

"You don't need to concern yourself with what I'm doing! Just answer the question."

I thought carefully before speaking. "Well, I suppose the thing about you that bothers me the most is the way you view the world and the people who live in it."

"What do you mean?"

"You're so angry. So full of hate, and your ego is gigantic. And because you view everyone else with contempt and disdain, you insult and demean them. The way you rant about the Jewish race is a prime example."

"Well, I've explained my politics to you, and it's obvious that the Jews—"

"Enough already with the Jews! You said you wouldn't mention them! And I couldn't give a damn about your politics. I'm sick of hearing terrible lies about my people." I caught myself and took a deep breath. "Look, I'm sorry, I don't mean to yell, but come on, Mack. You're not stupid. I was raised in a Jewish household. You can't possibly think hearing all your anti-Semitic garbage is going to endear me to you."

He had no response, so I continued. "But your hatred doesn't stop with the Jews. You can just as easily focus your anger on Blacks, or Hispanics, or Queer people, or anyone else you're in the mood to lash out at. If you want my advice, let go of your anger. That egotistical, racist, hateful mentality isn't going to get you anywhere. Anger just breeds more anger." I paused, anticipating some rebuke, but again he was silent. "This became very clear to me while I was at the monastery.

"Oh, excuse me, oh great enlightened being!" he huffed. "And what other deep insights into the nature of the human condition did you discover while sitting on your ass for two weeks at some pretentious Buddhist monastery in hillbilly heaven?"

My head dropped. *Why do I even bother trying to talk to him?* Against my better judgment, I continued in a soft tone, hoping he might actually be interested in my answer. "It'll probably sound crazy to you, but one of the things I realized is that I'm no better, no worse, and no different than anyone else. We're all in the same boat. We all suffer, and we're all going to die. So, the only response we can have to life's joys or life's pain is to treat ourselves and everyone we meet with loving-kindness, compassion, and respect. And be helpful if we can. And because this concept is so completely alien to you, I quite honestly have a very difficult time being around you and your nasty, hateful behavior."

"Oh, Christ! You're in worse shape than I thought! I cannot sit here and listen to you spout a bunch of pretentious New Age diversity bullshit! 'We're all the same! We're all the same!' What horseshit! Give me a break! The average jerk-off on the street hasn't read Chaucer, or Dante, or Donne! And he hasn't done anything of any consequence to earn my respect, let alone my loving-kindness. Am I supposed to have compassion for a cold-blooded murderer? Or a rapist?" He leaned forward in his chair. "Is *this* the crap those monks have been drilling into your head? Christ, Lulu, you're so fucking gullible! Those phony-assed Buddhists have brainwashed you!"

The words flew out of my mouth before I could stop them. "You have no idea what you're talking about! And the only person who's been trying to brainwash me is *you!*" Furious, I stood up to go.

"Okay, okay," he said. "Look, I'm sorry. Sit back down. Let's not argue."

"My God, Mack, that's all we've *been* doing for the past twenty years!" I sat down and covered my face with my hands. "This isn't getting us anywhere."

"Listen, I know I can't stop you from going back to West Virginia.

But beware, Lulu. I'm warning you: Things are not always the way they seem. If you stayed at that monastery long enough, you'd begin to see all its flaws."

For a split second, I worried he might be right. "Well, I'm not planning to stay there indefinitely."

"No?"

"Of course not!"

"You're not planning on becoming a nun?"

"No! I told you that before. I don't want to become a nun. It's nothing like that. You don't understand."

"Just remember, Lulu, you have responsibilities here. Namely me! You can't keep trotting off playing enlightened Buddhist princess whenever the mood strikes you, and abandoning me like some piece of old furniture."

"I'm not abandoning you, Mack. I'm just going to West Virginia for a weekend retreat. I'll be back in time to teach my cooking class." Behind him, the gold-framed photograph of the two of us hung on the wall above the buffet table. In the photo, Mack and I are standing on the front porch of the old farmhouse we rented before moving to Trex's place. My mother took that picture ten years ago, the summer she and Dad came out to visit. Mack has his arm around me, my big, yellow-blossomed begonia baskets hanging above our heads. Shortly after that photo was taken, Mack discovered Dr. Sharpe's anti-Semitic broadcasts on the short-wave radio.

"Lulu," Mack said, "I can see that you've reached a point in your life where you're going through some sort of spiritual conversion. This kind of thing happens all the time. Perhaps going on this retreat will help you deal with your father's death, and I won't stand in your way. But I have an idea. If you'd really like to spend some quality time at that monastery, like several months or a year, tell them you'll cook for them. You couldn't be more qualified for the job! They'd be lucky to have someone as skilled as you in their kitchen. Of course, they'd have to pay you a salary, which you wouldn't need since you'd be getting free room and board."

"What are you getting at? Are you trying to get rid of me?"

"Not entirely. You could do your thing at the monastery, and send me your salary to pay the rent and feed me and the pets until you decided to come back home."

Although my jaw dropped open, I shouldn't have been surprised. His "idea" confirmed everything I already knew: Mack had no desire to share his life with me. He cared for one thing and one thing only: himself.

I stood up. "I've answered your question, so there's nothing more to discuss. I hope you take my advice to heart. For your own sake." I expected to hear some nasty comment or insult, but instead he turned his freshly shaved head toward the window. I climbed the stairs to my room, silently counting the days until my return to the monastery.

25

Gifts of Gratitude

I was out of bed extra early the Wednesday morning before the retreat, excited for my food delivery trip into Pittsburgh. I had plans. I ate a bowl of oatmeal to fuel me for the day, wrote out the invoices, packed all the food containers into cardboard boxes, and called for Mack. We'd hardly spoken over the past week, but he'd volunteered to help me load the car on delivery day. Because of all the snowdrifts surrounding the house, the car was parked over at the barn. But the path leading from the house to the barn had blown shut during the night, and Mack had to shovel another path through the drifts to reach the vehicle.

"What a fucking ordeal!" Mack grumbled as we both trudged along the narrow path, each carrying a heavy box filled with food containers. "All this bullshit in order to earn a few lousy bucks! Couldn't you have picked some other line of work, like selling real estate, or insurance? I mean, come on, you Jews are natural born salesmen. Running a god-damned vegetarian cooking business way out here in the middle of cow country is insane!"

The sky was gray, threatening. The forecast predicted snow showers mixed with freezing rain. I had no doubt the car would make it down the hill to the road, and down the mountain into Pittsburgh, but coming back up at the end of the day . . . well, that would be an entirely different story.

We loaded the boxes into the car. Before I drove away, Mack knocked on the driver's side window. I rolled it down. "Now, listen," he said, "if you can't make it up the driveway when you come back, just leave the car down at Trex's house and walk up. I can go down later with the sled to get any groceries."

"I might have no choice. The forecast is calling for—"

"I know what the goddamned forecast is calling for!" he snapped. "Christ! All this fucking energy and effort wasted on a bunch of rich assholes who can't be bothered to cook for themselves!"

Obviously, he hadn't absorbed a word I'd said to him when he'd asked me why I found him so abhorrent. I was a fool to believe he might make an effort to soften his language and control his anger. Nothing had changed.

In Ligonier, I bought my first present. I'd been secretly thrilled by the idea of bringing little tokens of gratitude to several people at the monastery, as I considered all of them my teachers. I was most excited about my gift for Charles. The coffee shop in Ligonier roasted their own beans, and I purchased a pound of "Dancing Goats Blend" and a single cup French press to brew it in. *Oh, won't Charles be surprised!*

In Greensburg I bought a bird feeder filled with thistle seed to give to Pete because he had the job of tending and refilling the monastery's bird feeders. In Pittsburgh, after delivering my food orders, I purchased two tall lavender-scented candles, one for Polly and one for Machee Nee. On the way home I stopped at a nursery in Latrobe to search for something special to give Bhante Upali for the greenhouse, and found the perfect gift: a gorgeous mini dendrobium orchid with fuchsia blossoms to add to the monastery's orchid collection.

Freezing rain pelted the windshield on the winding drive back up the mountain, blurring my vision. I drove slowly, both hands gripping the steering wheel for dear life, my gaze glued to the taillights of the car in front of me. To ease my nerves, I kept repeating, "Only two more days. Only two more days until I'm back at the monastery."

After what seemed like an eternity, I reached the crest of the mountain, and turned onto Route 985. Almost home. The road was clear, but *would I be able to make it up the driveway?* Although I got a running start and tried twice, each time, about a third of the way up the hill, the tires started spinning on the fresh coating of ice and I had to give up, put the car in reverse, and ease it back down the hill. Even parking the car in Trex's icy driveway was difficult, and I nearly fell getting out. Except for the orchid, I stashed my presents in the trunk under a tarp so Mack wouldn't find them, explode, and give me hell. Clutching a weighty grocery bag in each hand for balance, the orchid wrapped in tissue stuffed inside my coat, I hiked up the slope, concentrating on one slippery step at a time.

As I came through the front door, Mack snarled, "I told you to leave any groceries in the car and I'd bring the sled down and get them later. You bitch and bitch that I don't help enough with the business, and when I offer to—"

"Please, Mack, don't start. I've had a long day." I placed the groceries on the counter, took off my coat, and set the delicate orchid plant on the kitchen table. "I didn't want to leave this plant out in the cold."

"*More* plants? Haven't I told you there are too many goddamned plants in this house? You need to start getting *rid* of plants instead of buying them. Plants are utterly useless! They just take up space, and you know how I can't *tolerate* being surrounded by clutter."

I ignored him and unpacked the five-pound bag of apples and a two-pound bag of flour.

"Did you hear me?" Mack said. "You've got to start getting rid of some of these plants! Why are you Jews so materialistic and desperate to buy useless things? How many times do I have to tell you? *Less is more! Less is more!*"

I turned to face him. He was wearing me down. He tried to provoke a fight by pressing the "Jew" button, and I was teetering on the edge. As luck would have it, before anger had a chance to consume me, I saw it clearly for what it was: simply the emotion of anger, and I was able to let it go. Seeing I had no response, Mack bolted up the stairs and slammed the door to his room.

A few minutes later the phone rang. When Robert told me that Trex was gone, my world turned dark. "The doctor said they think a blood clot broke loose and went to his brain. It must have happened sometime during the night. I wanted to let you know as soon as possible. I know how close you were to him."

I could barely breathe and collapsed onto the kitchen chair, my body suddenly cold and numb as though I'd fallen into a pool of icy water. Bombarded by incomprehensible thoughts and emotions, I tried to digest the sudden, awful reality: *Trex is dead.* "But, but I just saw him last week."

"Oh, I'm glad. I'm sure he enjoyed your visit."

Tears welled in my eyes. I thought about my dad. The moment of his sudden death came back full force, and I relived the horrific images imprinted in my mind forever: the paramedics entering the bedroom, me standing beside the bed, the paramedic fastening a blood pressure cuff, me watching my dad's face wince and go blank.

"I'm so sorry, Robert," I finally said. "I'll miss him. Trex was a good soul. One of the best. Thanks so much for calling."

The blood drained from my cheeks. I hung up the phone and cried and cried. When my sobs finally quieted, I stood up and stared out the window. The sight of mountains on the horizon—those solid, reliable, magnificent mountains that never died—comforted me. I recalled Trex's prophetic words when I'd visited him in the nursing home. He'd said, "I'd be more comfortable in heaven." Initially those words frightened me, but now I understood what he meant, and a tremendous sense of relief washed over me.

Mack came down the stairs and into the kitchen. "How am I supposed to get any work done with all your goddamned blubbering down here? Who was on the phone?"

I turned to face him. "Trex is dead."

He didn't respond.

"Did you not hear me? I said, Trex is dead."

"That's too bad."

My gaze turned back to the mountains. "No," I said. "It's good. He was ready."

"No one's ever ready. We're born, we live our lives in quiet desperation, then we die with fear and regret. People shed a few crocodile tears over the dead at their funerals, then they go back to their own miserable lives and problems. No one cares."

My face contorted. "I cared about that old man! I cared about him a lot! But why would I expect you to understand? What do you know about those kinds of feelings?" I rubbed my eyes. "Look, I'm tired. I'm going upstairs. I have another long kitchen day tomorrow, and a cooking class to teach tomorrow night."

Inside my little room, I sat on the edge of my bed and thought about Trex. I grieved his passing as though I'd lost a family member. How strange that he happened to die right before I left for a Death Awareness retreat! Now I'd have both my father's *and* Trex's sudden death to contemplate over the long weekend. The sound of Mack's footsteps up the stairs and the slamming of his bedroom door gave me chills. *How can that man be so heartless?* My palms came together at my chest. Silently,

I thanked the unknown person who'd canceled their registration for the Death Awareness retreat, allowing me to attend. Because if I had to keep listening to Mack's vile remarks all weekend long, I wasn't sure how much longer I'd be able to turn the other cheek.

The next morning, I started a busy kitchen day with some baking. After several hours, two trays of apple crisp were cooling on the counter, and two loaves of spelt bread were rising near the radiator. I planned to take these homemade natural treats to the monastery as an offering to the monks. After a quick lunch, I spent the rest of the afternoon prepping the ingredients for my cooking class. Thankfully, Mack stayed out of my way, and we didn't actually speak until I was packing up to leave for class.

"I'll take that box down the hill for you," he said, entering the kitchen.

"That's all right, I can manage." I went over to the coat rack.

"You *think* you can manage. But the truth is, you'd be lost without me, Lu. You need me to keep you on track. You'd screw up royally if I wasn't constantly watching your back. Christ, you'd *never* be able to make a living way out here in the boonies all by yourself. Your laziness would run this business into the ground."

I bit my lip and put on my coat.

Mack followed me down the hill carrying the heavy cardboard box filled with plastic bags of cut-up vegetables, jars of herbs, bottles of seasonings and oils, cans of beans, a couple of saucepans, sheets of recipes, and utensils. Standing in Trex's driveway, he asked me what time I'd be home.

"I don't know, Mack," I sighed. "The usual time. Somewhere between nine and ten." I got into the car and started the engine. Mack placed the box on the back seat.

"I'll leave the porch light on for you," he said. "You know I'll be in bed, so don't make a lot of racket downstairs when you get home."

⸙

Susan was my best and most loyal student. She attended every cooking class I taught, arrived early, and stayed afterward to help me clean up. She was middle-aged and divorced, with shoulder-length brown hair and large brown eyes. She usually sat in the front row, taking copious notes. Last month when I told my class I'd be attending a silent retreat at a Buddhist monastery, it was Susan who'd expressed the most interest.

The class lasted two and a half hours. At the conclusion, while the dozen women seated in folding chairs in front of the demonstration table sampled the three-bean casserole, broccoli and beet salad, walnut pâté, and fried brown rice I'd just prepared, I started to clean up. Susan ate quickly, then joined me behind the table and volunteered to wash dishes while I put things away.

"So," she said, scrubbing the sticky rice pot, "you're going back."

I was puzzled. "Back where?"

"To the monastery."

I placed a bottle of olive oil into my box and turned to face her. "I'm leaving tomorrow. How did you know?"

"I could just tell," she said, smiling.

"Come on, Susan. How did you know? I haven't told anyone."

She set the clean pot in the drain and turned around. "I just sensed it," she said. "I saw the difference in your face when you came back."

I laughed. "You, too? You saw that my face had changed?"

"You were beaming! And your whole demeanor was different. You seemed so . . . so content. So happy. I figured something wonderful must have happened while you were there. And whatever that 'something' was, I just *knew* it would draw you back."

I picked up a dish towel and started drying. "I *have* to go back, Susan," I whispered. "I don't know why."

In a voice not quite her own, she said, "You'll find out."

"I will?"

"Of course you will!"

"Well, I sure hope so."

"You have unfinished business there."

"Unfinished business? What do you mean?"

Susan took off her rubber glove and placed her hand on my shoulder. "I'm not exactly sure, but I just know you'll find out." She smiled sweetly, her face practically luminescent. "Now you're finally ready to be good to yourself."

Warmth spread from the tips of my toes up to the top of my head. I was suddenly back in the meditation hall on that magical morning when Kuan Yin appeared to me in Jessica's form. Maybe Kuan Yin was close to me right now, in Susan's form. She'd said, *Be good to yourself.* How strange. Those were Charles's parting words to me when I left the monastery.

"Are you all right?" Susan asked.

"Yes, yes, I'm fine," I nodded. "Thank you, Susan. Thanks so much for staying. And for helping me." I placed my palms together and bowed my head. We finished putting the rest of the pots and pans away, wiped down the stove, the counters, and the long demonstration table.

"Well," Susan said, "I guess that's it. Will I be seeing you again next week for class?"

"I think so."

"I'm not so sure."

"But why?"

"Oh, you never know," she said, grinning. "You might get snowed in again!"

We both laughed. "Yeah," I said. "Wouldn't that be wonderful!"

PART FOUR

Open to Love

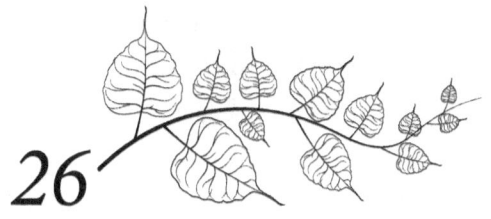

26

Sunshine in a Dark Place

(Day 18)

The covered porch was empty and warm. Someone had built a roaring fire in the woodstove. Retreatants were instructed to arrive at 5 p.m., but I made sure to arrive an hour before the crowd. I wanted to distribute my presents and reserve a cushion near the front of the meditation hall close to Machee Nee and Polly. First, I headed to the library. Maybe Charles would be there, reading as usual. Instead, I found Pete on a stepladder, wearing his usual black ski cap.

"Welcome back," he said descending the ladder, a book in his hand. "Good to see you again."

That morning I'd dressed in my favorite pink and blue floral skirt, blue turtleneck sweater, and navy tights. I'd even slipped on the round crystal earrings my mother had given me a year ago for my birthday. Typically, women retreatants wore no earrings, but these little sparklers were barely noticeable—no bigger than a fingernail. Besides, the only monastery rule concerning jewelry forbade the wearing of "noisy" jewelry, so I was in the clear.

"How are you, Pete? Are you still bald?" I joked.

"Still shiny," he said removing his cap. "At least for now."

I gave him a big smile. "Oh, it's so good to be back!"

"Good to have you back. But you haven't missed much." He leaned close and whispered, "This place can get pretty boring when there's no retreat."

"Well, I doubt we'll have any big excitement during a Death Awareness retreat."

"Not unless we get another snowstorm!" We both laughed.

"Oh, I have a present for you! Actually, it's also for the monastery. I didn't see any finches the last time I was here, so I brought you a bird-feeder filled with thistle seeds. The finches love thistle, so maybe they'll come around. The male finches turn bright yellow in the spring. Wait till you see them!"

"Gee, thanks."

"I'll bring it to you once I unpack the car. Oh, and since I'm in the library, I was wondering . . . Do you happen to know if you have a copy of the twenty-fifth chapter of the Lotus Sutra?"

"I think so. The Lotus Sutra is a Mahayana Buddhist text. I'll look for it, but if you want to know more about the Lotus Sutra, you should ask Charles. He knows all about Mahayana Buddhism. Not long ago Charles came very close to becoming ordained as a Mahayana monk."

"Wow. Seriously?"

I found Charles in the kitchen leafing through a cookbook. "Hi," I said, startling him.

When he looked up and realized it was me, a playful smile adorned his face. "Well, hello, Laurie! It's good to see you again!"

"It's good to see you, too. Thank you for your lovely card. And for the picture of Kuan Yin."

He approached me. "I hope my card didn't cause you any problems at home. I probably shouldn't have sent it. I had the envelope in and out of the mailbox several times."

"No, no, it wasn't a problem at all." His eyes were a darker shade of blue than I'd remembered.

"Well, don't you look lovely," he said. "How have you been? I hope things were pleasant for you at home."

"Oh, things at home were about the same as they always are. But I'm not home now. I'm actually here! I can hardly believe it!" I giggled like a schoolgirl. "You know, Charles, it's weird. I don't know why, but something kept telling me that I had to come back."

"I was hoping you would. This monastery can be a rather dark, melancholy place. It's not very often someone walks through that front door who laughs and smiles and sparkles like you do."

Blushing, I averted my gaze. "Oh, I didn't do anything special."

"Yes, you did. You brought a ray of sunshine into a very dark place." His smile deepened the creases in his rugged, handsome face, and his eyes, full of sincerity, took my breath away.

I picked up the cookbook and leafed through a few pages. "Hey, we had a lot of fun cooking together last time, didn't we?"

"That we did!"

"I suppose you're cooking for this retreat?"

"Polly's cooking breakfast and I'll be cooking lunch. Including the monks and lay people, we'll have close to sixty mouths to feed. At least it's a short retreat. Once I had to cook breakfast and lunch for sixty-five people over the course of a nine-day retreat. By the time that retreat was over I was ready for a thick, juicy steak and a six-pack of beer!" He laughed that infectious laugh of his, and I joined in the mirth.

"Listen, Charles, I'll be glad to help you. I can volunteer for kitchen duty."

"You do as you please, but I won't refuse your help."

I moved closer to him. "Now, Charles, what's this I just heard about you almost becoming a monk?"

He glanced up at the ceiling. "That's a rather long and complicated story."

"That's okay. You don't have to explain."

Polly entered the kitchen carrying a clipboard. Charles stepped away from me. "Polly, hi!" I squealed, giving her a hug.

"Well, I see you're back for more," she said.

"It's hard to stay away! Oh, I brought you a little present. It's in the car with the rest of my gifts. I brought something for Machee Nee, too."

"She's no longer here," Polly said.

"Oh, no! I was really looking forward to seeing her again."

"She left for Thailand several days ago," Polly said. "It was a bit of a shock to us, but she said that she needed to go back home."

"I knew she was struggling with her feelings for home. I'm sure she made the right decision. But I'll miss her."

"We all miss her," Charles said.

"Oh, Polly, I baked apple crisp and a couple loaves of bread to offer the monks. The crisp is all natural and sugar free, and the bread is made of spelt flour, an ancient whole grain."

"Sounds yummy. I'll set out a loaf of bread for the monks' breakfast tomorrow, and I'll put the second loaf in the freezer for later. I'm sure they'll gobble up the dessert by end of day tomorrow!"

"That'd be great, Polly. Thank you."

Polly consulted her clipboard. Squinting behind her wire-rimmed glasses, she addressed Charles. "Now, do you have everything you need?"

"I'm all set," Charles said. "At least for the first two days. I may have to make a run to the store later on."

"Polly, does that clipboard happen to tell you where I've been assigned to stay? I'd like to unload the car and unpack."

Polly shuffled papers on the clipboard. "Let's see, you're in Parami kuti. That's the second kuti on the left as you're going up the main path. It has a gas heater which I can show you how to use if you'd like."

"Oh, I'm sure I can manage." Just as I turned to go, Bhante Upali and Barry entered the kitchen from the dishwashing room.

"Good afternoon, Bhante Upali," I said, turning to face him, palms pressed together. "It's good to see you again."

He jerked backward. "Uh, hello. So, you've come for the retreat?"

"Yes, Bhante. And I brought some plants for the greenhouse. I hope you like them." In addition to the orchid, I'd clipped some cuttings from my wandering Jew plant back home.

He nodded, then turned to Polly. "Where is that case of soymilk that arrived last week? That soymilk was sent here for me, and I haven't had any of it."

Polly's brow furrowed. "You mean the Westbrae fortified vanilla-flavored soymilk?"

"Yes," Bhante Upali said. "Some people I know sent it here specifically for *me*, to keep in *my* kuti, you know, for days when I'm in seclusion."

"Oh, I'm sorry, Bhante," Polly said. "I thought that case of soymilk was just more dana for the monastery. I put it in the attic because the pantry was so full."

"Well, you were mistaken. That case of soymilk was a gift sent exclusively for *me.*"

"I'm sorry for the mix-up, Bhante," Polly said, palms pressed together.

"I can go up to the attic and get it for you, Bhante," Barry said. "And take it to your kuti."

Had I heard Bhante Upali correctly? Confused and disappointed, I stared at the emaciated monk's long, oval face. Was this the same monk who hiked through the Himalayas with no possessions, asking for nothing, taking only what was given? Was this the Buddhist monk and teacher who had conquered his ego, desires, and attachments? During

his dhamma talks, Bhante Upali spoke about the importance of cultivating "anatta" or "no self." He'd cautioned against thinking in terms
of "I, me, or mine." Yet here he was, like a demanding child, whining
for "MY" soymilk, which was sent specifically for "ME." Obviously,
his sense of self was still strong, and very much attached to this case
of soymilk.

Parami kuti was a one-room hut about nine feet by twelve covered by
a room-sized rug. I placed my sleeping bag and suitcase on the hard
mattress. Beside the wooden bedframe was a low nightstand with a
thick candle and a pack of matches. Against the opposite wall was
another low table with an oil lamp and another pack of matches. A
round meditation cushion sat in the corner. Hanging on the wall above
the cushion was a large poster of a smiling, cross-legged Buddha with
gigantic ears. I opened the bamboo shade covering the kuti's solitary
window above the bed. Then I played with the dial of the gas heater to
make sure it worked.

I liked the little hut. It had a clean, sparse energy to it, and I could
see how living in this tiny space with few possessions would be condu-
cive to cultivating a spiritual life. After checking to make sure there was
indeed a pee bucket and toilet paper beneath the bed, I left the kuti,
headed back down the path toward the main building where I'd parked
my car, then drove the car down to the parking lot.

Vehicles with license plates from Maryland, New York, Virginia, North
Carolina, Georgia, and Tennessee filled the parking lot. I reached into
the back seat of my car and plucked a few carnations from the bouquet
I'd brought, keeping my promise to show Barry how to arrange flowers
for the altar. Then I hurried through the woods, heading directly for
Kuan Yin's statue. When I entered the bamboo grove, my heart raced.
And then there she was, smooth, shiny-white and beautiful, holding

out her hand to me. I stood motionless before the lovely marble woman, overcome with gratitude and love for her. Beside her delicate bare feet, someone had placed a vase filled with white and lavender mums.

My palms pressed together at my chest, tears of joy slipped down my cheeks. How wonderful it was to be close to her again! I bowed my head. "Thank you. Thank you, dear Kuan Yin, for all your help and guidance," I whispered. "I know you are watching over me. Please continue to be with me, in any form you choose, and please continue to give me strength and courage." I paused, then added, "I have a feeling I'm going to need both." I bowed again and placed the carnations by her feet. Then I reached into my coat pocket, removed an orange I'd brought with me, and set it beside the vase of flowers. In the distance, a group of people walking up the driveway were talking in loud voices. Suddenly self-conscious, I started for the main building, but then stopped abruptly and turned around. I couldn't leave Kuan Yin until I touched her smooth marble fingers, which fit so perfectly in my hand.

There were several dozen people congregated on the covered porch, and a queue of retreatants at the registration table in the dining hall. Bhante Upali sat on one of the chairs reserved for monastics. Three young men knelt on the floor in front of him, offering boxes of gifts. Charles sat on the bench opposite the stove. I made my way through the crowd and sat down beside him. We didn't speak for a good five minutes. Although our lips remained closed, a communication beyond words connected us. Finally, Charles turned to face me and said, "We have to stop meeting like this."

I burst out laughing. Everyone on the porch turned and looked at us with critical faces, especially Bhante Upali. I leaned toward Charles and whispered, "Is there some sort of rule against laughter around here?"

"Well, there is a Buddhist injunction against giddiness. You're allowed to laugh, as long as you don't become carried away by it. And, because this monastery tries to maintain a certain serious, reflective atmosphere, a lot of giggling sort of stands out."

"We sure did a lot of giggling and laughing after the snowstorm."

"Yes. That was an unusual exception. I suppose everyone involved was happy and relieved to have made it out the other side of the storm. Even the monks let their guard down."

We were silent for a little while longer, then I asked, "Charles, were you the one who put the vase of flowers by Kuan Yin's statue?"

He smiled. "Guilty as charged."

"I just knew it!"

"Don't tell anyone."

"Why not?"

"Bhante Upali won't like it," he whispered. "I'm sure when he sees the flowers, he'll make some remark."

"But why would he do that?"

"Well, although Kuan Yin isn't formally recognized in the Theravada tradition, many people who come here and who, I might add, donate heavily to the monastery, worship Kuan Yin. Last summer when three older Burmese women stayed here, they placed offerings of fruit and flowers by Kuan Yin's statue each morning. I thought this was a splendid thing to do. So, after the women left, I took on that responsibility. I kept the area neat and tidy, and set out vases of flowers every few days. It was my own way of paying homage to the Bodhisattva of Compassion. But it didn't take long before Bhante Upali put a stop to it. He's funny about that area."

I shook my head. "But that doesn't seem right. What harm could there be in placing flowers or fruit beside Kuan Yin's statue? He didn't stop the old women from doing it."

"No, he didn't, because those offerings are part of their tradition.

Those women believe that with every good deed and every offering they make, they accumulate merit. Merit contributes to their growth toward enlightenment, and determines the quality of the next life."

"The next life?"

"Reincarnation. It's a tough concept for most Westerners to accept."

"Do you believe in reincarnation, Charles?"

With a smile and a wave of his hand, he said, "Why not? I believe the world is full of infinite possibilities."

"Yes, I suppose it is." I stared at the dancing flames inside the firebox. "Well, if reincarnation does exist, what would you like to be in the next life?"

"Oh, I think I'd like to come back as a dandelion," he said.

"A dandelion? You've got to be joking!"

"Not at all. Dandelions are such pretty, tough, bright yellow things. People treat them like weeds, but in my opinion, they're one of the most beautiful flowers on earth. And dandelions don't harm anyone."

More people entered the building. A tall young man with greasy auburn hair and a long beard set down a filthy knapsack on the low bench near the door. He removed his coat, exposing tattered jeans held up by a thick rope for a belt and a faded tie-dye T-shirt. He ambled toward the registration table and stood in line behind an elderly Asian man dressed in khakis and a white button-down shirt.

I turned to Charles. "I brought you a present. It's nothing much. Just a little something I thought you might like."

"You didn't have to go and do that."

"But I wanted to! I really appreciated and enjoyed our conversations."

"And I have to admit I feel the same way."

Almost breathless, I blurted out, "Isn't it weird? I mean, I've literally just met you, yet I feel as though I've known you for ages."

"In another life, perhaps?" He laughed.

I laughed, too. Maybe a little too loudly, because again, disapproving faces turned in our direction. But I wasn't going to let those condemning eyes prevent me from enjoying myself and Charles's company.

"You know, it's getting pretty crowded in here," I said. "How about walking down to the parking lot with me? Your gift is in the trunk of my car."

We stood close together in the parking lot as Charles unwrapped his gift. "This is the best present I've received in years," he said, containing a flush of emotion. "Thank you for your thoughtfulness. I can't wait to go back to my kuti and brew my first cup of real coffee!"

"Yes, now you have the real thing!" I searched a small clearing in the forest behind him. "Which one is your kuti?"

He turned around and pointed. "Beyond those trees and to the left."

"What's it like living in a kuti?"

"It's adequate. I'm used to small spaces from my years living on the sailboat. I have everything I need to maintain my own meditation practice in that kuti. I have an altar, a Buddha statue, incense, and a bell."

"You have a bell? Oh, it must be wonderful to have a bell! Would it be all right if I came to your kuti sometime? I'd love to see your altar and hear your bell."

He backed away. "Heavens, no, child! That's strictly against the rules."

"Oh, I'm sorry. I didn't think—"

"No women are allowed in the men's kutis and vice versa. If anyone found out you were inside my kuti, I'd be tossed out of here on my heinie, pronto!" Then he laughed, his eyes sparkling like sapphires. "Although I must say the thought of you visiting my kuti is quite a lovely one."

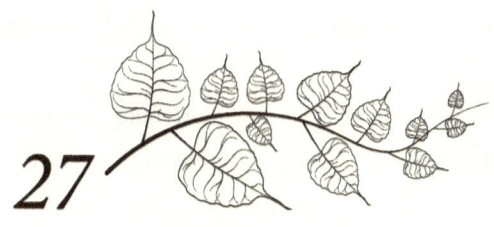

27

Forgotten Treasure

(Day 18, Evening)

Dusk was settling in. A dozen or so retreatants sat on the covered porch drinking hot beverages, waiting for evening meditation to begin. I sat opposite the woodstove. The weather had turned mild, and the fire was low. Bhante Upali appeared in the doorway to the dining hall and approached me.

Before I could greet him, he said, "Were you the one who put the orange and the vase of flowers by the statue?"

"Uh, well, I put the orange there, Bhante. But not the vase of flowers."

"Would you please remove the orange? It attracts rodents."

"What about the flowers? They're so pretty."

"They should be removed also. We like to keep that area free of all debris."

My heart sank. "All right, Bhante," I said with a shrug. "I'll remove them." I turned toward the window and watched the birds at the feeders.

"Would you look at that cat!" Bhante Upali said, irritated. "Look how he's hiding behind that bush waiting to attack that squirrel. Just last week we found a mutilated squirrel in the hallway leading to the

Women's Dorm. We're going to have to do something about those bird-feeders. They're like bait for our cat. We should probably take them all down."

Alarmed, I stood up. "But you *can't* take them down, Bhante! I mean, a lot of people find pleasure in watching the birds at the feeders."

Bhante Upali's playful little boy face came out of hiding. "Oh, so you're another one around here who's attached to the birds."

"Well, yes. I suppose I am. They're such beautiful, amazing little creatures. I keep birdfeeders at home. I have several cats, so I've seen plenty of mutilated mice, moles, chipmunks, and the occasional squirrel. At first, I was horrified, but then I realized it's just nature doing her thing."

"Yes, yes, I know," the monk said, nodding. "But it becomes a different matter entirely when nature comes into the Women's Dorm in the form of a bloody, half-eaten squirrel."

"You could put a bell on the cat's collar."

Bhante Upali looked skyward. "That's already been suggested."

The meditation hall was filled to capacity. Bhante B sat on the cushion below the altar. He and Bhante Upali would co-lead the retreat. During the hour of meditation, I had difficulty concentrating, distracted by the multitude of human bodies surrounding me and filling the large hall to capacity. It was a diverse group of males and females—young, old, thin, heavyset, robust, frail, Asian, Caucasian, African American. People were breathing loudly, shifting positions noisily, coughing, sneezing, farting. Toward the end of the session, I recognized the familiar nature sounds outside the hall, and couldn't keep from smiling. Those sweet seasonal tones were the peepers chirping their first love calls. How wonderful it was to hear them again toward the end of a long winter!

The sound of the bell being struck three times echoed throughout the hall. I opened my eyes, uncrossed my legs, and rose to my knees. With palms together, I gazed at the golden Buddha seated high on the altar, grateful to be back in his benevolent presence. His smiling face illumined by soft candlelight was like a warm, giant hug, welcoming me home.

After everyone bowed three times, Bhante B spoke a few words of welcome, then turned the microphone over to Bhante Sabbakittika, who was again the retreat coordinator. The African monk welcomed everyone and reviewed all the rules. He explained that the library would be open during the entire retreat because it contained visual aids Bhante B and Bhante Upali would refer to during the long weekend. He concluded by wishing everyone a "wonderful retreat."

I was the last person to leave the meditation hall. Before exiting, I slipped into the greenhouse. Bhante Upali was there watering the Bodhi Tree. I pointed to the plants I'd placed on the potting bench earlier. "Did you see these, Bhante?" I asked.

"Oh. Did you bring those?"

"Yes." I smiled. "When I saw the color of that orchid, I simply couldn't resist. And these cuttings in the jar come from one of my plants at home. It's called a wandering Jew plant." I chuckled. "Sort of like me. Once the cuttings root, you can pot them up. It's a very easy plant to take care of."

He glanced at the cuttings, then moved toward the door as though he hadn't heard me. He stopped abruptly, turned around, and wearing his serious monk face said, "So, you know this retreat will be quite different than the last one. Due to its subject matter of course."

"Yes, Bhante. I figured it would be."

"And because this retreat lasts only a few days, we aren't scheduling any personal interviews or dhamma discussions."

"I see." I supposed he was making it clear there would be greater distance between us this time around.

"But, of course, if you have any questions, just write down your question and place it in the question box in the dining hall. We've scheduled a Q & A period at the end of each day."

"All right, Bhante." Head bowed, my palms came together at my chest. "I understand."

⚬⚭⚬

That evening the covered porch was jammed with retreatants milling about or sitting on the low benches sipping from mugs labeled with their names. The majority of them moved about the monastery in an awkward, halting manner, as though lost, confused, or frightened. Most wore baggy pants and oversized sweatshirts. Many faces were sad, pale, wistful, or expressionless, and to my disappointment, there were no beautiful smiling young girls dressed in white like Jessica. After a while the crowd thinned as people said good night and retired to their rooms. Charles exited the kitchen and went to the beverage area. I joined him.

"Would you like something to drink?" he said.

"Yes, that would be nice." I selected a blue mug and wrote my name on a piece of masking tape. As I brewed a cup of chamomile tea, I read the words written on the chalkboard near the kitchen door:

Wisdom tells me I am nothing
Love tells me I am everything
And in between these two
My life flows.

I recognized the cursive handwriting. "Charles, did you write this poem on the chalkboard?"

"Guilty as charged. Occasionally while I'm reading, I'll jot down some interesting thought or quotation. Lately, I've been writing some of them on the board for others to ponder. But I honestly don't think anyone around here pays much attention to my scribbling."

I read the poem a second time. "How lovely. Where did you find it?"

"Oh, I don't remember. It's not Buddhist." He laughed. "In fact, that's why I put it up there."

"I don't understand."

"Oh, you know, to go against the party line. Shake them up a bit."

The mischief in his tone emboldened me. "I have an idea. Would it be okay if I wrote something on the board as well?"

"By all means. Here, wait, let me get rid of this. It's been up there for three days." He erased the poem and handed me a piece of chalk. "Have at it!"

I giggled. "I hope this is all right. It will probably sound silly." I wrote: *Can you hear the peepers?* Excited, I smiled. "Well? Can you?"

He squinted. "Ah, yes," he finally said. "Yes, I can hear them."

I laughed with delight. "Aren't they wonderful? You only hear these tiny tree frogs once a year. Their mating calls are a sure sign spring is just around the corner." I paused. "You know, it's strange that I'm hearing them for the very first time tonight. At the monastery."

Just then Bhante Upali appeared from out of nowhere. The monk inspected the chalkboard, then glared at us. "Who's been writing these things on the board?"

His words stung like a slap in the face. I turned toward Charles. He remained silent. I mustered my courage, faced Bhante Upali and declared, "I wrote that, Bhante."

"This chalkboard is to be used for monastery business only." He turned to Charles. "You ought to know this is not a place to be writing such things."

"It was my fault, Bhante," I said. "I'm sorry."

"Make sure one of you erases that chalkboard," the monk said. He turned with a swish of his robes, and headed swiftly down the hallway.

Dejected, I ambled toward the woodstove. Charles followed me. "I don't understand it," I said. "Ever since I got here, Bhante Upali's been acting differently toward me. All he's done is complain, demand, and try to ruin or belittle everything I find enjoyable. He didn't act that way before."

"He's just put up his armor," Charles said.

"Hi armor?"

"The monks can't tolerate too much enjoyment around here. They're afraid of it. The slightest amount of fun, excitement, or strong emotion might lead to desire, and since Buddhism teaches that desire leads to suffering, the monks here are extremely cautious when it comes to their interactions and behavior, especially around women. One crack in their armor could lead to completely natural feelings and emotions they try to suppress and avoid at all costs."

"Charles, are you saying that . . . ?"

"Well, I think it was obvious Bhante Upali felt close to you during the last retreat. After the snowstorm he relaxed and let himself go a bit, and that scared him. So, this time he's keeping his distance emotionally. Just my personal observation."

It was true I'd relaxed around Bhante Upali during the last retreat. We'd had such fun after the snowstorm that I almost forgot he was a monk. Had I behaved too casually with him? So casually that he was now afraid of me?

"You know, when I was here the last time, it was the most magical experience of my life. By the time I left, I felt so wonderful. So happy. Like a completely different person. And Bhante Upali's teaching had a lot to do with that. But now . . . I don't know. Things feel different." I looked at the oversized woodstove, the one thing that had remained the same. "And it probably sounds silly, but the last time I was here, I didn't let the fire go out. Not once."

"I know. You're quite a competent and clever woman. From what you've told me, you're the one who keeps everything going at home."

"Well, I've had to think outside the box to keep our heads above water."

"And you're doing an amazing job."

"I guess living out in the country all these years has brought out the pioneer spirit in me," I chuckled.

"Would you like to sit outside?" Charles said. "It's rather mild out tonight and there's a bench on the porch."

I searched his eyes. "That might be nice."

✿❀❁❀✿

We sat close to each other, our backs resting against the siding. Somewhere in the darkness beyond the big brass gong were the peepers, their shrill calls echoing throughout the forest. I inhaled the moist, earthy aroma of the sleeping forest—that rich, recognizable smell when decay gives way to new life. My body and mind relaxed into the peace and comfort of the night. At the same time, I was aroused by Charles's close presence.

"Are you warm enough?" he asked.

"Yes, I'm fine."

"Here, put this over your legs." He draped his jacket over my skirt. "There, that's better."

There was a congenial, unspoken language between us—the kind of silent communication that comes from years of familiarity. All was quiet except for the peepers' calls piercing the night air.

"Noisy little critters, aren't they?" Charles said.

"Oh, yes."

Beyond the darkened bamboo grove, the lovely white statue of Kuan Yin stood on her lotus flower pedestal, hearing the cries of the wounded world. Did she hear my cries? *Did she bring me back to this magical place to help me find something I lost many, many years ago?*

I took Charles's hand in mine. Squeezing his thick, fleshy fingers, I said, "You have the hands of a farmer."

"Don't I though!" He laughed. "Thick ugly things."

"No. They're just working hands."

I sighed and melted into the tranquil night. How pleasant it was to simply sit on a porch with a kind man on a lovely evening filled with the promise of spring! I couldn't remember the last time I'd felt so safe, content, even loved. "This is really nice," I whispered.

"Yes, it is."

Without warning, something deep inside me suddenly exploded. I sat bolt upright, shellshocked, panicked, confused, as though a bomb had just detonated inside my chest. Numb with fright, my heart pounded fiercely and I jumped to my feet.

"I think I'd better turn in," I said, handing Charles his jacket. Before he could respond or stand up, I was down the stairs and hustling up the main path to my kuti.

As soon as I was inside, sobs burst from my lips, and for the next ten minutes I could not stop the avalanche of tears. I paced the length of the kuti, wailing as though death had snatched a loved one away. *What's wrong with me? Where is all this grief coming from?* Gradually my breathing slowed and my cries quieted. I sat on the edge of the bed and dropped my face into my hands, confounded by my own hysterical behavior.

After several minutes of deep breathing, I understood what might have happened. Sitting beside Charles on the porch, I'd tasted a lost and forgotten treasure—a delicious and vital treasure that had been absent in my life far too long. With that sweet taste, the icy fist that had squeezed my heart shut for over a decade suddenly shattered, leaving me face to face with a devastating reality: The delicate flame of love struggling to survive inside my broken heart had, in reality, been snuffed out for nearly half my life. Back inside my kuti, I'd wept uncontrollably, grieving the long-lost years deprived of that most precious treasure: an open, loving heart.

Of course, I blamed Mack. He was the monster who had ripped me to shreds and hardened my heart, turning it to stone. I wiped away a few stray tears, prepared for bed, and told myself to remain positive. Maybe now there was a chance to heal my damaged heart. Maybe now I had a clue to the mystery of why it had been so crucial for me to return to the monastery. And maybe that reason had very little, or nothing, to do with my father's or Trex's death.

Snuggled in the warm folds of my sleeping bag, I peered out the window at the stars shining like brilliant white lights of hope against the dark sky. When my eyelids finally closed, I had a premonition. A major shift in my life was forthcoming. Although I had no idea what it would be, where or when it might occur, or how this monumental change might come about, I was certain my return to the monastery was a crucial piece of the puzzle.

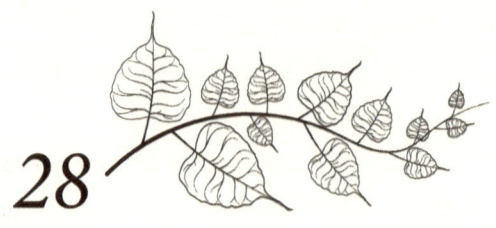

28

Mama Nature's Intention

(Day 19)

The alarm clock awakened me at 4 a.m. I dressed quickly, anxious to sip my tea alone on the covered porch in the pre-dawn stillness before the new group of retreatants drifted in. The retreat schedule was similar to the one I'd followed during my first visit, except there was no time allotted for dhamma discussions, yoga, or personal interviews. Most of the time was to be spent in the meditation hall and the library. I tried to imagine how one was supposed to meditate on death, but figured Bhante B and Bhante Upali would give us detailed instructions. I just hoped it wouldn't be too gruesome an affair.

As I prepared my tea, the kitchen door opened and Polly came toward me with a steaming mug in her hand. She leaned in and whispered, "I was afraid one loaf of your bread wouldn't be enough to serve for the monks' breakfast this morning, so I defrosted the second loaf last night."

"Okay," I whispered. I wasn't sure why she'd told me this. She'd always been so strict about observing Noble Silence.

One by one the new retreatants moseyed in. As the swarm of

bodies milled about the narrow space, I grew cramped and uncomfortable. I headed for the shelter of the meditation hall, where I stood alone beside my cushion in the second row, dropped to my knees, and bowed three times to the golden Buddha. Someone had already lighted the candle. I settled onto my cushion, crossed my legs, and gazed at the magnificent statue. Silently, I asked, *Do you know why I've come back?* Although he made no response, the Buddha's serene smile illumined by soft candlelight told me, beyond a shadow of a doubt, he knew the answer.

Charles was bustling about the kitchen when I entered after breakfast. "What can I help you with?" I whispered. "It's my job now. I volunteered for kitchen duty."

"Well, I'll have to up my game now that I have a professional helping me in the kitchen," he joked.

"Want me to make the salad?"

"By all means. Thank you. Use anything you'd like from the cooler."

Although Polly had finished her work clearing the serving table, she lingered in the kitchen, observing us. Ten minutes later, evidently satisfied, she stuffed her hands deep into the pockets of her white trousers and left the kitchen. Charles shut the door behind her.

"If you need me to prep anything else once I'm done with the salad, just let me know."

"How long are you here for?"

"The work period is over at 8:45. We have to be back in the meditation hall at nine."

As I put the finishing touches on the salad, Charles came toward me. "That's gorgeous. So colorful!"

I'd topped the two huge bowls of mixed lettuces with radish slices, purple cabbage, grape tomatoes, cucumber, bean sprouts, black olives, and grated carrot. "Do you think this will be enough for everyone?"

"It's perfect."

Being so close to Charles gave me butterflies. I checked the clock. "Can you pull everything together by eleven all by yourself? I can stay longer and help if you'd like."

"No, no. You go back to your retreat. That's what you came here for."

I wondered. *Is it?*

Back in the meditation hall, Bhante Upali sat on the cushion below the altar. He placed a stack of paper on the carpet in front of him and pinned the small microphone to his robe.

"I'd like to begin this morning by reciting a verse from the Visuddhimagga: 'When a person is truly wise, his constant task will surely be this recollection about death, blessed with such mighty potency. For people who have not developed mindfulness of death fall victim to fear, horror, confusion, as though they are seized by wild beasts, spirits, robbers, or murderers. But the person who has developed, to a high degree, mindfulness of death, they die unconfused and undisturbed and open to the universe.'"

For the next hour and a half, Bhante Upali spoke about death—reading directly from his notes. He advised us not to struggle against death, but instead to observe death with detachment, to acknowledge and accept the resistance and fear of death, to soften and relax around it, letting it flow through us.

I tried to pay attention, but his tone and manner seemed mechanical, forced, and inauthentic compared to the easy-flowing, contemporaneous speech of his former dhamma talks. The time dragged as I tried to listen, bored and distracted by my own whirring thoughts. Plus, it annoyed me that no one was meditating. Instead, everyone had to sit still and listen to Bhante Upali talk and talk and talk, reading from his stack of papers. I was grateful when the brass gong outside sounded three times and I uncrossed my aching legs.

Upon entering the kitchen for lunch, my eyes lit up like a kid at the candy store. Half a dozen hot vegetarian dishes crowded the long lunch table, including my huge bowl of salad plus an array of pickles, olives, and chutneys. Charles stood beside the big black stove observing the lunch procession, ready to jump in and refill an empty bowl. I caught his eye, and with a huge grin I whispered, "Everything looks scrumptious!"

Serving herself in the line in front of me, Polly turned around with irritation. *What's her problem? Polly broke Noble Silence herself this morning when she mentioned the bread!* I ignored her and heaped my plate with servings of rice almandine, mushroom gravy, green bean casserole, roasted broccoli, spinach-mushroom quiche, and a separate bowl for my salad. I waited for Polly to exit the kitchen, then I turned to Charles and whispered, "You've got to eat some of your own delicious food. Please make a plate for yourself."

"I'll eat later," he said with a wink.

I shook my head. There was a tray of brownies at the end of the table, and I grabbed the biggest piece on my way out of the kitchen.

After lunch I helped Charles clear the serving table while volunteer retreatants washed dishes in the adjacent room. Polly entered the kitchen, grabbed a broom, and started sweeping the floor. Had she come into the kitchen to spy on us? Charles edged close to me and whispered, "When we're done, would you like to take a walk?"

If Polly had heard us, she didn't let on. "Sure," I whispered. "I'll meet you in the parking lot."

The blacktop of Winding Creek Road was a welcome sight. Mounds of snow on both sides of the road now appeared as mini hills instead of mini mountains. The sun was shining, the sky bright blue, and the fresh smell of early spring in the air was intoxicating. Charles and I walked slowly, side by side. I didn't know much about his life, and was curious.

"Charles, how long did you live on the sailboat?"

"Let's see, actually living on the boat, not counting the years I kept an apartment on shore, I'd say, all together, it amounted to about ten years."

"Wow, that's a long time."

"I spent twenty-five years living in the Keys, not counting my various forays into other parts of the country. Although I always considered the Keys to be my home, I'd go through periods where I'd get tired of the Keys, and question what I was doing there. Then I'd get some insane notion to pursue another direction, and strike out for parts unknown. I'd be gone for months, sometimes years at a time, off on some crazy adventure." He paused. "But I always came back to the Keys. I'd be somewhere up north, cold, hungry, or sick, and the Keys lured me back with her warmth and beauty. It was a place that accepted everyone, no matter your background, attitudes, or addictions. Plus, I knew I could always survive there."

"It must be a beautiful place to live."

"Absolutely gorgeous."

"I can't imagine what it must be like to actually live on a boat."

"It may sound romantic, but living on a sailboat has its downsides like anything else. My boat was small, so right there you're limited. Not just in terms of actual space, but simple things like cooking meals, washing dishes, and bathing can become a chore. And of course, you always had the weather to contend with. I spent many sleepless nights curled up in my bunk during rough weather worrying if my mooring lines would hold or break loose as the boat slammed me up and down all night long."

"Wow, that must have been frightening."

"It was. But the worst part was when I'd have to row to shore in bad weather. It would take half an hour pulling on those heavy oars and fighting that strong current to move the dingy three feet forward. And I'd be totally soaked once I reached shore!" He laughed. "Then I'd curse and ask myself, 'Charles, what the hell are you doing?'"

"How often did you have to row to shore?"

"Oh, when I had to go to work, or to the laundromat, or to buy food. Sometimes if I felt the need for some company I'd row in and go to the bar for a couple of beers."

"Do you drink?"

"Not much anymore. Occasionally my friend Drew who lives close to the monastery will come pick me up late at night and we'll drive to the local watering hole."

I stopped walking. "Are you allowed to do that? I mean, being a resident of the monastery."

"Of course not!" He chuckled. "But if I didn't do something like that every once in a while, I think I'd go crazy in this place."

I giggled. "Oh, Charles, you're such a rulebreaker! Were you ever caught?"

"I'm pretty careful. I leave my kuti late at night after everyone's gone to sleep. I walk down to the road, to a certain spot where Drew picks me up. After the bar closes, he drops me off on the road and I walk back to my kuti. I figure if I bump into anyone, I'll just say I was out for an early-morning stroll, and hope they don't smell alcohol on my breath!"

We both laughed. "Oh, you naughty boy!" I teased. "But don't worry. Now that I know your secret, I won't turn you in!"

"Sad to say, there's some people around here who would."

"You mean, like Polly."

"No comment."

We continued along the road in silence. Charles checked his watch. "We'd better turn around. I don't want you to be late for meditation."

The sun disappeared behind a cloud. My hands grew cold and I slipped on my gloves. "Charles, you said you had to row to shore for work. What kind of work did you do?"

"The question is, what kind of work *didn't* I do? Let's see, I spent time employed as a cook. I was a landscape foreman for many years. I worked for a while as a commercial fisherman. I was a small engine mechanic, a plumber's assistant, a welder. I was a charter captain on my own boat, and hired myself out as a deck hand on other charters. I worked for a construction company renovating houses. I airbrushed and sold T-shirts and clothing, was a copy editor for a medical publisher, and worked for two private police forces. I was even employed for a short time by a company that cleaned out septic tanks!" He burst out laughing. "Talk about a humbling experience!"

"Wow, you've certainly packed a lot of different experiences into your life. But how did you come to Buddhism?"

"I was twelve years old when I first discovered meditation. Back then, there weren't many books available about Buddhism like there are today. But I found this one book at the library. I read it, and I was immediately interested in meditation. I used to go hide in the closet and practice meditating so my mother wouldn't catch me at it. Now, you have to understand this was in the slow, backward South—redneck country, rural Georgia about 1952. Just to mention the word 'Buddha' would have you labeled a crackpot."

"So, you were a closet meditator!" I laughed.

"Yes, I suppose I was!" Our pace slowed. "Oh, but here I am talking only of myself and babbling like an idiot! I apologize. I lost my head. I guess that's what happens when a man walks along a peaceful country road in spring beside a beautiful woman."

My cheeks flushed. "Do you really think I'm pretty?"

"Dear child, you're an exquisite creature! Don't you know that? You have a lovely figure, a beautiful face, gorgeous dark eyes, thick dark hair, lovely skin. Anyone who tells you otherwise is either blind or a fool!"

I shook my head. "My husband never compliments me."

"Your husband's a stupid man. He doesn't see what's right in front of him. He doesn't know what a treasure he has."

His words were like warm, soft blankets comforting my soul. "Well," I said, "my husband's made it pretty clear he prefers his own company to mine. He's not even interested in sex anymore." I don't know why I said it. The words tumbled out of my mouth before I had a chance to think. "I'm sorry, Charles. I shouldn't burden you with my troubles."

"Don't apologize."

"And I shouldn't have mentioned the sex thing. It's embarrassing to admit that your own husband doesn't want you in his bed." I stopped walking and turned to face him. Craving reassurance, I asked, "Is it wrong of me to want that kind of intimacy?"

"Not at all. It's Mama Nature's intention," he said. "It's what we're designed for."

I made it back to the meditation hall just in time for the two to five o'clock session. Now it was Bhante B who sat on the cushion below the altar. Thick books had been placed on each meditation cushion. Bhante B directed us to the first page and said, "Forgiveness and loving-kindness are very important wholesome aspects to cultivate within ourselves in order to prepare ourselves for death. So, we are going to read, out loud together, these loving-kindness and forgiveness meditations starting on page one."

Disappointed, my head dropped. Word, words, and more words! Why aren't we *meditating*? When the recitations reached page thirty,

Bhante B instructed us to close the books and proceed to the library. "There you will study the visual aids," he said. "We use these to promote the idea of human impermanence, and to contemplate and reflect on the transient nature of human life."

Two long tables had been pushed together in the center of the library. When I scanned the items on display, I thought I might throw up. There were photographs, in full color and graphic detail, of corpses in various stages of decay. We were instructed to examine the photos carefully, but I couldn't bring myself to do it.

⚬⚭⚮⚯⚬

As I exited the meditation hall after the evening Q & A session, a delicious, familiar aroma was in the air. Chocolate! I headed for the kitchen, opened the door a crack, and saw Charles pulling a tray of brownies from the oven. He was alone. I giggled and went inside to join him.

"Brownies! Yum! My favorite!"

"I saw you take one at lunch, so I made some more."

"That was sweet of you."

"So, how's the retreat going?"

"Uh, okay I guess."

"Just okay?"

"Well, so far this retreat is proving to be *very different* than the one last month."

"I suppose you saw the photographs today."

"You've seen them?"

"Oh, yes. I've studied them extensively. But perhaps my years working as a surgical assistant at the medical school prepared me for them. I've seen many corpses. I've even dissected a few."

"My God, Charles. When was this?"

"In the Navy I was trained in surgery. I thought I wanted to be a doctor. Later I worked in various hospitals and operating rooms."

"There doesn't seem to be a field in which you *didn't* work!"

He laughed. "And I've only told you about the ones you'd approve of. I've neglected to tell you about the other side of my life—the times when all I did was commit pillage and mayhem!"

"Oh, so there's more?" Our laughter was unrestrained, and I worried we might get in trouble. "We probably shouldn't be talking so much. I mean, this is a silent retreat, so technically we're breaking the rules."

The kitchen door opened and Polly entered, grimacing. Charles placed the brownies on the cooling rack and left the kitchen, leaving me to face Polly alone. "You seem to be getting along quite well with Charles," she said.

"Oh, yes. He's a very nice man."

"I have trouble talking to him. Sometimes he gets downright hostile with me." She scowled. "Would you please tell him to stop corrupting the retreatants?"

Shocked, I blurted, "What on earth are you talking about?"

"Well, for one thing, he talks to everyone. Retreatants are expected to observe Noble Silence."

I hesitated. Weren't we both breaking Noble Silence right now? I didn't want to argue with her so I said, "Well, all right. I'll tell him." I left the kitchen in a huff, put on my coat, and exited the building. Charles was waiting for me on the path leading up to my kuti.

"What did Polly say?" he asked.

"Oh, nothing important." All of a sudden, I wished I hadn't returned to the monastery. Something wasn't right. That morning I was bored beyond belief as Bhante Upali read from his papers. In the afternoon, instead of meditating, I was expected to recite verses and study decaying corpses. And now, instead of enjoying a clear, tranquil mind, I was flustered and irritated, and doubted I could sleep. Then I had an idea.

"Charles, would you like to join me on the porch again tonight? But later, after everyone's gone to sleep. I'm feeling a bit unsettled, and I'd appreciate some company."

"It'd be my pleasure."

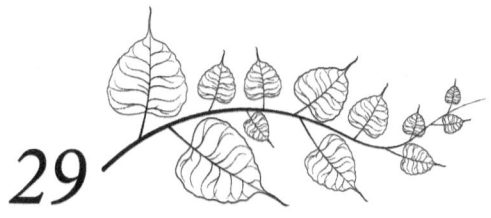

29

Even Misery Gets Comfortable

(Day 19, Evening)

At ten o'clock I left the kuti and headed down the moonlit path with my flashlight. So far, my time at the monastery was not turning out the way I'd expected. I'd hoped to rediscover that blissful place deep inside of me, that sweet emptiness where judgment and ego dropped away leaving my mind clear, calm, content. Instead, everything about this retreat felt wrong or upside down. I was disappointed there was no optional yoga, no dhamma discussions, no personal interviews, and much less time scheduled for actual meditation. Plus, it irked me that Bhante Upali and Polly were behaving so coolly toward me. To top it off, I wasn't even allowed to put flowers beside Kuan Yin's statue! Still, I remained convinced there was an important reason behind my irresistible urge to return to the monastery. I doubted that reason was to recite verses and study photographs of decaying corpses.

At the bottom of the hill the sight of Charles sitting on the porch bench lifted my spirits, and I skipped the rest of the distance to the main building. Wouldn't it be nice to savor that bubbly life energy instead of having to focus all my attention on death!

"Good evening," Charles said as I came up the stairs. "I brought an extra jacket in case you got cold."

"Thank you." I sat beside him. "It's pretty chilly tonight, isn't it?"

"Yes, it is."

The forest was incredibly still, quiet.

"I guess it's too cold for the peepers," I said softly.

We sat in semi-darkness. Only the far edge of the porch was illumined by the glow of the security light above the entrance to the Women's Dorm. All lights were out in the main building. "Do you know if everybody turned in for the night?"

"I think so. Bhante Ganda was wandering around the kitchen earlier, but I think he's gone to his kuti."

"Well, I don't mean to sound paranoid, but sometimes I feel like we're being watched. But we're not doing anything wrong."

"No, of course we're not. But remember, this is a Buddhist monastery, and you are on retreat."

I sighed. "I know. But it doesn't feel like I'm on retreat. Everything is different this time. I can't seem to settle into the structure of this retreat. And I'm having a lot of trouble concentrating. Plus, I've seen a side of Bhante Upali that makes me a little sad. I thought he was enlightened. I thought he'd conquered his ego and desires, but I see glimpses of it every day."

Charles laughed. "He might be a monk, but he's still human!"

"Yes, you're right about that. I just wish I'd see more of his human side. Like last time."

We were silent. A soft breeze brushed my cheek. "Oh, I don't know, Charles. Maybe it's my own fault this retreat isn't going well. Maybe I'm not trying hard enough, or giving it a fair chance. Polly sort of reprimanded me today. I really should be keeping Noble Silence, but, I . . . well, it's just that talking with you has done me a world of good! More than you can imagine. I mean, what's the harm in having a little friendly conversation?"

Charles's eyes flashed. "What did Polly say?"

I didn't want to tell him that she'd accused him of corrupting the retreatants. "Oh, you know, just that we might be talking too much."

"I'm getting rather sick and tired of Polly's holier-than-thou attitude and her obsessive need to control everything that goes on around here! She's accused me many times in the past of talking too much, and personally, she and all those men parading around in bed-sheets can kiss my arse! A lot of retreatants come and talk to me. We engage in harmless, light conversation in and out of the kitchen, and I'll be damned if someone says 'good morning' to me that I don't re-spond! This place would benefit from more congenial conversation and light-heartedness. It would help soften that heavy, austere, depressing, almost deathlike atmosphere they try to create. Good grief, everyone here walks around like a zombie! Like they're dead! Somebody has to try to instill a little life into this place."

Surprised by his outburst, I said, "Wow, you sound pretty angry."

"Oh, I suppose I've just been here too long. I really ought to leave. Many years ago, down in South Florida, anger was my middle name. I was a different man back then, complete with ponytail and earring, and dressed entirely in leather. You wouldn't have recognized me. I cruised all over the country on my motorcycle. I owned a bunch of firearms and didn't hesitate to use them if necessary. I was hostile to the world, in constant combat, and totally caught up in that hard, male ego trip. And I was terribly unhappy. If you had met me back then, you would have run the other way. Fortunately, I was exposed to a few exceptional women who helped straighten me out. I consider myself very lucky to have had such wonderful female teachers. They wouldn't put up with any of my stupid male bullshit." He paused. "It took me a while, but over the years I managed to let go of all that anger. Anger doesn't get you anywhere. It's a waste of time and energy. And it can ruin your life."

"My husband is consumed by anger," I said in a shaky voice. "He's fueled by it. I mean, I know he's had a difficult life and feels rejected by the world. That's probably why he's so hostile to it. But deep down, although he'd never admit it, I think he feels like he's a failure. He's just so resentful, and full of bitterness, and, and—" Tears formed in my eyes. "And he takes all his anger out on me!"

Charles placed his hand on my knee. "According to Buddhism, regardless of the circumstances, if you have anger, you're lost. Your husband's a lost man."

We didn't speak for several minutes. I shivered, and Charles placed the jacket he'd brought around my shoulders. I was afraid that if we kept talking, I might lose it.

"I've come to believe," Charles said, "that the real challenge in this life is to minimize trauma. If you can walk through your life softly and gently enough to bring as little harm to yourself and others as possible, only then can you say you've accomplished something."

My teeth clenched recalling the gut-wrenching battles Mack and I had fought over the years and the resulting trauma it had caused me. My muscles tensed with loathing for him, my hands formed fists. I'd been keeping every ounce of that trauma to myself for so many years, and now the floodgates burst open.

"Oh, Charles, my husband doesn't give a shit about me! That selfish bastard has to be the cruelest man on earth! His language and behavior have ripped my soul to shreds! His viciousness has cut me down so low it's a wonder there's anything left of me! Sometimes I feel so lost, so hopelessly empty, alone and broken, I, I . . . Oh, it's no wonder I can't seem to find my way out of this mess!" I started to cry. "I feel like I'm in prison."

"It's all right." Charles reached into his pocket, handed me a tissue, and I wiped my eyes.

"Oh, I'm sorry. I didn't mean to explode like that. Things were pretty awful when I was home."

"I was worried they might be."

"And it's not just me he attacks. Mack lashes out at everyone: my mom, my sister, a neighbor, even the plumber! And . . . well, oh, I might as well say it. I haven't admitted this to anyone. If I did, people would think I've totally lost my mind. Mack is a raging anti-Semite. It's true! And I'm Jewish!" I shook my head. "How can I stay with someone like that? Do you think I'm insane?"

"Of course not!"

"I can't tell you how many times I've wanted to pack a bag, get into the car, and go. Just leave. But it's so difficult to walk away from your home, your income, everything you know."

Hot tears dripped down my cheeks. Charles put his arm around my shoulder. "Unfortunately, staying becomes a habit," he said.

"Sometimes I blame myself for not having the courage to leave. I feel so stupid."

"Don't. You're just caught in a trap. I know what it's like. Many years ago, I was entangled in a bad marriage myself. When that happens, you see no way out, so in order to survive, you resign yourself to the situation and adjust, no matter how painful it may be. Even misery gets comfortable after a while."

"But you got out?"

He laughed. "By the skin of my teeth!"

I took a deep breath, exhaled slowly, and glanced at a cluster of bright stars high in the night sky. "Charles, was it really your association with women that helped you let go of your anger and hostility?"

"Oh, most definitely. But it was also related to the two years I spent in New England living alone in the middle of a pine forest in a ramshackle hut half the size of my kuti with no electricity and no running water. Although that experience almost killed me, I learned a lot about myself."

"My God, Charles! What in the world were you doing there?"

"Seeing if I could survive," he said with a chuckle. "I spent my days cutting firewood to feed an old stove which was my only source of heat and on top of which I boiled all my water which I fetched from the stream. I cooked rice and beans on top of that stove, which was basically the only food that kept me alive those two years. What I remember most about the entire experience was that I was always cold. My whole life, it seemed, revolved around how to get warm. I practically lived in my ski suit."

I shook my head. "You never cease to amaze me, Charles. What a full, adventurous life you've lived."

"Most people would say I'm mad as a hatter!"

"Not at all! Most people only dream about living on sailboats, or taking off for parts unknown on a motorcycle, or living in a Buddhist monastery. You know, I used to be pretty adventurous myself when I was younger. I wasn't afraid to take risks or break the rules. Looking back, I did some pretty wild things." I gazed into the darkness of the forest and shook my head. "I don't know what's happened to me. I've lost my confidence and my rebellious spirit. My life has become so stale, so dull and tedious. God, I wish I had more adventure in my life!"

The sound of heavy footsteps alarmed me. I bit my lip, hoping it wasn't Polly or, worse, Bhante Upali. Soon the lumbering figure of Bhante Ganda appeared under the security light. Wearing a black jacket over his orange robes and a black watchman's cap, he approached us from the direction of the office. As he stepped onto the porch, he nodded and said, "Good evening, Charles."

"Good evening, Bhante Ganda," Charles said with a slight bow of his head.

"Nice evening tonight, isn't it?" Bhante Ganda gave us his crooked jaw smile.

"Yes, it is," Charles replied.

"I was just in the office answering some emails," the monk said in a sing-song voice. "And I thought I'd get myself a cup of hot chocolate before turning in." He opened the front door, then turned back to Charles. "Enjoy the rest of the evening." Before he disappeared inside the building, Bhante Ganda gave Charles a noticeable wink.

Charles laughed softly. "Oh, that Bhante Ganda!"

"He's a strange monk," I said. "How did he ever get ordained?"

"Yes, Ganda's different. He really has no business being a monk. But I like him. He's a character. He's had a colorful past. He's lived on the streets, done some crime and drugs. But he turned the corner, abandoned his old life and decided to become a monk. Actually, it's not very difficult to find someone who will ordain you if you're set on becoming a monk."

"Do you know him well?"

"Fairly well. He likes to ride into town with me when I go for groceries. He tries to get away from the monastery whenever he can. The first time he asked to come with me, I said, 'Of course.' Then when we were a few miles away from the monastery, he asked me to pull the truck over, which I did. Then he took a knapsack from the back of the truck, disappeared into the woods, removed his robes, and put on a pair of jeans, a flannel shirt, and a pair of sneakers. When he got back into the truck, he explained that he always changed into these clothes when he left the monastery. That way, when he returned, no one would smell cigarette smoke on his robes!"

Through my laughter, I could barely say, "I knew it! Bhante Ganda's a rulebreaker too! Just like us!"

30

The Real Heroes

(Day 20)

The next morning, sipping tea alone on the darkened covered porch before dawn, I admonished myself. There were only two more full days left of the retreat, and I wasn't making any progress. I berated myself for my lack of effort to follow the monastery rules and retreat guidelines. I had to try harder if I wanted to discover what called me here. I had to immerse myself fully in the retreat experience. After all, that's what worked for me the last time.

For starters, I promised myself to keep Noble Silence for the rest of the retreat, and fight the temptation to talk and laugh with Charles. While in the meditation hall, I would pay close attention to the verses we were instructed to read, and recite every single one. I'd even make another stab at viewing those horrid photographs in the library.

But once I was inside the meditation hall, my attempts to concentrate on the verses Bhante B had us recite proved futile. Instead of focusing on the words coming out of my mouth, my agitated mind bounced like a ping pong ball from one meaningless or alarming thought to another. After everyone closed their books, only ten minutes remained in the morning session for meditation. I tried to focus on my breath coming in and going out. I tried to watch my thoughts arising and passing away, but failed miserably.

In the kitchen after breakfast, as Polly cleared breakfast items from the serving table, Charles gathered ingredients to prepare for lunch. I tied an apron around my waist. Charles informed me what was on the menu, and I set to work on the salad. Polly hovered over us until she was satisfied with our calm, quiet behavior, then she exited the kitchen.

As Charles and I worked, our eyes met at intervals. A couple of times his playful smile made me blush, and I quickly turned my gaze away.

"Okay, the salad's pretty much done," I said to him. "I could mince some garlic for your stir-fry."

"Uh, yes, that'd be helpful. Oh, and if you're chopping garlic, would you mind making extra? Bhante B likes to eat raw garlic with his meal. He says it's good for his blood pressure."

"Oh, sure. I'll put some aside in a little bowl. Where do you keep the small bowls?"

"In the dish room on the wire shelves. There ought to be something there you can use."

I wiped my hands on my apron, entered the dishwashing room, and scanned the selection. The choice was obvious. My hand grabbed a small glazed blue bowl with a lovely, intricate design of white flowers.

Back in the kitchen, I asked Charles, "Is it okay to use this bowl? I mean, it's really beautiful. Far too good for chopped garlic."

"Funny you should choose that bowl."

"Why? It's the prettiest bowl on the shelf. I wish I had one like it at home."

"I'm the only one in this place who ever uses that bowl. No one else will touch it."

"That's odd. I wonder why."

"People aren't attracted to beauty around here. I suppose they're afraid they might get *attached* to it!"

I suppressed giggles.

I minced a mound of garlic, then checked the clock. "What else can I prep for you, Charles? I still have about fifteen minutes before I have to be back in the meditation hall."

"Anything you'd like. There should be plenty of produce in the cooler. Chop up whatever suits your fancy!"

Charles was right. The cooler contained an abundance of fresh, colorful produce to choose from. "My goodness, these veggies are gorgeous!" I gathered firm red and yellow peppers, bright orange carrots, a big white cauliflower, some little round Brussels sprouts, and a bunch of the greenest parsley. "I can't imagine what life must be like for people who don't eat vegetables," I said, rinsing the parsley at the sink. "Honestly, I think I'm addicted to vegetables. I love eating them, growing them, cleaning them, chopping them, cooking them! It probably sounds crazy, but I've been known to walk into the produce section of a grocery store, and be blown away by a bunch of kale!"

Charles laughed. "Sounds to me like you have a love affair with the entire vegetable kingdom!"

I laughed again, this time a bit louder. "Okay, it's true! I won't deny it. But as much as I adore Brussels sprouts and kale, deep down, I carry a real torch for broccoli!"

"Aha! Now I understand your true nature!" Charles joked.

I couldn't resist. "Oh, help me, Charles! Help me! I think I'm attached to vegetables!" Tickled by my own joke, peals of laughter gushed from my lips and I doubled over. When I straightened up, Bhante Upali's shaved head and sallow face appeared in the kitchen doorway.

"Oh, I'm sorry, Bhante!" I apologized. "I didn't realize. Was I being too loud?"

He nodded. "The windows in the dining hall were rattling."

After lunch I grabbed some carrots for the horses and took off on my own down Winding Creek Road. With each step, I scolded myself. *You imbecile! You moron! You did it again. You have absolutely no self-discipline!* Although I had every intention of keeping Noble Silence, I could not stop myself from joking around with Charles. I had to rein myself in. I had to complete the retreat in silence if I hoped to gain any insight into what had drawn me back here with such intensity.

The chilly mountain air invigorated me as I hiked along the creek. Several puffy white clouds dotted the bright blue sky. When I finally reached the familiar bend in the road, the horses stood in their usual spot by the fence. The sight of their long faces, velvet noses, tangled wisps of mane, and shiny, muscular bodies filled me with delight.

"Well, hello, my friends," I said, approaching. "Look what I have for you today. Aren't you lucky!"

On my way back I spotted a figure walking toward me. As the figure came closer, I recognized Charles wearing a dark-green army jacket and blue baseball cap. When he reached me, he stopped walking, and we stood facing each other.

"Mind if I join you?" he asked.

"Oh, sure. I'm just on my way back."

We continued several dozen yards down the road before speaking. Then I said, "Maybe we should try not to talk to each other so much."

"Is that what you want?"

I stopped in my tracks, unsure. Then it just came out. "Yesterday Polly asked me to tell you to stop corrupting the retreatants."

His eyes became slits, his hands tightened into fists, and his face turned rigid. "That bitch!"

"Oh, Charles, please don't be angry! I shouldn't have told you. I thought maybe we could laugh about it."

"What the hell does she mean by 'corrupting' the retreatants?!"

"I'm sure she didn't mean anything. She just said that you talk to everyone."

"Oh, for heaven's sake! Talking or no talking, Polly can't tolerate seeing a man and a woman enjoying each other's company. I've had just about enough of Polly and her sanctimonious, male-hating bullshit!"

"Charles, please don't be upset! I'm sorry I mentioned it. Polly's just being Polly. Don't take it personally. I mean, all she probably meant was that you do seem to engage in a little more conversation than most people around here."

His lips pursed and his eyes caught fire. "I'm still a living, breathing human being, and, as such, I refuse to die to the world prematurely and walk around here like some indifferent, half-dead tongueless zombie!"

With that comment, the conversation ended and we continued along the road in silence. After a few minutes Charles said, "Polly and I have had our share of conflicts in the past. But Polly has a problem with all males. It's difficult because I have to share kitchen duties with her, and she's the type of person who always has to be in control."

"I'm all too familiar with that type of behavior." The sky darkened. I spotted a thick band of gray clouds in the distance. "Can't you just talk to her and try to get along?"

"Polly and I can't talk. She has her own ideas about how the kitchen should be run. She's adopted the role of the beneficent mother superior here at the monastery and orders everyone around. Even the monks. She absolutely refuses to listen to a male point of view, so I don't bother trying to communicate with her."

"She does seem to keep a close eye on things."

We rounded a bend in the road. The babble of the shallow creek made pleasant music. The wind picked up. Dark gray clouds were closing in.

"Charles, do you mind me asking why you decided against becoming a monk? Is it because of some of the experiences you've had here?"

He stopped walking and glanced skyward. "There were many reasons I didn't go through with it. One was my family. How would my kids feel about me coming to visit them showing up with a shaved head and wearing a dress? And if I were ordained in the Theravada tradition, I couldn't even hug my daughter or my granddaughter. But I suppose the main reason I couldn't go through with it had to do with a quotation I once read. A foremost Buddhist scholar said that there is one reason and one reason only for becoming a monastic. And that is to seek liberation. Nothing else."

"And you don't want liberation?"

He started walking and I stayed by his side. "I've never been very good at lying to myself, and I was forced to admit that seeking liberation was not *my* reason for wanting to become a monk. Besides, I'd make a terrible monk! I wouldn't be able to follow all the rules. I'd be sneaking off somewhere and doing things I shouldn't be doing like Bhante Ganda. Or worse!" He laughed.

"But if you weren't seeking liberation, you must have been seeking something else, right?

He bit his lower lip. "You might say I was searching for an identity, a place to be. I was trying to answer the questions, 'Who are you? What are you? Where are you going?' I suppose I toyed with the idea of playing dress-up and seeing what kind of figure I might cut as a Buddhist monk." He laughed. "But, of course, I've been asking myself these same questions for forty years, and I still haven't come up with any answers!"

I chuckled. "I think we all ask ourselves those same questions at some point."

"For me, becoming ordained as a Buddhist monk would be sheer hypocrisy. In order to do something like that you have to be a believer, and I'm not a believer. Never have been. In order to dedicate your life to the Buddha's path, you have to take this leap of faith—you have to actually *believe* there is some other level of existence out there to attain—call it liberation, or enlightenment, or nibbana."

"And you don't?"

"Enlightenment, ENSHMITENMENT!" Charles huffed. "We don't know if anyone has attained it! If they have, they haven't said. And if they've claimed it, they certainly haven't attained it."

"I'm not sure I'm following you."

"My dear child, there is no other state or level of existence outside of ourselves and what we see and experience all around us. Everything is *right here*. Right in front of our faces, there is nothing else. There's no other 'Charles' waiting to emerge and be carried off to Nibbana. This very existence, with all its joys and sorrows, is all we have to deal with. I don't believe the meaning of our existence can be found hiding out in some monastery torturing ourselves, sitting on hard cushions for hours upon hours, detaching ourselves from natural pleasures and desires, practicing austerities, and renouncing the world in order to attain something I don't even know exists! I believe we suffer when we go *against* our true nature. But that's exactly what you're expected to do when you become a monk. Suppress and deny your true nature."

My brain was buzzing with confused, tangled thoughts and emotions. Charles sensed my uneasiness. He glanced at his watch. "We'd better pick up the pace or else you might be late for meditation."

At that point I didn't care if I was late, or if I missed the entire meditation session. My pace slowed as I struggled to digest all that Charles had said. "I get the impression you're not happy with the way Buddhism is practiced here. If that's the case, what kind of Buddhism *do you* practice?"

He stopped walking again and turned to face me. "You mean, personally? For myself?"

"Why yes, of course."

Once more he looked skyward, as though the clouds contained the answer. "I believe we are not separate from existence. I'm here. Existence is here. And as far as I know, there is no other existence besides the one I'm in right now. So, by rejecting this world, by withdrawing my senses, I'm rejecting and cutting off a piece of existence. And if we have any chance of understanding this crazy life and death cycle we're born into, I believe we can't leave any of it out. People who renounce the world have no respect, no trust in Mama Nature, in the way things flow naturally. In my mind, to withdraw from the world is like giving Mama Nature a sharp slap in the face. It's like a whiny child refusing a precious gift, crying, 'Take it back! I don't want it!' As though Mama didn't know what she was doing. What audacity!

"I believe the real arahant, the truly wise one, is the one who participates in the world and everything in his life is nicely balanced. Those are the real heroes. The Zen monks say, 'Dive in.' There's a line in the Lotus Sutra that advises, 'Joyful participation in the sorrows of the world.' To find harmony amidst all the chaos—that's the real struggle."

My overloaded brain quit functioning. We continued walking in silence. When we reached the monastery driveway I stopped at the entrance and asked, "Is that why you want to leave here, Charles? To go and participate in the joys and sorrows of the world again?"

"I've lived here at Bodhi for almost three years, and despite all my hopes and expectations to the contrary, I've come to see that this monastery is just another institution with all the built-in flaws and foibles any institution has. And the monks and residents who live here, no matter how much they starve themselves, no matter how many hours they sit in that meditation hall and fall asleep, no matter how many suttas they study and recite, although some of them may put on a good act, they are just as human as you and me. They still have their irritations, jealousies, likes, dislikes, and attachments. They haven't attained anything except a sore buttocks and severe weight loss. And they possess no greater knowledge, understanding, or wisdom than the bag lady sleeping on the street corner!"

"Charles, you don't mean that!"

"Yes, I do!" His voice intensified. "How much do you think Bhante B has had to struggle in his life? He's been fed, clothed, sheltered, and bowed to since he was twelve years old. He's never worn a pair of pants, never touched a woman, never been in love, never been drunk, never in his life put in a full day's hard labor, never had to worry about earning money to pay the rent, or where his next meal was coming from. What could he possibly understand about suffering? He doesn't know the first thing about what he's trying to escape from!"

I couldn't believe my ears. The wind tousled my hair. A few raindrops wetted my cheeks. Stunned, I just stood there, my feet stuck to the ground like two blocks of cement.

"I'm sorry," Charles said. "I hope I didn't upset you. If it's any consolation, this realization was a great disappointment to me. I came here expecting to find some high degree of spirituality. I imagined seeing the monks floating a foot off the ground, the meditation hall glowing gold and brilliant, exuding otherworldly peace. And what I've come to see during my years here is that the people who live here are just as sad, crazy, fearful, and disillusioned as you and me. Just because you've shaved your head, put on a dress and a pair of sandals, and you walk around like you're half-dead, doesn't automatically mean you're a spiritual being."

Behind Charles, the hand-painted wooden sign at the entrance to the driveway came into focus. *Bodhi Community.* Now I viewed those two words through a slightly different lens. Just then, Mack's prophetic warning popped into my mind: "If you stay at that monastery long enough, you'll begin to see all its flaws." I cringed.

We continued up the drive toward the main building. The rain fell harder, its soft, soothing patter echoed in the adjacent woods. I pulled the hood of my jacket up over my head and started down the path toward the bamboo grove.

"Where are you going?" Charles called. "Aren't you going inside for meditation?"

I turned around. "No. Not yet. I have to go and see Kuan Yin. I need to hold her hand."

"This is your retreat. You do what you need to do."

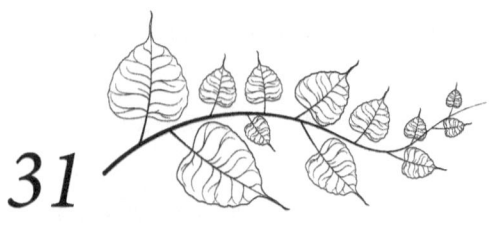

31

I Will Hear It

(Day 20, Evening)

The rest of the day passed as a blur. After visiting Kuan Yin I went back
to my kuti, changed into dry clothes, and turned the propane heater up
to high. I had no desire to go to the meditation hall and recite passages
or hear Bhante Upali read from his papers. Instead, I tried to meditate
on the cushion in my kuti, but my mind refused to settle. Charles's
cryptic words replayed inside my brain like a broken record as I struggled to process all he had said. Ultimately, I gave up and took a long
nap.

At six thirty I grabbed my flashlight and headed to the meditation
hall for the evening dhamma talk and Q & A session. The retreat
was almost over; I was determined to pay close attention. Bhante
Upali sat straight and tall upon the cushion below the altar. During
my first retreat, he'd been livelier, talkative, and relaxed, especially after
the snowstorm. But now he moved about the monastery restrained,
silent, stone-faced, and unemotional. In the fading light, I made out
his pale, sunken cheeks, the dark circles beneath his eyes, and his bony,
wasted frame hidden beneath orange robes. At that moment, instead

of a revered Buddhist monk, Bhante Upali appeared like a cadaver. Still, I considered him to be my teacher and maintained great respect and admiration for him. Without his instruction during my first retreat, I might never have experienced such a blissful, transformative state of consciousness, or been blessed with that precious insight into impermanence.

Once everyone was settled on their cushions, Bhante Upali cleared his throat and began his dhamma talk on the importance of loving-kindness and forgiveness.

"Contemplating death arouses the sense of urgency—that's its primary function—the urgency to 'get your act together,' so to speak. That means purifying the mind of any negative states that prevent our minds from floating free at the time of death. The whole point in the contemplation of death is to be prepared, to be ready when it happens so you don't die confused or remorseful.

"So, in order to prepare yourself for death, first of all we must realize death can happen at any time. And second, if it does happen, we must ask, am I ready? What am I still clinging to? Do I have anger, hatred, ill will, grudges, resentment, greed, lust, or desire for things? If you still have those things strong in your mind, then you're not ready to die. But you may die anyway. And you'll die in an unprepared state."

He took a long drink from his mug, then continued.

"So, it's important to ask yourself, am I ready to die right now? Is there any unfinished business I need to take care of?"

My back stiffened. *Unfinished business? That's what Susan said after cooking class! She told me the reason I had to return to the monastery was because I had unfinished business. But what could it be?*

"Forgiveness," he continued, "is an active type of mental purification. Forgiveness renews life by finishing unfinished business. We've all had encounters with people who cause us anger, hatred, and other unwholesome mental states. By not forgiving other people, our minds are prevented from floating free at the moment of death. If we're holding others out of our hearts, then we'll never be complete. Even an unsuccessful attempt at forgiveness has the considerable power to heal the forgiver, and sometimes the forgiven. So, even if you're not able to forgive that person entirely, if you can find loving-kindness in your heart, you can take that small step toward the intention to *want* to forgive them—and that's really the first step to breaking that hard shell, that barrier of *never* wanting to forgive them."

Is it possible for me to forgive Mack for his cruelty? He'd caused me such terrible, heartbreaking pain over the years, I couldn't even imagine having the intention to *want* to forgive him.

"And in the same way as we want to forgive others, we also want to forgive ourselves. We've all done things we're not proud of. Things we might wish we'd done differently, or with more awareness, and we hold on to self-loathing or unkind thoughts toward ourselves. But we're just another being. So, we need to be kind and gentle with ourselves. We need to send loving-kindness to ourselves, and forgive ourselves."

During the Q & A period following the dhamma talk, a question was asked about suicide, and I thought of Mack. Over the years, he'd threatened to kill himself multiple times. Once, during a heated argument when I told him if he continued to berate me I would leave, he grabbed the pistol he'd bought for protection. Right in front of my eyes, he placed the barrel of the gun against his forehead and shouted, "I swear I'll do it, Lu! If you dare walk out of this house, I swear I'll blow my brains out!" I'd never been so terrified in my life until he finally put the gun down. Later, I came to the conclusion that threatening to kill yourself when someone refuses to obey your demands is the ultimate form of control any one person could impose upon another. *How could I forgive him for that?*

Later that evening, as I sat on the low bench opposite the woodstove, my restless mind tried to piece together all that Bhante Upali had said during his talk, as though it were a gigantic jigsaw puzzle. It was almost 10 p.m. The majority of the retreatants had left the main building for their beds, but I was wide awake.

Voices sounded from inside the kitchen. Charles came through the kitchen door, sat down beside me, and whispered, "If you're not too tired, I'd like to show you something tonight."

My head turned right, then left. We were definitely alone. "Okay, sure. I'm not tired at all."

"But Polly's still messing around in the kitchen. Let's wait until she leaves."

"You two weren't arguing, were you?"

"No. She's trying to work out the schedule for next week. After this retreat is over, I'm supposed to have two days off."

"That's great, Charles."

Ten minutes later, the kitchen door opened. Polly exited wearing an expensive-looking hiking jacket with all sorts of flaps, zippers, and drawstrings. Before she left the building, she gave us a long, cold stare.

As soon as Polly closed the front door, I asked Charles, "What do you want to show me?"

"It's outside. Put on your jacket and come with me." He stood up. "Wait a minute." He stepped outside, scanned the area, then poked his head inside the building. "I'm going to start walking down the driveway. Wait a few minutes, then follow me. I'll meet you in the parking lot."

"Okay." My skin tingled with nervous anticipation. *What could he possibly want to show me?*

Halfway down the driveway I spied Charles's shadow waiting for me at the edge of the driveway near the parking lot. When I reached him, he put his arm around me, drew me close, and told me not to speak. But I couldn't refrain from asking, "Where are we going?"

"I'm taking you to my kuti."

I shuddered.

"You said you wanted adventure. Well, here it is. We'll go around the back of the parking lot through the woods. Just stay close to me and keep quiet."

I didn't speak another word. We moved like thieves in the dead of night. Part of me was slightly fearful, but another part of me was secretly thrilled by this spontaneous, clandestine activity. I just kept moving one foot in front of the other until we reached the door to his kuti.

Quietly, we crept inside. The tiny space was dark. Charles lit a few candles and an oil lamp. I was shocked by this simple hut he called home. "Please," he said, "sit down."

There was no chair, just a few milk crates stacked on top of each other. Against the far wall a wide wooden plank supported by cinder blocks served as a desk. Against the opposite wall was a low bed covered by a sleeping bag and blankets.

"Please sit on the bed," he said. "It's the only comfortable place here. Would you like something to drink? I have a little propane stove for heating water, and I'll start a fire. You're probably chilled."

"I'll pass on the drink. I've already had several cups of tea tonight." I sat on the edge of the bed. *What am I doing here? How did I even get here?* It was all happening so fast.

The kuti itself wasn't much bigger than a walk-in closet. I couldn't imagine anyone living here for any length of time. The small wood-stove sat directly opposite the door. While Charles fumbled with some newspaper and kindling, my attention was drawn to an exquisitely carved, ten-inch-tall white Buddha statue on a low table beside the bed. The Buddha was seated cross-legged on a lotus flower. Also on the table were several rocks placed close to the statue, a vase of dried flowers, and a bamboo incense burner. "Oh, Charles, your Buddha is absolutely gorgeous!"

"I couldn't resist him. I found him at a Vietnamese Buddhist festival I attended several months ago. When I saw him and asked the vendor how much, I was prepared to give him all the money I had in my pocket!" Charles approached the bed, lifted the statue, and handed it to me. "Look at the lines. The delicate expression on his face, the detail of the headdress. And look at his little fingers. Isn't he amazing?"

"Oh, yes. He certainly is." I examined the lovely white sculpture resting heavy and smooth in my hands. The Buddha's right arm hung loose and relaxed over his crossed right leg, his left hand poised gracefully on his lap, palm up. Every detail, from the folds of his robe to his bare feet, from his tiny fingernails to his serene smile, was sheer perfection. "Honestly, Charles, this is the most beautiful Buddha statue I've ever seen. Really, he's amazing. Is this what you wanted to show me?"

Charles sat on the bed beside me. The candlelight cast shadows across his face. "My dear girl, I must apologize to you for everything I said this afternoon. You shouldn't listen to me. I didn't mean half of what I said. I was just grumbling. Something was irritating me, and when I get irritated, I tend to criticize and complain. I have to be careful because I seem to be getting increasingly jaded as I grow older. Please forgive me. And I shouldn't have said those nasty things about Bhante B. That was unkind of me. And petty."

"Well, I'd be lying if I said your words didn't have an effect on me. I was a little upset for a while, but I—"

"I knew it! I *did* upset you. Damn it! I worried about that all afternoon. You had a positive experience during your first retreat here and my stupid, exaggerated, unkind remarks spoiled something for you. When will I learn to stop running my damn mouth! I've been here too long. I should have packed up and left after my first year." He stood up and paced the length of the kuti.

"Oh, Charles, please don't feel bad! You haven't ruined anything. I understand, and I forgive you. Being here so long, you've seen a lot. You've made some observations, and you're entitled to your opinions. But please don't be concerned about me. I'm a big girl, and I can make up my own mind about things. And you're right. I did have a positive experience here last time. It was wonderful, and I'll never forget it. Nothing anybody says can take that away from me. Ever. Something incredible happened to me during that last retreat, and I'm beyond grateful for it. I still don't know how it happened or why, but I do know it had a lot to do with Kuan Yin." I paused, wanting to tell him everything, knowing he'd understand. Instead, I said, "I sensed she was very close to me."

"You wouldn't be the first person to have felt that. Some people claim to have actually seen her, that she's appeared to them."

My heart fluttered. *So, I'm not the only one! Had she appeared to Charles too?* Unsure what to say next, I held out my hand to him.

He took it and said, "Good heavens, child, your fingers are like ice! It's still cold in here. That damn stove isn't worth a dime!" He bounded back to the stove and added more wood. "Please forgive me for bringing you here. I hope I haven't offended you."

"Offended me? No, no, of course not!" I smiled. "After all, I did ask if I could come see your kuti, didn't I?"

"Yes, yes, you did." He returned my smile, went over to his desk, picked up an object wrapped in newspaper about the size of a softball, and handed it to me.

"What's this?" I asked.

"Open it. It's just a small token. Something to take home with you."

"Charles, you don't have to give me anything."

"It's nothing much. Go ahead, open it."

I unwrapped the newspaper. There in my hand was the little blue bowl I'd used for Bhante B's minced garlic. "Oh, Charles," I gasped, "how did you? I mean, it's so lovely, but I can't accept this!"

"Don't worry, I didn't steal it. I put ten dollars in the dana box with a note saying this money was from Charles and was to be used to replace a bowl I'd broken in the kitchen."

"Oh, Charles!"

"I saw how much you admired it, and I wanted you to have it. Don't worry, no one around here will miss that bowl. Please, take it home with you and enjoy it. And when you use it, remember your time here at Bodhi."

My fingers caressed the smooth glaze of the bowl. "Oh, well, all right. Thank you, Charles. You really shouldn't have. It's just so pretty, and it's the perfect size for my morning oatmeal. I'll use it every day, and it will definitely remind me of my time here." I shivered, suddenly anxious that my time at the monastery was nearly over.

"Are you still cold? Here, let me put a blanket around you."

"No, that's okay. I'm fine. Really. It's just that the time here has gone by so fast. And I worry I've haven't learned or found anything that could help me once I'm back home." I looked down at the dusty brown rug beneath my feet, then back up at Charles. "It's weird. I knew deep in my bones that I had to come back. But I don't know why."

"I'm sure there's a reason," he said.

"You really think so?"

"Of course." His smile reassured me. "There's just one more little thing I'd like you to have," he said.

"My goodness, Charles, please! Why all the presents?"

"No reason in particular. But I'll be leaving this place soon, and during my time here I've accumulated more things than I can carry in a backpack. So, lately I've been giving my possessions away and I'd like you to have this." He reached underneath the bed and pulled out a slender wooden block about a foot long with a shiny gray cylinder suspended on top of it. He placed the object in my hand. A walnut-sized wooden ball protruded from one end of the block. "This is what I wanted to show you. And what I want you to have as a remembrance of me."

"What is it?" I asked. "I have no idea."

He flashed his impish grin and pulled the wooden ball, sliding an attached wooden mallet out of its sheath inside the block. "Go ahead and strike it," he said, handing me the mallet.

Smiling from ear to ear, I took the slender mallet in my hand. I scrutinized the solid silver cylinder, then focused on Charles. "Oh my God. It's a bell!"

"Have at it!"

I raised the mallet directly above the center of the cylinder, then dropped it swiftly. *Ping-ing-ing-ing-ing-ing-ing.* Sitting perfectly still, eyes closed, I focused on the pure, echoing tones. They lingered for a full minute before softly fading into nothingness. I opened my eyes and giggled with delight, happy as a child on her birthday. "Oh, Charles, this is the best present in the whole world! Really, it's wonderful! But I can't accept it. This is your bell. You keep it. It's too precious."

"No," he protested. "I want you to have it. I insist."

His sincerity, kindness, and generosity penetrated the roots of my soul. "But, Charles, if I take it with me, you won't be able to hear it!"

"I'll hear it." He placed his hand on my thigh. "I promise you, no matter where I am, no matter where you are, when you strike that bell, I will hear it. You can count on that."

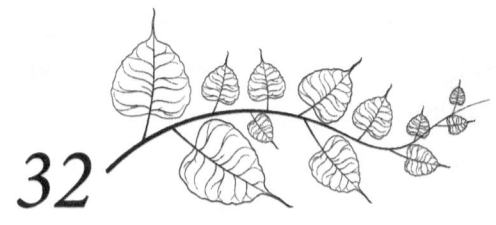

32

They All Start with B

(Day 21, Morning)

The gong awakened me, but I lingered in bed. It was after midnight when I finally left Charles's kuti. He'd insisted on walking me halfway back to my own kuti, where he handed me his flashlight, said good night, and disappeared into the darkened forest. Half asleep and worried I'd be late, I dressed quickly. Before leaving my kuti, I pulled the mallet from its sheath beneath the bell Charles had given me. Standing very still, I struck the metal cylinder. The exquisite vibrations filled every inch of the small hut before gradually fading away. Bathed in peace, I wondered if Charles had heard it too.

I made it to the great hall in the nick of time. Sitting cross-legged on my cushion, I didn't hear a word Bhante Upali said. The only audible voice was the frantic one inside my own head torturing me with anxious thoughts and unanswerable questions. *What in the world is this mysterious "unfinished business" I need to complete? Why did Susan say that was the reason I had to return to the monastery? If I don't find out what I need to do before I leave tomorrow, will my unhappy life continue once I'm home? The only positive thought I could come up with was,*

Maybe Kuan Yin can help me.

I didn't see Charles until after breakfast. When I entered the kitchen for the morning work period, we smiled at each other occasionally, but didn't speak. Again, I volunteered to make the salad. With a heavy heart and troubled mind, I chopped mounds of vegetables, convinced this retreat had been a waste of time. I hadn't had any profound insights about death, and I hadn't gained any deeper understanding of how to navigate my troubled life with Mack. As I placed cling wrap over the two large salad bowls, Charles approached me. "I owe you an apology," he said.

"For what?"

"Taking you to my kuti last night. What's wrong with me? I don't know what came over me. You're a married woman, and this is a Buddhist monastery with strict rules of engagement between men and women. I ought to be ashamed of myself!"

"Oh, Charles, stop! Why do you keep apologizing for everything? Nothing happened! You didn't do anything wrong. *We* didn't do anything wrong. I'm not ashamed, and you shouldn't be either. All we did was talk. Nothing's wrong with that."

"I'm sure your husband would disagree."

"He disagrees with me about *everything!*" I snapped. "And don't you worry about my husband. Just let me worry about him, okay?" The sharpness of my tone surprised me, and I composed myself. "Look, to be honest, my marriage died a long time ago. It's dust and ashes. I haven't had a real husband for over ten years. Instead, I've had a whiny child to take care of, a screaming, nasty, egocentric, dependent child who hates everyone and everything!"

"I'm sorry," Charles said. "I didn't mean to—"

"Nothing to be sorry about. I should be the one to apologize for my outburst. I guess I'm a little uptight about having to leave tomorrow. So, let's get lunch together. What's on the menu?"

"Aren't you going back to the meditation hall?"

I was well aware of what awaited me in the meditation hall. Bhante B would be seated on the cushion below the altar, and he'd instruct us to continue our recitations as he'd done every day of the retreat.

"No. I think I'll stay here in the kitchen and help you get lunch ready. Okay?"

"That's entirely up to you."

"Well, that's what I want to do."

"Suit yourself."

The kitchen door opened and Bhante Tagarasikhi, the Thai monk, entered. He gave us both a big smile, went over to the cooler, took out a carton of milk, and poured himself a glass. His smooth, high-cheeked face always expressed serenity and deep understanding, and he moved about the monastery with the grace and fluidity of a ballet dancer. I'd forever cherish the silent connection we'd forged the day we both gazed at the gigantic sparkling icicles hanging from the roof, and he spoke those two little magic words. At that moment we'd become like comrades sharing a precious secret that bonded us for eternity.

The monk finished his drink, washed his glass at the sink, then approached me. He pointed to my ear. Smiling, he repeated those two miraculous words. "Like diamonds."

My hand rose to the little crystal earring hanging there. Hearing him speak those words once more ignited my heart with hope. I returned the monk's smile, and with palms pressed together, bowed deeply to him.

Charles and I got to work. He planned to make eight different dishes, plus his usual bowls of condiments. I volunteered to make the chickpea curry stew and the roasted squash and Brussels sprouts. We worked on opposite sides of the counter chopping mountains of cauliflower, carrots, mushrooms, green beans, squash, peppers, and onions.

"Oh, Charles, do you have any sesame oil? The recipe you gave me calls for olive oil, but I really think sesame oil would work better."

"Of course. There should be a new bottle in that cupboard to your left. Use whatever you like. You know much more about vegetarian cooking than I do. I'm really not a good cook. I just fumble my way through everything. Thank goodness the monastery has an extensive collection of cookbooks. Otherwise, I'd be completely lost."

"Oh, come on. You turn out wonderful meals," I protested. "Everything's always delicious."

"Pure luck!" He laughed.

"Oh, I have some extra garlic cloves here. Should I mince some to put aside for Bhante B?"

"Yes, thanks. We mustn't forget Bhante B's blood pressure medicine. I have a small bowl right here you can use."

"Speaking of bowls, I really love that little blue bowl you, well, acquired for me." I laughed. "I still can't believe you did that! And, of course, I love the bell. That's the best present of all." I paused. "You've been so kind to me, Charles, and I just want you to know . . . well, how much I appreciate it."

His knife stopped moving. With his soft blue eyes locked on mine, he said, "It's my pleasure."

My heart melted. My gaze fell to the cutting board. I smashed a garlic clove, blinked a couple of times, then set down the knife. "You know, I just realized something. **B**lue **B**owl. **B**ell. That's three **B**s. "What do you make of that?"

"**B**odhi Society," Charles said. "And I gave you a **B**ook."

I giggled. "That's right! Two **B**s for you! What else?"

"**B**oddhisattva!"

"Oh, yes, absolutely!"

Now it was a game. Eager to play, I skipped around the counter and stood beside him. "What else?"

"How about **B**hante **B**?"

"No," I laughed merrily. "He doesn't count! My turn. Let's see. Didn't I mention my love affair with **B**roccoli?"

"Indeed, you did. And I think you also mentioned your affinity with **B**russels sprouts!"

I laughed some more, leaned in, and whispered, "And do you know what else I truly love, more than anything else in the world, and with all my heart? My **B**ig, **B**road-chested dog. My **B**eloved **B**ooter!" I poked him in the ribs. "That's four more **B**s for me! Your turn!"

"Let's see, I used to live on a **B**oat," Charles said.

"Yes, very good. My turn. "Oh, I love watching the **B**irds. And . . . Oh darn! It's too bad 'peepers' begins with a 'p.'"

"Well," Charles said, "instead of peepers, we could just call them **B**eepers."

Unable to contain myself, I burst out laughing. "Oh, beepers! Yes, let's call them beepers!" Doubling over with mirth, I said, "Oh, Charles, we're being so silly, but it's fun. It feels so good to laugh!"

Polly burst into the kitchen. I straightened up, pursed my lips, hurried back to my side of the counter, and started chopping squash. Polly went directly to Charles and said, "Are you going for groceries after lunch?"

"I think I'll have to in order to feed everyone lunch tomorrow before they leave."

"There are a few items I'd like to add to the shopping list," Polly said. "I've got my menus planned for your days off and I need some specific items." She handed him a piece of paper. "I've written everything down on this list. Bhante Upali said to take the black truck. Do you have the keys?"

"I know where they are," Charles said.

Before Polly left the kitchen, she pulled me aside. I expected to be chastised for laughing so loudly with Charles. Instead, she surprised me and said, "Pretty earrings."

"Uh, thank you." *Wow. Maybe Polly isn't that upset with me after all.*

⚬❦⚬

Charles and I finished our lunch preparations with ten minutes to spare. The vast array of colorful vegetarian dishes on the table resembled an exquisite still life painting. "We did it, Charles!"

"I don't think I could have finished it all on time today without your help."

"Oh, it was fun. I had a blast." I wanted to give him a hug but I didn't dare. Instead, I said, "By the way, I've been meaning to ask you something for a while now. What was it exactly that motivated you three years ago to come to Bodhi to live and possibly become a monk?"

His face turned stone serious. "I've always wanted to wear a dress."

Again, I burst out laughing.

"Calm yourself," Charles said, opening the kitchen door. "It's almost time to ring the gong."

The orange cat appeared in the kitchen doorway, his tail high in the air. Someone must have let him in by accident.

"Oh, I'll go get him," I said. The cat scurried down the covered porch and into the darkened dining hall. I ran after him. Just as I was about to scoop him up, I practically bumped right into Bhante Upali, half hidden in the shadows, and immediately backed away. The monk bent over, lifted the cat in both arms, and hugged the warm, furry animal to his scrawny chest.

"Leave my cat alone," he said.

I stood deathly still, staring at the monk embracing his beloved pet. The thought that this cat must be Bhante Upali's only source of physical affection saddened me. "I'm terribly sorry, Bhante. I was just going to put him outside. I know you don't like him wandering around inside the main building."

300

"It's all right. He can stay inside for a short while." Bhante Upali lowered his head and his slender fingers stroked the cat's furry neck.

"Certainly, Bhante."

He raised his head. "You're missing the retreat."

I hesitated, unsure if I should apologize or speak the truth. "But Bhante," I finally said, "I'm enjoying my own retreat. I've been meditating in my kuti, taking long walks, and I've been practicing mindfulness and generosity in the kitchen."

He squinted, doubtful.

"Bhante, I don't think you understand how much work is involved in preparing a nutritious vegetarian lunch for close to sixty people. It's an enormous job! And Charles is in that kitchen all alone with no one to help him get lunch together. And here I am, a professional vegetarian cook. I feel compelled to help. And, since I can't afford a big donation to the monastery, helping in the kitchen is my way of giving dana."

Still stroking the cat, Bhante Upali's little boy smile came out of hiding. "Well," he said, "then I suppose I should thank you for your generous contribution."

After lunch, Charles left the grounds in the black pickup truck with his shopping list. I mopped the kitchen floor, then headed for the covered porch. As I sipped a hot cup of green tea, I scanned the bulletin board. *What's this?* A folded piece of paper was tacked there with my name on it. My gut told me it was bad news. I removed the note from the board, unfolded the paper, and read: "Your husband called and wants you to call home."

"Oh, great," I moaned. Here I was trying to forget all about Mack and my troubles at home, and here he was, popping up in front of me as usual, probably with some demand, insult, or criticism. *What could he possibly want that can't wait until tomorrow when I get home?*

I glared at the handwritten words on the paper. I saw my anger rising. I had no desire to speak to Mack. I'd said everything I had to say to him hundreds of times before. I'd begged him to treat me with respect and stop ordering me around. I'd pleaded with him to quit insulting my family and maligning the Jews. All to no avail. No, I would not call him. I had nothing left to say to that man. Furious at his intrusion, I crumbled the piece of paper and threw it in the trash can. But then I panicked. He said he'd only call in case of emergency. *What if, on the off chance, there was an actual emergency?* I threw my hands up in the air and headed for the telephone in the hallway leading to the Women's Dorm.

As I dialed home, I cautioned myself against being lured into an argument. I told myself, rather than trying to *talk* to Mack, I would *listen.* I doubted he'd tell me he was looking forward to me coming home, or that he missed me and was sorry for all the hateful things he'd said to me in the past. Still, I'd give him the opportunity to express something positive, although I was convinced the chances of that happening were slim to none.

"Oh, Lu, I'm glad you called," he said.

"I just saw your message. Is everything all right? Is Booter all right?"

"Booter? Yes, yes, of course. He's fine. You don't have to worry about the pets when you're gone. I take extremely good care of the pets. Seriously, half my day is taken up attending to their needs, feeding them, cleaning up after them, making sure they have fresh straw in their beds. They've never had it so good, the ungrateful mongrels! But I'll tell you, they'd be in a terrible spot if I weren't around and they had to rely on you to take care of them. You're such a birdbrained space cadet and you'd forget to feed them."

My grip on the phone tightened. I reminded myself not to lash out or argue. "That's not funny, Mack."

"What's your problem, Lu? Can't you take a joke? Honest to Christ, you have absolutely no sense of humor."

"Yes, I know. You've told me that a thousand times. Look, why did you call? Is everything all right at home? You said you'd only call in case of emergency."

"This *is* an emergency! I'm out of yogurt! I ate the last bit of it yesterday. I've been rationing myself. You didn't leave me much in the way of food before you took off on your little so-called spiritual retreat. At least you could have made sure I was well-stocked with yogurt before you left. I did not appreciate that."

I closed my eyes and was silent.

"Lu, are you still there?"

"Yes, Mack. I'm here." I sank into the chair beside the phone, suddenly chilled; my body brittle and hollow as though my blood and saliva had dried up.

"I'm sure there's a store on your way home that carries that brand of organic yogurt I like—you know the one. The organic full-fat. Pick me up a couple of quarts, will you? And make sure you get the organic. I'm not going to eat that other crap."

Stunned, I could barely speak.

"Lulu, do you hear me?"

Almost to myself, I managed to say, "You called here and interrupted my retreat just to tell me to stop at a grocery store and bring you two quarts of yogurt?"

"For Christ's sake, Lu, you sound as though I've just asked you to climb Mount Everest! I do hope this little request doesn't put too much of a strain on you. I know you've been working so hard sitting on your ass all weekend. Look, I'd go get it myself but I'm stranded here, remember? You monopolize that car. You think you can take off with it any time you feel like it without the slightest regard for your husband! I need my yogurt! If I don't eat yogurt every day my bowels don't work properly, and if I can't take a shit in the morning, I have to take an enema and that screws up my writing and I end up losing a whole day!"

My head dropped. I'd heard this same complaint countless times in the past, but this time it seemed beyond ridiculous. "Mack, if there's nothing else you want to say to me, I really have to get back to the retreat."

"Oh, so you claim."

"And what's that supposed to mean?"

"Take it for what it's worth. I don't know what the hell you're doing there in hillbilly heaven! You could be partying every night, or screwing one of the monks for all I know. I wouldn't put it past you!"

My teeth gnashed. I wanted to hurt him, to say something spiteful. Instead, I said, "Mack, how did you get so mean?"

"*You're* the mean one! Leaving me stranded here in the middle of godforsaken nowhere with no food, no money, no car! Trotting off on your so-called 'spiritual' vacations and coming home all haughty and superior! Hey, if you want to screw a monk, that's your business, but it's bad karma. It'll come back and bite you in the ass! Remember, Lulu, what goes around, comes around."

My eyes narrowed. "Yes, you're right, Mack. That's very true. Those wise words apply to *everyone*, including you!"

There was silence at the other end of the line. Finally, he said, "What time will you be home tomorrow?"

"I don't know."

"What do you mean, you *don't know?* What time is the retreat over?"

"Sometime after lunch."

"Well, don't piss away the afternoon screwing around with your monk friends. After lunch, get on the road as soon as possible and get your ass home before dark. I definitely will *not* appreciate it if you come waltzing in here after dark expecting me to come downstairs and help you unload your bags when I'm preparing to retire for the evening."

"Mack, I have to go now. Is there anything else you'd like to say to me before I hang up?"

"Don't forget to stop and get the yogurt!"

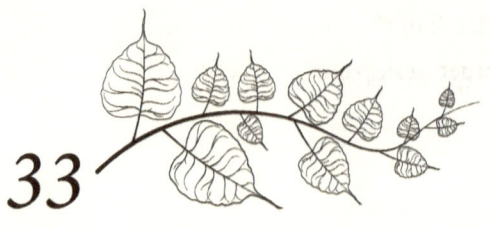

33

Just Be You

(Day 21, Evening)

I sipped cup after cup of tea on the covered porch waiting for Charles to return from his shopping trip. I'd skipped meditation, figuring the afternoon would be better spent helping Charles put groceries away rather than studying decayed corpses.

At half past four, Bhante Ganda came lumbering down the hall. "Excuse me, Bhante, shouldn't Charles be back from town by now? He's been gone an awfully long time. I hope nothing's happened to him."

Bhante Ganda gave me his sly, crooked smile. It was no secret Charles and I had been spending a lot of time together. Sometimes I worried our laughter and friendly behavior had drawn too much negative attention among the monks and retreatants. But Bhante Ganda didn't seem to care. "He's probably hit some traffic," the monk said and continued down the hall toward the kitchen.

Ten minutes later I heard the truck's engine in the driveway. I put on my coat and went outside just as the black pickup parked in front of the main building. Charles got out and opened the tailgate.

"You were gone a long time," I said, grabbing a grocery bag from the front seat. "I was beginning to worry."

"I had to run all over town in order to get everything on Polly's list."

Once all the bags and boxes were inside the kitchen we started to unpack. I removed two big bunches of kale, three broccoli crowns, and two mesh bags of Brussels sprouts. "Oh, Charles!" I squealed. "You bought all my favorite vegetables!"

"I'll use them to cook you a fine lunch tomorrow before you leave." He reached inside a cardboard box and removed something wrapped in tissue. "I also thought you might like this."

I shook my head. "Charles, you have to stop giving me things!"

"Please. You must indulge me. Giving brings me pleasure, and I haven't enjoyed this kind of pleasure in many years."

"Oh, I wish I had something to give you in return."

"You already have."

My heart went out to him. "Have I really?"

"No question. Now, go ahead. Open it."

Excited, I tore open the tissue paper. Inside was a plant with shiny green leaves and delicate pink blossoms growing in a blue ceramic bowl. "Oh, Charles, it's lovely!"

"I picked the one in the blue pot because I know you like that color."

"It's perfect. Thank you. Really, it's so sweet of you to—" I paused. Staring at the shiny green leaves, my face lit up. "Charles, do you know what kind of plant this is?"

"I have no idea. What is it?"

With a huge grin, I said, "It's a begonia!"

"Begonia," he repeated. Then he chuckled. "Ah, yes, of course! Another **B**!"

After all the groceries were put away, I grabbed my coat. Outside, I hurried down the path, through the bamboo grove and across the little bridge to visit Kuan Yin. The retreat was practically over, and if I'd truly come here to contemplate death, I wasn't doing a very good job. And I hadn't once thought about my father or Trex. So, why was I here? Maybe coming back was a mistake. All I'd gained from my return to the monastery was a big fat zero. But I couldn't give up. I remained convinced there was some purpose for my return—some important "business" I had to finish. *But what?* I'd had one clue the night I sat on the porch with Charles, but there had to be more. Maybe Kuan Yin could help me solve the puzzle.

My heartbeat quickened as I stood before the marble Boddhisattva, white and beautiful as always. My palms came together at my chest. *Were you the one who lured me back here?* Unexpectedly, I dropped to my knees. "Oh, dear Kuan Yin," I whispered. "Is there some special message you have for me? Some life-changing lesson I need to learn?" I didn't expect an answer. I just needed to be near her, to feel her loving presence. The wind rustled through the bamboo stalks. Carried upon the breeze, a woman's soft voice spoke these three words: Just be you.

Surprised, I rose to my feet. *Just be me? Is this another clue?* My palms pressed together, I bowed deeply to the wise woman. Then I placed my fingers in her outstretched hand. "Thank you, dear Kuan Yin, for your guidance," I said. A smile broke onto my face. I had an idea.

Charles was sitting on the front porch as I came up the path. I climbed the porch steps and sat on the bench beside him, our shoulders and arms lightly touching. A cool breeze brushed my cheeks. The sun was low in the sky, spreading a warm, rosy glow upon the forest. We were silent, watching the birds at the feeders. A big red cardinal alighted on the feeder closest to us, scaring the chickadees away.

"Charles, do people who come here on retreat ever take off for a little while in their cars?"

"You mean leave the grounds?"

"Yes. Is it ever allowed? Do you need some sort of special permission?"

"Well, technically, retreatants are told not to leave the grounds. But if you absolutely must, you should let someone know when you're leaving and when you're coming back. But, of course, not everyone does. Why? Would you like to go somewhere?"

"Oh, I'm thinking about it. Actually, there is something I might like to do." Sneaking off to Charles's kuti the other night had reawakened my adventurous spirit. And since I'd already broken one of the biggest rules by visiting Charles's kuti, what did it matter if I broke another big monastery rule tonight? Nothing I'd done so far had solved the mystery of my return, so I figured all options were on the table. Besides, I was supposed to *be me.*

"Well, if you do decide to go anywhere, I'd go soon," Charles said, "before the afternoon meditation session is over. That way, you'll be less likely to be seen and you can come back after dark."

I laughed. "You seem to be quite familiar with these little clandestine adventures."

"Yes," he chuckled. "I'm an old hat at this sort of thing." He faced me. "If you don't mind me asking, what is it you have in mind for tonight?"

"Oh, I might have a little party with an old friend."

∞⌒⌒⌒∞

Without a glance behind me to see who might be watching, I hurried down the driveway heading straight for the parking lot, sure of myself. I had a plan, but I had no idea where to find what I was looking for. I got into my car, started the engine, turned right onto Winding Creek Road, and reached for the map on the front seat.

A beat-up red Ford pickup was parked on the side of the road in front of the horse pasture. I pulled up beside the truck, rolled down my window, and addressed a heavyset bearded man in bib overalls unloading hay bales from the cab of the truck.

"Excuse me," I said. "Hi."

He gave me a big, tobacco-stained grin. "You visiting at the temple?" he asked.

"Uh, yes. I was here before, during the big snowstorm. But now I've come back."

"People tend to do that down at the temple. I see the same cars comin' and goin' down this road a lot. That big snowstorm was somethin' else, wasn't it?"

I laughed. "Oh, you can say that again! But I was worried about the horses."

"Oh, I take care of 'em. Brought 'em into the barn for a coupla days."

I smiled. "I don't really know my way around this area. Could I ask you for directions?"

"Sure. Where you wanna go?"

"Where's the closest place I can buy a bottle of wine?"

～～～

I had no trouble finding the 7-11 in Wardensdale. I bought a bottle of merlot, a corkscrew, and an oversized plastic cup stamped with a University of West Virginia emblem. I didn't agonize or struggle over the decision. I didn't try to justify or defend my liquor purchase as I'd done in the past when I dared to bring a bottle home for myself despite Mack's ban on alcohol entering our house. For that horrible offense, I was castigated for days. Well, tonight would be different. Tonight, I would *be* me. Tonight, I planned to enjoy an evening with my old friend, a dear companion I used to turn to when confused, upset, or searching for answers.

I made it back to the monastery around dusk. Instead of heading straight for my kuti, I waited in the parking lot until it was dark enough to walk up the hill unnoticed. Once safely inside my kuti, I lit the oil lamp and the candle. Then I spread my sleeping bag on the floor. On it, I placed the meditation cushion, wine bottle, plastic cup, and corkscrew knowing perfectly well I was breaking a huge monastery rule and not caring in the slightest. Even though I hadn't kept Noble Silence, even though I'd skipped meditation sessions, refused to study the photos of decaying corpses, dismissed the boring recitations, laughed too loudly with Charles and even visited him in his kuti, somehow, I was certain everything was all right. I wasn't doing anything wrong. In fact, I had no doubt that at that particular moment in my life, I was exactly where I was supposed to be, doing precisely what I was meant to do.

I sat on the cushion, opened the wine bottle, poured the red liquid into the plastic cup, and took a sip. It tasted wonderful. I took another sip. Then another. Soon I welcomed that warm, fuzzy swirl of unwinding which was, at one time, my only friend and comfort during those sad, lonely nights when Mack abandoned me, retiring to his room immediately after dinner and slamming his door shut.

There were a few muffled knocks on the kuti door. *Oh, shit! Someone spotted me and is coming to turn me in!* I hid the bottle, then opened the door a crack.

"Charles! What are you doing here?"

"I was worried about you. I just came to make sure you were all right."

I laughed. "Oh, I'm fine! I'm definitely fine!"

"Is that alcohol on your breath?"

I giggled. "Oh, what's a party without guests! Come on in!"

He placed his coat on the bed and rolled his sleeves up to his elbows. "It's warm in here. Much better than my kuti."

"I can turn down the heater if you like."

"No, no. It feels nice. Warm and cozy."

"I only have one cushion, so you'll have to sit on the floor. I'm having a little picnic on the floor. Only there's no food. Just wine." I laughed and pulled the bottle from its hiding place behind the bed.

"I see," he said.

"But I only have one cup, so we'll have to share." I sat on the cushion, and he sat on the floor beside me. "I couldn't help myself, Charles. I haven't had a drop to drink for ages. I hope you don't think badly of me."

"Not at all. Not at all. One can only practice austerities for so long before our natural human impulses rise to the surface. How do you feel?"

Grinning broadly, I said, "Wonderful. I feel wonderful!" I poured more wine into the cup and handed it to him.

"Good. I'm glad. You *deserve* to feel wonderful. You're a beautiful woman. You're a joy to be around. You're capable, intelligent, kind, resourceful. You keep a household going with very little money all on your own. Your husband should be down on his knees every day, grateful for all you've done for him."

"Well . . ."

He took a sip from the cup. "I've met dozens of men like your husband. Small, angry men playing the role of bully. People like that need scapegoats to blame for their own failures. They need someone or something to criticize, to belittle, to hate. But they're all bluff. Inside they're nothing but cowards. Frightened, they hide themselves away from the crowd and lash out in anger and contempt. I've come to see that the man who's most angry is the man who's most terrified."

"Wow. That's a perfect description of Mack." He handed the cup back to me and I took a sip. "You know, he thinks he's this great literary genius. I mean, his ego is huge. It's out of control. I mean, he actually considers himself a vastly superior human being. What a joke!"

"I've come to see it really doesn't matter what we do."

"What do you mean? Certainly, what we choose to do with our lives has meaning."

"Only to you. And that's legitimate. But in terms of our effect on the grand scheme of things, no. Because the universe goes on in the way it wants. No matter what we do. The universe doesn't care if we write a book of literary genius or we don't. Life continues doing its thing whether we stand on our heads, sit on our butts on hard cushions all day long, climb Mount Everest, or run a marathon. There's nothing to be 'gained' or 'gotten' from this life because everything crumbles and fades away. We can maintain the illusion that we're actually 'accomplishing' something while we're here, that we're 'getting' somewhere. But that kind of thinking only feeds the ego. And if you're brave enough to look death in the face and realize what a short time we have here, you come to see that what you 'do' doesn't really matter. The depth of the grave is the same for paupers, kings, and sages."

Blown away by his words, my jaw fell open. "But, but, if what we do doesn't matter, what's our purpose for being here?"

"Other than to procreate, I'm not sure. I suppose the best we can do is to be kind, to walk through life softly, gently, with compassion, and without causing harm or pain to ourselves and others."

I sighed. "Gee, Charles, maybe you should be the one leading the Death Awareness retreat." I poured more wine into the cup and handed it to him. The bottle was almost empty. In the soft candlelight, I was surprised to see streaks of thin white scars on his forearms. "Oh, my! What happened to your arms?"

He took a sip from the cup. "Oh, those stupid scars. I resemble a roadmap, don't I? They're souvenirs from a time in my life when I had to feed the alligators at the museum."

"Alligators?"

"For a time, I was curator of exhibits at the Museum of Science in Miami. We had a big glass cage where we kept some alligators and caimans. Part of my job was to feed them cans of dog food from a pole. I had to go inside that cage and face those mean critters. They were always hungry and snapping at the food. Needless to say, sometimes they missed the dog food and instead nibbled on chunks of my arm! The kids who came to the museum loved watching it, and feeding time became quite an attraction. Actually, I think most of the kids were rooting for the gators!"

We both laughed. I leaned my head against his shoulder. "You know, earlier today I thought attending this retreat was a mistake. But now I'm really glad I decided to come back."

"Yes, but that decision may well have been your undoing."

"How do you mean?"

"Ah, you poor, dear child. Little did you know that when you came to this monastery an innocent, unsuspecting retreatant seeking refuge and spiritual fulfillment, that you'd meet and fall prey to"—he paused dramatically—"The Corruptor!"

I laughed and snuggled closer to him. My mouth rose to his ear and I whispered, "Yes, but you can only corrupt the corruptible!" My lips settled on his soft, warm cheek.

"Oh, you delicious woman!"

Zipped inside my sleeping bag, I was wide awake. It was past midnight. Alone on the hard mattress inside my kuti, I smiled at the empty wine bottle and hard blobs of wax on the nightstand where the candle had dripped. Maybe there *was* some benefit to this retreat after all. I'd experienced joyous, sensual emotions that had been dormant for years: the thrill of being desired and the warm excitement of forging an intimate connection with a kindred spirit.

I snuggled inside the folds of my sleeping bag. The forest was silent as death. Had this retreat taught me anything about death? Bhante Upali said that because death could happen at any time, we must ask, "Am I ready?" He also said that in order to die in a prepared state with our minds open to the universe, we must use loving-kindness to forgive ourselves and others.

Had I forgiven myself for aborting my own baby? I thought I had, but maybe I hadn't. Could I find enough loving-kindness in my heart to forgive Mack for his cruelty to me? I didn't have to think long. The answer was no. Absolutely not. So, according to the Buddhists, because I couldn't forgive Mack, I still had unfinished business. And because I still had unfinished business, I wasn't ready to die.

I peered out the window at the stars shining in the black sky above the tree line and I thought about dying. I thought about my father. His death was so sudden, he must have died in an unprepared state. I thought about old man Trex. He said he'd be more comfortable in heaven, so he must have died prepared. Prepared or unprepared, I loved them both and now they were gone. The cheerful woman I used to be was also gone. Even though she was alive, that woman had disappeared off the face of the earth. Then it occurred to me: living with Mack was like death. I turned over on the hard mattress and pulled the sleeping bag over my head. *Yes, the Buddhists are right. I still have unfinished business, so I'm not ready to die.* **Not yet.** Instead of coming back to the monastery to contemplate death, maybe the reason I'd come back was to learn how to start living again.

34

The Key

(Day 22)

The next morning my head ached, my eyes burned, and my mouth was dry as cotton. Upon hearing the wake-up gong, I fumbled in the dark finding my clothes. Unsteady on my feet, I was lucky enough to grab the pee bucket in time, and thank goodness my aim was on target.

I opened the door and stood on the porch of the kuti. In the beam of my flashlight, fluffy snowflakes tumbled down from the darkened sky. I inhaled deep breaths of cool, crisp air. The fuzziness in my brain began to clear as my flashlight panned the sleeping forest floor covered by a thin dusting of white. One thing I'd learned from my years living through long winters in the mountains, was that snow could come at any time right up until summer. These early spring snows were different than the expected snowstorms of winter: spring snows came as a surprise, coating the ground with a few inches which usually disappeared quickly on the warmed earth.

I leaned over the porch railing, stretched out my hand and caught several snowflakes which immediately melted in a cool puddle in my palm. I smiled softly, then put the liquid to my mouth. It tasted sweet.

Or was that just my imagination?

Inside the main building there were about a dozen retreatants sitting on the covered porch drinking hot beverages, waiting for the morning meditation period to begin. I would have loved a cup of hot coffee, but since I couldn't tolerate the taste of instant coffee, I brewed myself a strong cup of black tea and sipped it on the low bench in front of the woodstove. Ah, warmth! Someone had started a fire on this chilly early spring morning. Thank you, mystery stovemaster!

As I watched the flames flicker inside the firebox, disappointment crushed my heart. Today was my last day at the monastery, and I hadn't discovered the important business I was supposed to finish. Soon I'd be on the road, face to face with the sad reality of returning to a wretched man, to a home that was a virtual prison, and to a lonely, isolated life where it was practically impossible to just *be me*. The only bright spot had been my time spent with Charles. But that pleasant dream was coming to an end. I shrugged my shoulders, pushed those depressing thoughts aside, placed my empty mug on the windowsill, and headed to a dark corner of the dining hall. I wanted to practice a few yoga poses and clear my head before the last morning meditation session.

As I rested in the butterfly pose, Charles's tall figure darted into the dining hall from the kitchen. He whizzed past me toward the covered porch and disappeared. I came onto my knees, lowered my head to the floor, and relaxed in child's pose for what seemed a long time. When my head finally rose to check the clock, I stood up slowly, my mind happily clear and spacious. The covered porch was empty. As I headed for the corridor leading to the meditation hall, the backdoor at the end of the hall swung open. Charles, wearing a heavy quilted jacket and with snowflakes in his hair, burst inside and jumped in front of me.

"Do you see what's happening outside?" he said.

I smiled. "Yes. It's snowing."

"I just heard the weather forecast," he said, wild with excitement. "They say we could get four to six inches by this afternoon, possibly more. Some secondary roads might be closed."

"Really?"

"Obviously, you aren't safe driving home in these conditions. You'll have to stay."

I caught his enthusiasm and turned toward the window. I couldn't see much because it was still dark. "How much snow is out there now?"

"Oh, maybe a couple of inches. But listen to this, I still don't believe it. I bumped into Polly early this morning and she was actually acting very pleasant toward me. She told me that because I'd done such a great job cooking for this large retreat, she'd take an extra day in the kitchen for me next week so that I could have three days off instead of two! Bless her heart! I don't know what came over her. It's unheard of for anyone here to have three days off."

"Wow, Charles, that's great."

"Right now, the snow's coming down fast. Obviously, it's too danger-ous for anyone to be out on the roads. Looks as though Mama Nature doesn't want you to go home today."

I caught his desire. I wanted to tell him the truth: that I, too, did not want to go home today.

With a raised brow he whispered, "Another **B**."

I was puzzled.

"**Blizzard**," he said.

We both laughed. "Yes, blizzard! Of course."

"Seriously, you can't drive home in such treacherous weather con-ditions. And, well, it certainly would be nice to spend another couple of days together. I have the time off, and well, it could be fun." He paused. "We could even go somewhere if you'd like."

My heart ached to tell him: Yes, I would stay! I could call Mack and lie. I could tell him I was snowed in again. But then Mack would flip out at the news, rave like a maniac, and possibly make trouble for the monastery. Plus, I'd return home to a nightmare, and suffer weeks of grief and demeaning accusations.

"I wish I could stay, Charles. Honestly, I do. But I can't miss another week of work. I've taken off so much time already, and the last snowstorm really set me back financially. You know Mack doesn't bring in an income, so if I don't work, there's no money. And right now, I'm just about broke."

He hung his head.

"I'm sorry. Really, I am. I'd love to stay. Maybe I could come back again sometime soon? That is, if you're still here. And please don't worry about me. I'm quite capable of driving in weather like this. God knows I've had lots of experience driving up and down snowy mountain roads. Besides, I don't think this little spring snowstorm will amount to anything. The temperature will rise in a few hours, the snow's pretty wet and it'll melt quickly."

He stared at me with puppy-dog eyes. I was sad too, because I honestly wanted to stay, and was sorely tempted. The snowstorm provided the perfect opportunity, the perfect excuse to give to Mack. But instead of seizing the moment, instead of saying, "Yes, I'll stay" and spending the next few days with Charles, I was telling him I had to leave. Once again, I was doing Mack's bidding, following his orders. At the same time, I was holding on to the only life I knew.

"Just think about it," Charles said in a soft tone.

I couldn't refuse him. "All right, Charles. I'll think about it. I promise. Look, we can talk later. Right now, I'd better get to the meditation hall. I'm already late, and I think it's important I attend this last session."

All eyes were on me as I walked down the center aisle of the great hall. Kneeling, I bowed three times to the altar, seated myself on my cushion, and crossed my legs. Bhante Upali sat on the altar facing us.

A kind and gentle understanding radiated from his oval, candlelit face. He pinned the small microphone to his robe, focusing on me as he spoke. I met his gaze, hoping for any wise parting advice.

Bhante Upali kept his comments brief. He encouraged us to continue our efforts to practice meditation once we returned to our homes, our families, our jobs, and the responsibilities of daily life. He reminded us that all meditation, including meditation on death, was a continuous process of letting go. And he reminded us once more, that because death could come at any time, it was important to practice loving-kindness and forgiveness.

I closed my eyes. *Yes. Practice loving-kindness and forgiveness. Perhaps that's my unfinished business. I have to find enough loving-kindness in my heart to forgive Mack.* Stillness permeated the darkened hall as everyone dropped off into silent meditation. I inhaled, and sent loving-kindness to myself. *May I be well, happy, and peaceful. May I be free from pain, suffering, and delusion.* As I exhaled, I sent loving-kindness to all sentient beings, but my heart still refused to release a jot of loving-kindness to Mack. *How in the world can I love and forgive a man who's deliberately caused me such excruciating pain and suffering?* Suddenly I was overcome with unexpected remorse. Tormented by pangs of guilt and self-hatred, I blamed myself for staying in a miserable marriage, putting up with Mack's abuse, and wasting the best years of my life.

A lone tear slipped down my cheek. I tried to focus on my breath: *breathing in, sitting, breathing out, sitting.* After a while my body and mind relaxed. When the birds announced the rising sun, and rays of peach hues brightened the windows of the great hall, the radiant image of Kuan Yin standing on the dragon appeared in my mind. But instead of being surrounded by a swirling ocean, the Bodhisattva and dragon were floating atop a calm sea of snow. All of a sudden, I was no longer in the meditation hall. I was with her, transported somewhere outside myself, embraced in the warmth of her loving arms, both of us snuggled in a peaceful snowy blanket of purity, compassion, and forgiveness. Embedded within this soft cocoon of unconditional love, I realized my task wasn't to forgive and send loving-kindness to Mack. First, I had to love and forgive *myself.*

When my ears caught the tone of the gong being struck once, twice, three times, I was back on my cushion inside the meditation hall, my entire being alert, awake, and riveted on each of the three echoing tones of the gong arising and passing away . . . arising and passing away . . . arising and passing away . . . passing away until there was nothing left. *Nothing at all.*

My eyes popped open. My heart stood still. *Yes. Annica. All things pass away and are gone.* **No sense in holding on to anything** . . . My lips broke into a jubilant smile. Through the windows, freshly fallen snow sparkled like diamonds under the soft morning light. At that moment my struggle was over and I knew exactly what I needed to do. The marriage I'd been holding on to all those years—the miserable life I'd been clinging to in fear and desperation—was actually nothing. *Nothing at all.* And I could let it go. It was gone, and I was free of it. I'd finally found what I'd been seeking: The key to unlock the prison door.

Epilogue

Upon returning home I told Mack our marriage was over.

"I'm staying here at the farmhouse and you'll have to leave," I announced. "I have an established business to run and I need that income to survive. You can easily find work elsewhere."

I was surprised when he didn't put up a fight. Looking back, I'm fairly certain it was the resolute tone of my voice and the steadfast confidence in my eyes that convinced him he'd lost. I'd finally seen through his hollow game of lies and intimidation, and he no longer had power over me. Three days later I dropped him off at the Greyhound station, where he boarded a bus to Boston. I even helped him pack.

Toward the end of summer, after months of letters and phone calls, Charles came to live with me. He helped me with the cooking business, encouraged me to pursue whatever path I chose, and told me every day what a sweet and lovely woman I was. We respected and accepted each other for who we were, and a cross word hardly ever passed between us. We laughed, we played, and there were plenty of hugs and kisses.

The deep winter snows came once more to the Pennsylvania mountains followed by the big spring thaw causing the woodland streams to overflow their banks. When the dandelions exploded from the earth with a profusion of sunny yellow faces, and when the peepers were peeping their annual love calls, Charles died one night in his sleep.

I didn't know until the next morning. I'd brewed a pot of his favorite coffee and thought he was sleeping late. After a while I climbed the stairs to the bedroom. The blood froze in my veins as I stood shocked and horrified beside the bed staring at his ashen face and slackened jaw, knowing immediately he was gone.

It wasn't until several weeks after his death, still numb with grief, that I managed to kneel on the rug in front of the small altar I'd set up in the spare bedroom. I lit a candle, then bowed three times to Charles's exquisitely carved white Buddha statue, and to the postcard image of Kuan Yin standing on the dragon. I sent loving-kindness to myself, then to all sentient beings. I was alone once more, but no longer lost or afraid. I gazed at the photograph of Charles I'd placed upon the altar beside the postcard of Kuan Yin. The twinkle in his eyes made me smile, and his impish grin smiled back at me.

"Annica," I whispered. "All things are impermanent." I reached beneath the altar for my beloved gift, cradled it to my chest, then set it on the rug in front of me. Slowly, I pulled the wooden mallet from its sheath and struck the cylindrical bell once, twice, three times, certain Charles would hear it.

About the Author

A graduate of Boston University with a degree in psychology, Laurie has been practicing and promoting natural health for over 25 years. Her work in the health and wellness field has been featured on television, radio, and in local and national magazines and newspapers.

During her varied professional career, she opened and managed several health-related businesses promoting physical, mental, and spiritual health. Laurie taught yoga, meditation, nutrition, and cooking classes for adults, children, and seniors. She also authored a monthly health and wellness column for the publication *Our Town*, created and facilitated the "Healthy Living" program for Somerset Hospital, and developed and hosted the tv segment "Cooking for Health" on WJAC-TV.

Currently a Certified Health Coach trying to age gracefully with the Buddha's teachings in mind, she enjoys a quiet, simple life in Virginia. You can find her at www.lauriesjacobson.com.

Thanks for reading. If you enjoyed this book,
please take a moment to post a review at your
favorite store, and tell a friend.